ZEALOTS

HOW A GROUP OF SCOTTISH CONSPIRATORS UNLEASHED HALF A CENTURY OF WAR IN BRITAIN

ZEALOTS

HOW A GROUP OF SCOTTISH CONSPIRATORS UNLEASHED HALF A CENTURY OF WAR IN BRITAIN

OLIVER THOMSON

AMBERLEY

To my wonderful wife Jean and anyone else who may be descended from the survivors of the wreck of the Crown of London, *1679.*

First published 2018

Amberley Publishing
The Hill, Stroud
Gloucestershire, GL5 4EP

www.amberley-books.com

Copyright © Oliver Thomson, 2018

The right of Oliver Thomson to be identified
as the Author of this work has been asserted in
accordance with the Copyrights, Designs and
Patents Act 1988.

ISBN 978 1 4456 7795 8 (hardback)
ISBN 978 1 4456 7796 5 (ebook)

British Library Cataloguing in Publication Data.
A catalogue record for this book is available from
the British Library.

Typesetting and Origination by Amberley Publishing.
Printed in the UK.

CONTENTS

A NOTE ON SPELLING
OF NAMES

People in this period were inconsistent in spelling their names, which occasionally causes confusion – for example Colonel John Brown may or may not have been the same person as Colonel John Browne; similarly, James Holbourn(e), and Spens or Spence, but less obvious is Neaves or Nevoy, the violent minister of Loudoun. Archibald Johnston became Lord Wariston or Warriston, but I have kept him with two 'r's as so many Edinburgh streets named after him have that spelling. Similarly, place names have variations such as Wormiston, Wormeston and Wormieston near Crail in Fife. Some of my spelling choices are arbitrary so I apologise for any that cause irritation.

The other problem readers face is the swiftness with which people changed their names and titles in this period. Charles I in particular gave new titles as a very cheap, if not always effective, way of buying loyalty, so for example Field Marshal Leslie becomes Earl of Leven whilst James Livingston becomes first Lord Almond, then the Earl of Callendar. Archibald Campbell starts in this narrative as Lord Lorn then becomes the first Earl, then the Marquis of Argyll.

PREFACE

It has long been accepted that the impetus for the three English Civil Wars came from Scotland, but this book narrows down the area to one small neighbourhood in Fife. With its strong North Sea contacts, Fife had more than its fair share of ex-mercenaries from the German wars. Add to this a close-knit local group of frustrated politicians, lawyers and angry church ministers, all living within a 20-mile radius, and you have the explosive mixture that led eventually to the death of Charles I and nine wars in fifty years that cost more than 600,000 lives. Apart from Fife, nowhere else in Britain at this time had such a combustible concentration of rebel priests, articulate politicians and unemployed mercenaries; the author has trawled local records to demonstrate how the Fife Conspiracy achieved such momentous outcomes.

In addition, there is a gazetteer of all the castles, churches, monuments and battlefields associated with these wars and the people who fought in them.

Four key questions are posed:

- Would there have been an English Civil War if the Scots had not invaded England in 1640?
- Would Cromwell have won the Civil War without Scottish help?
- Why did the Scots change from the winning side to the losing side?
- Why did Fife play such an important role in starting these wars?

Warning: In narratives such as this it is hard not to take sides, to sympathise with underdogs, to enjoy the downfall of persecutors. This is particularly dangerous when the combatants belong to different religious sects and nearly 400 years later these issues remain sensitive, so throughout the pages which follow I have done my best to remain unbiased and I apologise if there are any hints of prejudice.

Perhaps the one acceptable emotion in this context is pity that so often members of different religious sects, often highly intelligent people, have felt the need to go to war with each other.

The rash and fatal experiment was made, 23rd July 1637 in the High Church of St Giles, Edinburgh.

Sir Walter Scott: *Tales of a Grandfather*

INTRODUCTION

The succession of wars begun in 1639 by the Scottish Church, egged on by a group of Fife conspirators, almost certainly represents the longest and most damaging series of conflicts between two branches of the Protestant Church in the whole of history. They also come second only to the German Thirty Years War and the French Wars of Religion in the list of all wars between opposing Christian sects. It has been a habit to blame Scotland's misfortunes on unfair treatment from the south, but the huge loss of life due to these wars greatly exceeded all the battles such as Flodden and Culloden put together, especially if you add to the casualties the large numbers of soldiers and civilians who died of malnutrition and plague, as well as the thousands of prisoners of war sent to the Americas as white slaves – a grand total of in excess of 60,000 people, or something like five per cent of Scotland's population at that time.

Similarly the damage done to trade and agriculture did far more long-term harm than the colonial disaster in Darien, which was blamed for the Union in 1707. There is no doubt that all this damage was essentially self-inflicted, the first seven wars recklessly undertaken in the name of a narrow ideological difference, acts of spiritual narcissism that led to massive human suffering and held back the progress of Scotland for at least half a century.

In addition, the fact that for religious reasons the Scots invaded England four times in ten years created a very unfortunate precedent for the Jacobites when they tried the same approach in 1715 and 1745. To this tally of guilt we should also add the huge damage inflicted on Ireland by the Scots in the 1640s; though Cromwell and

English troops get most of the blame for Irish genocide, the Scots mounted two invasions of northern Ireland that were characterised by extreme brutality and collateral damage leading to disease and starvation.

It is not the purpose of this book to show any bias in favour of one Christian sect or another; in fact Catholicism played only a small part in these events and the wars were almost entirely between two different branches of Protestantism. Nor is it the intention to condemn individuals for behaviour that might these days suggest war crimes, only to reflect on the obsessions that have in all ages contributed consequential human misery.

What this book does, however, is emphasise the importance of Fife in starting this conflagration. It was perhaps perversely the fact that St Andrews was both the location of Scotland's then largest university and also the seat of archbishops that resulted in such a concentration of rebel church ministers and rebel noblemen who were motivated to start an armed rebellion and were uniquely able to do so. This was because a number of Scotland's most respected professional generals, particularly the two Leslies, had homes in Fife so were easily able to recruit many of their colleagues who had earned their livings fighting for the Protestant side in Germany. The coincidence that so many talented churchmen, lairds and professional soldiers were concentrated in such a relatively small area, many sharing strong family ties, gave them the opportunity to share their ideas and passions and mount a series of successful co-ordinated attacks on the Stuart dynasty within a remarkably short timeframe. Despite the unpopularity of Charles I in England, there was no comparable concentration of opponents south of the border such as occurred in Fife. It was thus the Fife Conspiracy that set in motion what became the English Civil Wars or the The Wars of Three Kingdoms.

There were only a few ministers and two or three Fife gentlemen in town and what need it all the sturr?

John Leslie, Earl of Rothes

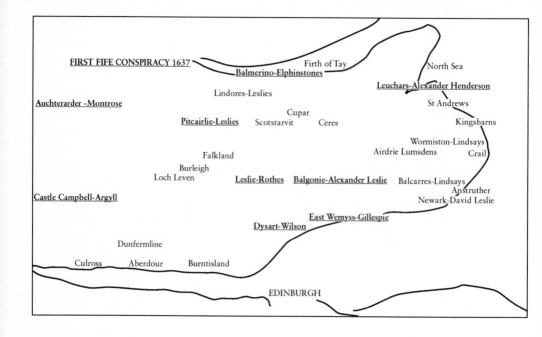

FIRST FIFE CONSPIRACY 1637

Firth of Tay

North Sea

Balmerino-Elphinstones

Leuchars-Alexander Henderson

Lindores-Leslies

St Andrews

Auchterarder -Montrose

Cupar

Kingsbarns

Pitcairlie-Leslies   Scotstarvit   Ceres

Wormiston-Lindsays

Airdrie Lumsdens   Crail

Falkland

Burleigh

Loch Leven   **Leslie-Rothes   Balgonie-Alexander Leslie**   Balcarres-Lindsays

Anstruther

Castle Campbell-Argyll   Newark-David Leslie

East Wemyss-Gillespie

Dysart-Wilson

Dunfermline

Culross   Aberdour   Burntisland

EDINBURGH

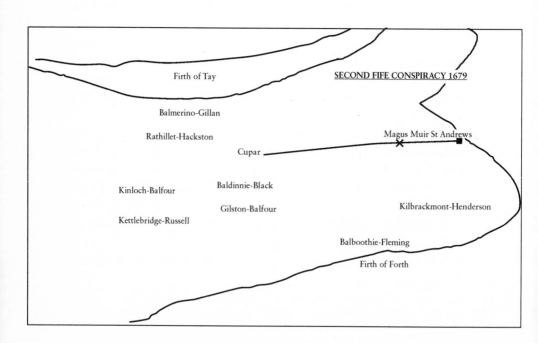

Firth of Tay   **SECOND FIFE CONSPIRACY 1679**

Balmerino-Gillan

Rathillet-Hackston

Magus Muir St Andrews

Cupar

Kinloch-Balfour   Baldinnie-Black

Gilston-Balfour   Kilbrackmont-Henderson

Kettlebridge-Russell

Balboothie-Fleming

Firth of Forth

FAMILY CONNECTIONS

Earl of Balmerino offends Charles I after 1633 coronation condemned to death but reprieved

His son marries Campbell of Loudoun's daughter

Walter Greig,his minister is close to Balcarres Lindsays

Alexander Henderson joint author of Covenant teacher at St Andrews, then minister at Leuchars

Argyll,Montrose and David Leslie all attend St Andrews, as probably also do Rothes and Loudoun

Leslies of Pitcairlie have three sons in Swedish army

David Leslie buys Newark Castle

John Leslie Earl of Rothes and Campbell of Loudoun both come to aid of Balmerino

John Leslie,Earl of Rothes.... *lives 3 miles from* .... Field Marshal Alexander Leslie, fostered as child by Campbells of Lawers

Rothes' daughter marries.....

Another daughter marries Scott of Buccleugh

Leslie's foster daughter marries.....

Family chaplain is James Wilson of Dysart

Leslie's son Col. Alexander Leslie of Balgonie.

Leslie's daughter marries Hugh Fraser of the dragoons

.....Alexander Lindsay Earl of Balcarres

his sister marries Robert Moray agent of Cardinal Richelieu

Family chaplain is Greig of Balmerino

Maitland of Lauderdale is close friend

Archibald Campbell Earl of Argyll

Wealthiest landowner in Scotland

Fostered by Campbells of Lawers

At St Andrews University

Cousin of Earl of Loudoun

Much influenced by Henderson of Leuchars.....

Has castle at Dollar close to Fife

Earl of Wemyss

his sister married to Campbell of Lawers so is uncle of Earl of Loudoun

.....family chaplain George Gillespie .....

Fife Conspiracy family connections.

PART ONE

THE FIRST FIFE CONSPIRACY

Chapter 1

THE LEGEND OF THE FLYING STOOL

The presence of numerous clergymen kept up the general enthusiasm and seemed to give a religious character to the war.

Sir Walter Scott: *Tales of a Grandfather*

The credit or blame for starting a succession of wars that cost an estimated three-quarters of a million British lives, including at least 60,000 Scots, is often given to Jenny Geddes, a woman of about forty who had a greengrocers stall in the High Street of Edinburgh. Plenty of important witnesses on Sunday 23 July 1637 allegedly saw her throw a folding stool on which she had been sitting in the crowded aisles of the High Kirk of Edinburgh – it was not fashionable at this time to call it a cathedral for that was a papist term, let alone call it St Giles, for he was then a largely forgotten French miracle-worker of Greek descent. These same witnesses, the great and good of Edinburgh, also saw the flying stool nearly hit its mark, the head of the Reverend Dr Hannah, dean of the church, just at the moment when he read out for the first time the new prayers from the new prayer book, just published by the Archbishop of St Andrews. Most of the witnesses perhaps also heard Jenny's accompanying remark addressed to Dr Hannah – 'The deil colick in the wame of thee, thou false thief! Dost thou say the mass at my lug?' (The devil give you stomach ache, you false thief. Are you saying mass in my ear?')

What the witnesses failed to record was whether Jenny Geddes made this brave and astonishing interruption of her own accord or whether she was put up to it by others who were just as angry about the new prayer book but perhaps less willing to indulge in such an undignified action. However, the fact that soon afterwards there were organised riots elsewhere in Edinburgh and in other parts of Scotland suggests that she was not operating alone. As a full-time street trader she had strong arms, a loud voice and a good turn of phrase, which no local laird or rebellious clergyman could have quite matched, so she was probably recruited for the incident by one of the rebel ministers or powerful lords who wanted to test public reaction to their plans. Certainly there is evidence of a number of secret meetings between rebel ministers and local lairds from Fife between April and July 1637. There was also quite a group of women further up the social scale, for example, the mysterious Mrs Barbara Mean, Euphemia Henderson and two women called Craig, who, if they did not play an active part, certainly encouraged women like Jenny. One account suggests that Jenny Geddes was a later invention and that Mrs Mean, one of the so-called Edinburgh matrons, was the real stool thrower. Another version implied that it was none of these women who flung the stool but an apprentice boy dressed up in a skirt.

Whilst Jenny or Barbara's outburst remained the iconic moment that provoked the two Bishops' Wars, and the English Civil War that was their offspring, there were a number of other incidents soon afterwards. Within hours the Bishop of Edinburgh, David Lindsay, was pelted with stones as he left the church and had to be rescued to help him reach his lodgings at Holyrood. Thomas Sydserf, the unpopular Bishop of Galloway, was attacked by crowds in Falkirk and Dalkeith; there were shocking rumours that he wore a crucifix round his neck. There were numerous bouts of stone throwing, which resulted in 23 July being referred to as Stoneyfield Day. In another incident, Alastair Gordon shouted angrily from his pew when a new minister insisted that the congregation knelt to receive communion. Walter Whitford, the belligerent Bishop of Brechin, was attacked by a mob when he announced that he was going to read from the new prayer book of which he was one of the authors. He then barricaded himself in his church and armed himself with two pistols in the pulpit. As the Aberdeen diarist John Spalding put it, 'the people got up a mad humour detesting that sort of worships and pursued him so sharply that he barely escaped out of their hands unslain.' William Annan, the minister of Ayr, had his surplice torn off by a crowd of screaming women, many of them apparently members of the most prominent families in Ayrshire. A witness wrote 'not satisfied with hooting and ranting they belaboured him with fists and sticks and tore his ruff, coat and hat to pieces.'

Such can be the anger of ordinary people whose daily habits are disrupted by unexpected change and perhaps – perhaps – this is, or was, often more keenly felt by women than by men. Jenny Geddes was not alone; other women, such as the Edinburgh prophetess Margaret Mitchelson, were to declare that the National Covenant had been dictated by Jesus himself. If Jenny and the other protestors seem extreme, it is worth remembering that a mere seventeen years earlier in 1620 a group of English Calvinists set sail from Plymouth in a tiny ship to cross the Atlantic to an unknown continent. It is also a fact that three generations had passed since the end of Catholicism in central Scotland and there had been nearly ninety years of aggressively anti-Catholic sermons. So the merest hint of a return to Catholic phraseology and imagery was enough to cause panic. It may seem ridiculous that fairly minor adjustments of a religion should cause such outrage, but they upset a pattern of life that provided psychological, spiritual comfort to ordinary people every Sunday. The ministers themselves perhaps had mixed motives, maybe a jealous resentment of the bishops or a fear of diminution in their personal authority, but they took it very seriously.

For the time being, this protest movement in Scotland did not seriously endanger people's lives, for no one was yet expecting it to turn into a war, but it just so happened that there was money available, ammunition dumps and a good supply of highly trained professional soldiers. So the least spark could cause a conflagration and it was the group of Fife gentlemen who were ready to fan the flames. As the anger and stress built up, the reaction to the new prayer book was eventually to cost thousands of Scottish lives and many more in both England and Ireland, probably at least 600,000.

The Lord of Hosts is With Us

Covenanter War Banner

Chapter 2

THE MINISTERS

Finding little warrant for force in the New Testament divines had recourse to the Old Testament where they discovered encouraging precedents ... for violent action.

John Buchan: *Montrose*

Amongst the candidates for the role of encouraging Jenny's (or Barbara Mean's) outburst and making sure it was well publicised are several of the men who soon afterwards followed it up with a well-orchestrated campaign of civil disobedience that was, in due course, to lead to civil war. And a large proportion of them were based in Fife.

Whether he was present on the day or not, one of the most obvious was Alexander Henderson (1583–1646), a Fife man probably born in Crail or Creich, who had studied and taught at St Andrews University before being appointed in 1615 as minister of Leuchars by Archbishop Gladstanes. Not surprisingly at that point he had been an ardent advocate of bishops, but his new congregation gave him a very cool welcome, so he thought again, perhaps converted by his fanatical neighbour James Bruce, the minister of Kingsbarns, and he quickly changed sides to become a leading opponent of all things episcopal.

Thus Henderson became in 1637 one of the prime publicists and promoters of the Jenny Geddes incident for he is known to have had a meeting with, amongst others, the Fife-based Lord Balmerino, an already established opponent of the Anglican version of Protestantism, in April 1637, four months before the incident. He was also at a meeting with other rebel ministers and the so-called Edinburgh matrons in June, so what Spalding called a 'clandestine band' was at work. A handsome, dark, scholarly-looking man with a fashionable Van Dyck beard, impressive with his white ruff and clerical breeches, Henderson was now in his mid-fifties. He was such an effective and articulate writer that he was rapidly able to draft the new National Covenant, a blueprint for a Church of Scotland that would be without bishops, without fancy surplices and without detailed orders as to how ministers should lead prayers or make sermons. He did this job so well that he was asked to write many other documents including the call for Scots to go to war against their anglicised king, Charles I, 'the necessity of resisting tyranny by arms in defence of the kirk.' It was to be a Holy War and he was later to accompany the Scottish army in its invasions of England. One of his earlier achievements was to turn the future Campbell Earl of Argyll into a dedicated Calvinist, which he did in a series of sermons in Glasgow – so effectively that Argyll became a regular preacher at Inveraray and a major supporter of the Fife Conspiracy. Surprisingly, Henderson must have acquired significant wealth for in 1642 he paid for the completion of what became the Parliament Hall at St Andrews University.

Perhaps the second most influential Fife minister, despite his youth, was George Gillespie (1613–48), born in Kirkcaldy. Another prickly St Andrews graduate, he refused a parish till after the removal of bishops but had already persuaded the Earl of Cassilis to join the conspiracy. He had also already, at the age of only twenty-four, published his *A Dispute Against English Popish Ceremonies* and preached to the Glasgow Assembly of 1638. He became minister at Wemyss, home of the influential Colvilles, one of whom was the mother of the Campbell Earl of Loudoun, another close ally of the Leslies, a family who would play a major role in the events to come. He was still only thirty when appointed as one of the negotiators in London for the alliance with the English Parliamentarians, the Westminster Confession and Scotland's third invasion of England in this period. He died of consumption in his mid-thirties but such was his reputation that his tomb, along with Henderson's, was vandalised by the new government in 1660.

Third in terms of influence was Robert Douglas (1594–1674), probably born in the Loch Leven area, educated at St Andrews and appointed minister of Kirkcaldy in 1628 where he must have met John Leslie of Rothes. Soon afterwards Douglas abandoned this post to serve as an army chaplain with the Scottish mercenaries fighting for the Protestant cause in Germany, thus giving an indication of his belief in the military solution for sectarian differences. He had then made important contacts with the Fife officers in the Swedish army and returning to Scotland about 1637, was in a strong position to advise men like Rothes and Henderson on the practicality of an armed rebellion in Scotland. Douglas supported the Covenant at the 1638 General Assembly and became an army padre with the Scottish forces invading England. He was negotiating in Westminster at the time of Marston Moor and publicly expressed his anger when the Scots contribution to that victory was downplayed by Cromwell, whose anti-Presbyterian stance he regarded as just as unacceptable as the Church of England. Whilst his contribution to starting the First Civil War can only be guessed, there is no doubt about his prime role in starting the Third, as he was responsible for the coronation of Charles II at Scone and thus for the disastrous Dunbar/Worcester campaigns after which he was imprisoned by his enemy Cromwell. He was the only minister to serve five times as Moderator, allegedly turned down the post of Archbishop of St Andrews at the Restoration and died at eighty as a parish minister.

The rest of Fife provided at least three dozen other ministers who had both strong anti-episcopal views and good contacts with their local lairds. James Wilson, for example, the minister at Dysart, north of Kirkcaldy, was not only a keen supporter of the Covenant but tutor to the Leslie family of Rothes. This family included both the Earl of Rothes, who as we shall see was to be one of the prime organisers of the war, but also General David Leslie, an extremely successful mercenary who had been born near Auchtermuchty. He was in turn connected with his superior officer Field Marshal Alexander Leslie who, though born in Perthshire, had recently bought Balgonie Castle in Fife and was now a neighbour of Rothes.

Another Alexander Leslie was the minister in Anstruther and later chaplain to General David Leslie, whilst John Duncan, minister of Culross, was chaplain to the Field Marshal. To square the circle the Field Marshal's son, another Alexander Leslie and already a colonel in the Swedish army, was married to Rothes' daughter, whilst to add additional muscle Alexander's daughter was married to Hugh Fraser, a dashing commander of dragoons.

Amongst other Fife ministers in the conspiracy a major supporter of Henderson in the 1638 General Assembly was David Dalgleish, minister at Cupar. Significantly, two Cupar women were hanged at Newburgh in 1661 for setting fire to his successor's manse.

Also important was Walter Greig, the minister at Balmerino whose earl was, like Rothes, an active early opponent of Charles I's religious policies. Greig was also chaplain for the Lindsay of Balcarres family, another powerful Fife earldom, and was like many other Fife minsters an army chaplain with the Scots army at Marston Moor, a post that involved both motivating the army to fight for its religion and sometimes giving advice on military matters, which was not entirely welcome.

Influential too were the two Row brothers, William who was minister at Ceres and patronised by the Lindsay Earls of Crawford and his brother the historian John, who was so precocious that he could read Hebrew at the age of seven, and who was minister at Carnock, close to the Leslie heartland. Also patronised by the Lindsays was Davit Forret who tutored Alexander Lindsay of Balcarres at St Andrews, became his local minister at Kilconquhar and served as his army padre, as did later Walter Greig, the minister of Balmerino who was with his horse troop at Marston Moor.

Also at Marston Moor and the siege of Newcastle as army chaplains were John Moncrieff, the minister at Kinghorn, and John Duncan from Culross, as was Andrew Donaldson, minister at Dalgetty from 1641, chaplain to the Dunfermline Regiment and a strong Covenanter who was dismissed as such from his charge in 1664. He was an army chaplain in the ill-fated Preston campaign.

Yet another padre at Marston Moor was John Govan the minister of Muckhart (close to the Fife border) who served with the Kirkcudbright Regiment and was a near neighbour of Castle Campbell at Dollar, a base of the other great anti-episcopal laird, Archibald Campbell, Earl of Argyll. As a virtual orphan, young Argyll had been fostered by the same Tayside Campbell family that had earlier cared for the future Field Marshal Leslie, thus creating a strong bond which they shared with the third major anti-episcopal laird, John Campbell Earl of Loudoun, himself also brought up by Loch Tay but with strong Fife connections through his mother, Jean Colville of Wemyss.

From 1641 the minister at Burntisland was the notorious Robert Blair (1593–1674) born in Ayrshire who was so ferociously anti-episcopal that he was excommunicated by the bishops in 1634 but found a parish in Bangor, northern Ireland, where he famously nearly matched the Pilgrim Fathers by filling a ship with Ulster Presbyterians which, but for a storm, might have made it across the Atlantic. He subsequently won renown preaching in London during the Scottish Army's participation in the First Civil War. His neighbour in Ulster was another Scottish minister, John Livingston, who like Blair was dismissed from both his Ayrshire and Irish parishes, accused of 'stirring up the Irish to extacies (*sic*) and enthusiasms' on a stipend of £40 per annum. Livingston collaborated in the doomed scheme to send oppressed Presbyterians to a new life in America. He was able to return to Scotland in 1637 and a year later was chosen to ride all the way from Edinburgh to London with the news of the Covenant. David Ferguson at Dunfermline and Henry Smith at Culross were also part of the ex-Ulster group of rebel ministers.

Other actively rebellious local ministers in Fife or nearby included William Spens of Fossoway who was later deposed, arrested and tortured for his support of the Argyll campaign in 1685, John Duncan who was at all the main Assemblies and with the army in England, and John Welway of Dron.

In all, there were as many as fifty Fife ministers who were strongly against the new prayer book and approved the Fife Petition against the book that was delivered three days before the stool-throwing incident. It just so happened that Fife, with its strong connections across the North Sea, also had the largest concentration of active mercenary officers serving in Germany. And in the Earls of Rothes and Balmerino, it had two of the most prominent parliamentary opponents of the new religious reforms, albeit both of them had a vested interest as owners of former church properties.

Moving south to Edinburgh, the other prime suspect as an early agitator against the church reforms dictated by the London and Canterbury regime was the much younger Archibald Johnston (1611– 63). A Glasgow law graduate, he had also studied some theology under the influential Robert Baillie. Born and brought up in Edinburgh, Johnston's sharp legal brain was to have huge influence over Scottish and English affairs for the next two decades, as he worked very closely with the Fife ministers. He had recently bought an estate at Currie, west of Edinburgh. Four years later at the age of thirty he was promoted to be Lord Warriston by Charles I, who was hoping to win him over. Dark with a fashionably pointed beard and the most elaborate of Puritan-style lace collars, Johnston was considered even in those days of religious fanaticism as being more fanatical than most. For him the prayer book was 'popish vomit'. The night before his execution in 1663 he was convinced that he would go to heaven and in his writings and speeches he claimed direct contact with God.

In 1637 he seems to have just suffered some serious bereavement and was desperate to forget his grief by frenetic activity for the church. It was said that he prayed for fourteen hours every day and needed only three hours sleep at night. Eight months after the Geddes incident, it was he who addressed a huge public gathering with a fiery response to a proclamation sent from London reprimanding the Scots for their insolent behaviour. He added the legal touches to the draft National Covenant being prepared by his friend Alexander Henderson. By the time Johnston was executed in his early fifties, he and his wife had produced twelve children and he left her so destitute that she had to beg for financial help. Yet she still faithfully tried to collect the parts of his dismembered body.

Amongst other active rebel ministers at this juncture were Andrew Ramsay, Harry Pollok and Andrew Cant (1590–1663). Cant was a strong Presbyterian, described as 'a profound enemy of bishops' who had been minister at Pitsligo in Aberdeen but at about this time was transferred to Newbattle outside Edinburgh, so he was able to take an active part and was one of many Presbyterian ministers who chose to accompany the rebel Scottish army and rally the troops. However, he was also available to return later on missions to try to convert the reluctant Aberdonians from episcopacy.

Cant's nephew was the notoriously bloodthirsty John Neaves, or Nevoy (*c.* 1616–72) who was minister of Loudoun and close associate of John Campbell of Loudoun (*see* below) who was to become one of the leading figures throughout the Civil Wars. Nevoy too became a regular army padre and famously insisted on the execution of all the 300 prisoners taken at the siege of Dunaverty, (*see* p129), against the wishes of General Leslie who had promised them clemency in return for surrendering the castle. As the *Fasti Ecclesiae Scoticanae* obliquely describes him, 'he was a man of great zeal and violence and did not object to the execution of the Macdonalds.' He was also to play a key role in raising the troops for the campaign of 1651 that ended in disaster at Worcester. After the Restoration he was dismissed from his parish and exiled to Holland, where he died.

David Dickson (1583–1663) from the Trongate in Glasgow had studied and later taught philosophy at the university before becoming a parish minister in Irvine in 1618. However, his preaching was so radical that he was discharged from his post and banned from preaching by the Bishop of Glasgow, whose title he naturally regarded as heretical. Thus for some time, like many ministers of his persuasion, he had been unemployed but trying to make ends meet as a wandering preacher. Like Cant he chose to be an army pastor and joined him with Montrose during the attacks on Aberdeen. After one bloody battle he was alleged to have said 'O Lord be praised, the wark of God gangs bonnily on.'

Samuel Rutherford (1600–61), a former professor of Latin at Edinburgh, had been sacked as minister of Anwoth in Galloway for his Presbyterian style of preaching and was sent to Aberdeen, where he became a successful unofficial preacher, later emerging as a prominent church powerbroker during the Westminster negotiations and Principal of St Andrews University until he was sacked by order of Charles II. He died whilst awaiting execution in Edinburgh.

Zachary Boyd (1583–1553) was the minister at Glasgow Barony famed for his belligerent sermons on 'the scarlet flood' and for later buttonholing Oliver Cromwell for a three-hour tête-à-tête, having already subjected him to a three-hour sermon and despite the fact that Cromwell had been advised to 'pistol the scoundrel'. He was a senior academic and poet, one of his poems being a paean for the Scottish army's victory over the English Royalists at Newburn. Significantly he had spent several years at the French Huguenot college at Saumur.

Robert Baillie (1602–62) studied at Glasgow University and was later Professor of Philosophy and Principal, where Warriston was one of his students. In 1637 Baillie took part in the condemnation of the new prayer book. Significantly, he bought muskets for a group of friends who were enlisting for the Holy War, later became a regular army chaplain during the invasions of England, a zealous preacher of Presbyterianism in London after the Battle of Newburn and was himself responsible for the negotiations that resulted in a Scottish army being wiped out at Worcester.

Other Glasgow and west coast supporters of the Covenant included Patrick Gillespie at the Cathedral who later opposed the Preston and Worcester campaigns and was dismissed in 1650, imprisoned in 1660 and narrowly avoided execution. John Bell at the Tron and Robert Wallace at Blackfriars were also pro-Covenant as were John Carstairs at Cathcart and Robert Watt at Cardross; but John Hay at Renfrew was against, as were John Maxwell at the Cathedral, James Hutcheson at Carmunnock, James Watt at (Old) Kilpatrick, and John Crichton at Paisley – he was deposed as 'a Papist' by the 1638 Assembly and moved to Dublin whereas his successor Alexander Dunlop served as an army chaplain in the Marston Moor campaign. Thus as compared with Fife, support in the Glasgow region was much patchier.

Perhaps the most unusual of the ministers was Eleazar Borthwick who, like Robert Douglas, had served as a padre for the Scottish mercenaries fighting in the Swedish army. He returned home in February 1637 and became the agent for the rebel Presbyterians in London, liaising with the English Puritans in the hope of their support against the king.

None of these ministers, apart from Robert Douglas, could be described as initially war-minded but they, and many like them, did hold such strong views on the details of church services and church organisation that even though their opponents were fellow Protestants they still could not conceive of any compromise. Kneeling at communion, bowing to altars, fancy vestments, prayers read from a book, bishops in palaces, crucifixes hung round the neck, fonts in the wrong place, all these things were anathema to them. For that reason they were willing to hazard their own lives but also those of many thousands of the lay population and on occasion to be merciless to their enemies. Perhaps they would have been hardly human if they had not at times resented the difference in their remuneration and lifestyle compared with the upstart bishops. Having been trained in a system where ministers could say their own prayers and read their own sermons it was hard to put up with criticism, orders and the threat of dismissal from bishops whom they largely despised as careerists and deviants from the principles of Calvin and Knox.

Despite these background temptations there is no doubting the sincerity of the vast majority of the kirk ministers or their determination not just to make Scotland a universally Calvinistic state but to spread the same presbyterian system to the less fertile territories of England, Wales and Ireland. It was for this reason that they dominated the politics of Scotland for the next dozen years and helped start a war that became a series of wars with disastrous results.

Though the majority of Fife and other lowland Scottish ministers were against the prayer book, there were exceptions. Some, such as George Dewar who was deposed from his parish at Anstruther in 1644, were genuinely in favour of bishops, others simply did not care: William Schetois of Falkland was sacked for drunkenness in 1627 and James Bennet of Auchtermuchty was accused of being 'ane frequent hunter with dogs and player at cards.' David Monro of Killochan was pelted with stones as a suspected anti-Covenant spy in 1638.

It is a fact that in this period of history with relatively low rates of adult literacy and minimal circulation of any form of newspaper, the pulpit was a major instrument of propaganda. This was one of the main reasons why the Stuart monarchy wanted control of the clergy as a means of enhancing its image and discouraging rebellion. By the same token once the clergy rebelled, as they now did in Scotland, they could exploit this same situation to enhance their own status and aim to dominate the political as well as religious life of the nation; thus they were to turn the southern half of Scotland for a while into a virtual theocracy.

In addition, once finding themselves dominating politics, the clergy also flexed their muscles in matters military, dictating the starting of wars or battles and at times even overruling their professional generals in the field, disastrously, for example, in the Battles of Kilsyth and Dunbar where unwise decisions by ministers turned expected victories into shocking defeats. At least on some occasions, as in the last bitter skirmishes of the Montrose campaign, they urged more savage treatment of defeated forces than was at this time customary amongst the professional soldiers, who regarded the offer of quarter as matter of honour. But spiritual renegades, particularly Catholics, were regarded as outwith any such code of behaviour.

The ministers, of course, regarded their role in supporting warfare as God's work, so they not only contributed to military decisions but also apportioned blame when victory was withheld by the Almighty. Thus defeats such as Preston were blamed on the fact that too many of the soldiers were not righteous enough. So numerous men who had perhaps been heard swearing or seen drinking or playing cards were dismissed with the result that Scotland's army was deprived of many of its most able officers.

The drive for righteousness became almost psychotic after the Battle of Preston, the result of which was blamed by the ministers on the ungodly soldiers. This desire to create a godly society with no trace of sin led amongst other things to the frenetic persecution of witches that began in 1649 when, largely at the behest of local ministers and their sessions, some 300 harmless women were executed without proper trial and often after torture. The most zealous of the witch-hunting ministers was Walter Bruce, the minister of Inverkeithing, who amongst others drove the wretched Lady Pitsligo to death in her cell.

There is no record of any of these ministers, even those who went to battle with the Scottish armies, dying a violent death except for those found in Edinburgh after the Battle of Dunbar when they were blamed by Cromwell's troops for causing the war and by Leslie's men for losing the battle. The majority of priests who were killed during the Wars of Three Kingdoms were Irish Catholics and on several occasions they were shown no mercy, despite having played a far smaller part than the Presbyterians in instigating the seven wars. It was to be different after the Restoration in 1660, when many Covenanting ministers were killed or executed.

Of the men who provided the intellectual rationale for the first and subsequent wars only two were executed. One was James Guthrie (1612–61) who ironically was against the Covenant till 1642 but then became minister at Lauder near Berwick; he was hanged for being a Remonstrant and daring to have tried to excommunicate General Middleton. Charismatically smart, he had an immaculately trimmed moustache and long hair. Having been warned off cheese by his doctor, he chose it for his last meal as no longer likely to damage his health. The other was Archibald Johnston, Lord Warriston, a lawyer by profession but as deeply fanatical as any of his contemporaries; he was captured and executed in 1663 as a long-term contributor to and promoter of the Covenant. Two other prominent ministers who died before the Restoration, Alexander Henderson and David Dickson, had their tombs defaced, as did George Gillespie as soon as Charles II came to power in 1660.

One young minister James Sharp (1612–79), born in Banff and therefore likely to be an episcopalian, changed his ideas for a while when he was made minister of Crail in 1642, but changed them again when offered the post of Archbishop of St Andrews in 1661. He too paid the penalty for extreme views and persecution when eighteen years later the frustrated Covenanters resorted to assassination. Yet apart from the bishops themselves there were a number of ministers who objected strongly to the Covenant, most notably perhaps the immaculately dressed George Wishart (1599–1665) who was deprived of his living in St Andrews by the 1639 General Assembly and was imprisoned in the notoriously unpleasant Thieves Hole of the Edinburgh Tolbooth. He was captured again when the Covenanters besieged Newcastle, and again after the fall of Montrose, of whom he was a great admirer and at whose state funeral he officiated when, at the Restoration, he was made Bishop of Edinburgh while still bearing the scars of prison rat bites.

Back in 1639, there were a significant number of highly articulate and strong-minded opponents of episcopacy, particularly in Fife and

Ayrshire and particularly amongst ex-students of St Andrews and Glasgow Universities. The fact that the chief bishop was based in St Andrews in some respects increased the hostility of the ministers who had studied there. Such strongly Calvinist ministers were a prime source of information and opinion forming for their large congregations and helped create the febrile atmosphere, which became a prelude to war. Locally they had considerable power in their own communities including that of excommunication, which was regarded as a very severe punishment. At this stage they also found a willing audience amongst many of the local landowners, both large and small, many of whom had other grievances against the bishops, particularly financial, so despite differences of class, the lairds and ministers found common ground. In the north east, on the other hand, where most of the ministers had studied at Aberdeen and where most of the lairds were still episcopalian, there was little sympathy with the rebel ministers to the south.

What was special about the Fife ministers, apart from their enthusiasm, was that they not only had like-minded lairds but also amongst them some of the most experienced soldiers in Europe, veterans of the Thirty Years War in Germany. King Gustavus Adolphus of Sweden, who had been the main employer of some 20,000 Scottish mercenaries, had been killed in 1632 whilst winning the Battle of Lützen; his successor Queen Kristina was, in 1637, only eleven years old, so Sweden's war against the German emperors was being downsized. The senior mercenary, newly promoted by Gustavus, was Field Marshal Alexander Leslie who had returned home to recover from his wounds and settled in his newly acquired castle in Fife at Balgonie. But at the age of fifty-seven, despite a bad back, he was far from ready to retire and he was a solid Presbyterian who had been fighting what he regarded as a holy war against the Austrian Catholics for twenty years. What is more, not only were other members of his family also talented soldiers but he had an entire nexus of former subordinates who would be only too happy to earn their salaries fighting in their own country instead of doing so in Germany, Russia or Holland. One of the reasons such a large number of mercenary officers came from Fife had been the entrepreneurial spirit of Sir James Spens of Wormiston (1571–1632), provost of the Fife coastal village of Crail, who established close contacts between the Baltic states and the uxorious lairds of Fife who tended to produce more sons than they could reasonably support, thus establishing a tradition of mercenary recruitment for the Swedish and Danish armies.

One of the other unsung intellects of the Fife Conspiracy was the St Andrews- trained lawyer Sir John Scott of Scotstarvit (1585–1670) who had spent time in Flanders and signed the Covenant promptly at Ceres in 1638. His knowledge of Scots law and history made him a very useful ally of the Fife lairds and ministers. By this time in his mid-fifties, he served behind the scenes on the Edinburgh war committees from 1640 to 1649 and lost much after the conquest by Cromwell. Significantly, his son George became a useful pro-Covenant propagandist and was imprisoned on the Bass Rock before helping to found a small colony in America, which he never reached as he and his wife both died on their ship crossing the Atlantic. Alongside the Scotts, the other expert communicator for the Fife Conspiracy was Peter Hay of Naughton, a neighbour of Balmerino's.

What was also perhaps special about Fife was the degree to which it had been internationalised. Its towns had adopted the Flanders style of building with crow-stepped gables. The farmers had planted flax crops using seed from Holland and there was now a prosperous community of linen weavers, including many Flemish immigrants from the Protestant Low Countries. Flemish fishermen looking for herring called regularly and the Fife coalmines had expanded with indentured miners to provide fuel for export but also to operate the saltpans on the coast, which produced an important export commodity. In addition, there was a regular flow of Scots mercenaries leaving the Fife ports and returning with money and new ideas. All this Continental interaction accounted for the fact that the people in Fife were more aware of European affairs than those further west.

Ministers in Fife, as elsewhere in Scotland during this century, had inherently fickle career prospects for with each change of fashion, they might be dismissed and evicted from their homes. This was true in 1638 for those who rejected the Covenant, in 1645 if they supported Montrose, in 1648 if they backed the Preston campaign, in 1662 if they opposed the return of bishops and in 1690 if they still supported James II. Many thus had to scrape by with outdoor preaching and in the later period this meant exposure to arrest, torture and sometimes execution. Even in a place as remote as Craignish in Argyll, three successive ministers were all deposed, the first in 1645 for opposing the Covenant, the second in 1662 for supporting it, and the third in 1690 for opposing it. A few of them even committed suicide including Edward Thomson, the Minister of Anstruther who drowned himself in the River Dreel after allegedly seeing a black beast. Many others naturally just kept quiet about their views and survived each change of fashion. Others ignored it all and concentrated on their other activities, for many of them owned farms or other properties. Some, however, went a little too far – such as the minister of Ardchattan, Colin Campbell, who was a fine mathematician but was suspended in 1676 for what the *Fasti* quaintly describe as indulging in 'prenuptial intercourse'. However, the ministers from Fife, particularly Alexander Henderson formed the prime driving force behind the rebellion and wars of 1639–40 and the large number of them who joined the Scottish army for the invasion of England that climaxed at Marston Moor demonstrates clearly their conviction that blood should be shed to spread Presbyterianism in both Scotland and England. Several of them were not only learned theologians but also talented publicists and negotiators capable of masterminding a war.

It is clear that the ministers who both studied and then taught at St Andrews University not only had a great influence on each other, potentially sharing the risks of rebellion, but also on the young lairds who went as short-term students. The university had become a sort of finishing school for noblemen's heirs so many were impressed by the Calvinist preachers as, for example, was the future Marquis of Argyll, who won the archery medal in 1623. John Leslie, Earl of Rothes, was there at about the same time and doubtless honed his debating skills. The future General David Leslie won the archery medal three years later, before joining the Swedish army, and the future Marquis of Montrose two years after that. The two Leslies were both Fife men and crucial to the Fife Conspiracy, whilst Argyll and Montrose, both with homes just outside the Fife boundary, were initially strong supporters despite their later fallout.

The Bishops' Doom

Title of a tract by Alexander Henderson

Piscy, Piscy, Amen
Doon on yer knees and up agen

Pro-Covenant street chant of 1638

Chapter 3

THE BISHOPS

A pope, a pope, down with anti-Christ
> Chanted by crowds outside St Giles
> as the Bishop of Edinburgh hid under the stairs

The first two wars were called the Bishops' Wars. Wars are often named after the losing side so if we blame the ministers and their flocks for starting them, then we must blame their opponents the bishops as much if not more.

Bishops had surprisingly not been abolished in Scotland with other institutions of the Catholic Church back in 1557 when Mary Queen of Scots was still clinging to her throne, but this did not sit well with a Calvinist regime run by assemblies. Mary's son, James VI of Scotland and James I of England had, however, been desperately keen to keep bishops, Protestant ones naturally, in order to give him some means of managing both Church and State, particularly as by this time he had moved to London. So he had rigged a vote at the General Assembly in 1618 for the Commissioners to abolish themselves and for their functions be taken over by the bishops. The next twenty years therefore saw an uneasy mixture of authoritarian episcopacy controlled from London or Canterbury and many Presbyterian ministers who did their best to ignore the instructions and in some cases were sacked.

There was an additional problem about resuscitating the bishops and their assistants, the cost. They had big expensive church buildings and lavish lodgings, if not palaces, and since their deans or archdeacons conducted the normal services, the overall cost of church manpower had greatly increased. This was why Charles I, as one of his first reforms in Scotland, had aimed to claw back the old tithe system which, since the Reformation, had been largely taken over by local lairds and aristocrats who then paid the ministers the bare minimum and certainly did not want the expense of bishops. Thus the Scottish land-owning class had strong reasons for objecting to the appointment of bishops and had a vested interest in supporting Presbyterianism.

In the decades leading up to the Bishops' Wars the older bishops had generally kept a low profile and avoided too much confrontation. It was not until William Laud was promoted to be Archbishop of Canterbury that the Anglican Church began to put real pressure on the Church of Scotland to conform. Laud was so much more a high Anglican protestant compared with the Calvinistic Scots that the conformity he demanded was very alien to most parishes.

In addition, Charles I was causing unrest amongst the Scottish noblemen by increasing the political power of the bishops, promoting the elderly Archbishop of St Andrews, John Spotiswood (1565–1639), the Primate of Scotland, to be Chancellor of the Privy Council and increasing the number of bishops on the council to seven. To make it even worse, the archbishop's son Robert was already on the Privy Council.

John Spotiswood, who had been Bishop of Glasgow back in 1610, now just wanted a quiet life and was very reluctant to organise the imposition of the prayer book, which he knew would cause so much trouble. In fact, he was by-passed and the job of editing it was given to four younger bishops, who were more of Laud's choosing. Meanwhile, he made himself unpopular with his local lairds by clawing back from them the income of the old Abbey of St Andrews to help meet his own expenses, which included the large bill for the prayer and service books being secretly printed in Aberdeen. On the one hand Spotiswood was seriously afraid of the effects of publishing the books and initially delayed it, on the other he changed his mind to curry favour in London as part of his plot to have one of his bishops take over from the Earl of Traquair (*see* below) as Treasurer of Scotland, part of the overall plan for churchmen to dominate the government.

One of these was James Wedderburn (1585–1639), the recently appointed Bishop of Dunblane, a Dundee man who had studied at Cambridge, spent time as a vicar in England and was regarded as Laud's 'confidential agent' in Scotland. He was one of the quartet that edited the controversial new prayer book for Scotland. The others were Adam Bellenden (1569–1647), newly appointed Bishop of Aberdeen, formerly at Dunblane; Thomas Sydserf (1581–1663), the aggressive Bishop of Galloway who was suspected of being a Catholic; and John Maxwell (d. 1647), former minister of St Giles and now Bishop of Ross, an example of whose fanaticism was his pursuit of the unfortunate Robert Blair. Blair was expelled a second time, on this occasion from his new refuge in Bangor amongst the Ulster Scots to whom he still preached in the traditional way, and allegedly advocated bodily convulsions as a feature of seeing the light. Sydserf had also dismissed several of his ministers for lack of orthodoxy, including the septuagenarian minister of Kirkcudbright, whose son, the local magistrate, refused to put his father in prison and was himself somewhat naively threatened with imprisonment in his own gaol. Bishop Sydserf's son, also called Thomas, was two decades later to found Scotland's first newspaper.

Similar in attitude to this group was the pistol-carrying Bishop of Brechin, Walter Whitford (1581–1647), who seemed to relish crowd violence and allegedly recommended to the king that he should use force to deal with the troublesome Presbyterians.

The Archbishop of Glasgow Patrick Lindsay (1566–1644), who had Partick Castle as his country residence, was less of a hothead and in poor health but, nevertheless, strongly promoted the new prayer book and was destined to be excommunicated and die in England and extreme poverty. The same fate awaited his slightly younger namesake the Bishop of Edinburgh David Lindsay (1575–1641) who had famously delegated the introduction of the prayer book in his church to his unfortunate deputy, Dr James Hannah. Edinburgh had only acquired a bishop in 1633 when Lindsay conducted the Scottish coronation of Charles I and was rewarded for writing numerous tracts in favour of the divine right of kings to run both Church and State.

Along with these two, the other elderly survivor was George Graeme (1565–1643) who, as Bishop of the Orkneys, could keep well out of trouble. The newest bishop was James Fairlie of Argyll who only had a year in post at Lismore before disaster struck, though he did manage without any resistance to conduct the morning service at St Giles just a couple of hours before the second disastrous one on July 23rd .

Of course none of these bishops were necessarily troublemakers any more than their Presbyterian colleagues, but they were just as fanatically enthusiastic as them to have a uniform religion for all four nations of the British Isles and were ready to impose this by force if necessary. For that reason they were already, like the English bishops, using new High Commission courts to impose their will. They were also claiming the right to supervise the appointment of all school teachers and extending their powers to control the nation's finance.

Eight of these bishops were to be excommunicated fifteen months after the St Giles incident but none of them were to die in battle, though they did have to suffer significant hardship and financial loss. Of the clerics on both sides of the divide, first the anti-Laud ministers were dismissed from their jobs and had to make do as freelance preachers, then after 1640 many of the pro-Laud priests were deprived of their livings and quite a number sought refuge in England.

Manipulating them all, though they resented it, was their master William Laud (1573–1645) who had become Archbishop of Canterbury only four years earlier at the age of sixty after a career mainly in academia. This had encouraged him to develop very fixed views about the style, discipline and dignity of church services, to be obsessive about details such as the decoration of altars, kneeling for communion, blessing baptismal waters, addressing the bread and wine, clerical surplices, stained glass and fixed formats for prayer. Apart from technically different views on original sin and the elements in communion, there were not any basic differences in doctrine between the Anglo-Lutheran and the Scoto-Calvinistic versions of Protestantism, but the English style was much closer to Catholicism. In addition, Laud in conjunction with his master Charles I of Great Britain and Ireland was desperate to make bishops not only the disciplinarians of a strictly uniform church, but to make them arbiters of State policy and public morality. Laud had used courts such as the Star Chamber to enforce his policies and similar procedures had begun in Scotland. The Fife earl, Lord Balmerino, had only just been reprieved from execution after his trial for daring to criticise the Anglo-style service at King Charles's Scottish coronation in 1633. Numerous ministers had been dismissed from their parishes and had to scratch a living for their families as freelance preachers.

One man who perhaps surprisingly was never appointed a bishop was Walter Balcanquhal (1586–1645), whose father of the same name had been a strongly Presbyterian minister in Edinburgh. Young Walter, by contrast, moved to Cambridge, became an Anglican priest and later chaplain, initially to James VI & I, then to the Marquis of Hamilton, at the same time being in 1639 made Dean of Durham. Regarded as one of the most virulent writers of anti-Covenant pamphlets, he became a hate-figure in Scotland and was specifically excluded from the Act of Oblivion in 1641, was harassed and maltreated even in England, and died in extreme poverty.

The dismissal of the bishops from their sees was followed in significant numbers by the dismissals of parish ministers who for various reasons supported the old regime, some perhaps because they had nursed hopes of being bishops themselves, others out of loyalty either to their old bishops or to the lairds who had given them their stipends. Over the next fifty years the job security of parish ministers was to be very limited as many were culled in successive changes of fashion, particularly as we shall see in 1638, 1650, 1660 and 1688.

Chapter 4

THE LAIRDS

Exorbitant powers were given to the bishops and the increased importance with which they were invested was calculated to excite the jealousy and alarm of the nobility.

Thomas Wright: *History of Scotland*

It was two Fife landowners who made the first serious stand against Charles I's religious policies and both of them were to play a key role in promoting the Bishops' Wars, which in turn helped provoke the English Civil Wars.

The first was John Elphinstone, Lord Balmerino (d. 1649), who had made a brave protest against the elaborate Anglican style of Charles's coronation in Edinburgh in 1633. A well-educated man, it seems likely he had attended St Andrews University briefly as a teenager as it was at that time seen as a finishing school for young lairds. He expressed disgust at the gold vestments of the bishops, the elaborate kneelings and bowings that day in St Giles. For this he was immediately arrested, then tried and condemned to death, only saved from execution because the king's advisers warned that such a punishment would cause public outrage. Balmerino also had a vested interest in objecting to the increased costs of the Church since he had to provide salaries for several ministers in his villages. Thus in 1637 he joined the team of Fife lairds and ministers who were drawing up plans for mass agitation, then backed the writing of the Covenant and, in due course, preparations for war. He played a personal role in demanding the surrender of the royal castle and important ammunition depot at Dalkeith and later helped write the controversial letter intended for the French king Louis XIII in which he referred to 'the tyrannical proceedings of Charles I'. He was perhaps too old for active military service but he did hand over a sum of 50,000 merks to help fit out the new Scottish army. As a man who had already shown his willingness to die for the cause, he was a significant force in providing credibility to the group of anti-episcopal lairds in Fife.

The second of the main Fife promoters of resistance, and later war, was John Leslie, Earl of Rothes (1600–1641), whose motives were perhaps not entirely idealistic – he was described as 'a man addicted to pleasure'. He too had done a short course at St Andrews, as we know had two other earls, Argyll and Montrose. Originally from a Speyside family but now based at Leslie in Fife, Rothes had been involved as a twenty-year-old in the protests against the policies of James VI & I when the king was trying to claw back for the Church lands that had been handed over to the lay gentry after the Reformation (the Five Articles of Perth). Rothes treated this as a matter of principle but basically he and his like did not want to see any erosion of their own wealth and resented the increased costs of the Stuart expansion of the ecclesiastical hierarchy. So it suited him to join forces with the local ministers who had quite different reasons for opposing the bishops, many of them simply contemptuous of what they regarded as the extravagant pomp and rigidity of Anglican style services that reminded them of Catholicism.

Rothes left a detailed account of the series of meetings he attended with fellow rebels between August and December 1637, and had also been involved in several secret meetings before the St Giles riot. By this time he appeared to have become a genuine and fanatical hater of the new style services. Thus, as leader of the Fife Conspiracy, Rothes formed a team with Alexander Henderson from Leuchars; James Wilson, his family chaplain based in Dysart; the lawyer Warriston, and others, to organise both the new Covenant and the meeting of the General Assembly in Glasgow in 1638. He also personally cultivated his new neighbour and distant relation Field Marshal Alexander Leslie, who had recently retired from the Swedish army and bought Balgonie Castle, just 3 miles from his own base at Leslie. To seal their relationship, Leslie's son, a colonel in the Swedish army, had married Rothes' daughter. Between them they then persuaded General David Leslie, who was his cousin from the Lindores branch of the family, to retire from the Swedish army, thus providing the Scottish rebellion with two highly professional and effective commanders and three colonels, Alexander Leslie's son Alexander, his son-in-law Hugh Fraser of the dragoons, and David Leslie's brother Ludovic. Rothes himself seems to have been short of money and in poor health, for he was granted a parliamentary salary shortly before he died in 1641. However because of his family connections and the location of his home, he probably had more influence in starting the succession of wars than any other single person.

In addition to the Leslies, Fife also had several branches of the Lindsay clan, which had produced two of the current bishops but also several who shared the views of Rothes. Indeed they shared churches with Rothes at Markinch and Dysart. Ludovic Lindsay (1600–1652), Earl of Crawford, had taken over the earldom from his unstable brother and was himself somewhat eccentric. Later a close follower of Montrose, he had an erratic military career, fighting for the English Royalists at Edgehill, an act for which he was stripped of his earldom by the Scottish Parliament. He was captured by the Scots at Newcastle, somehow escaped execution and died in exile in Holland. His earldom meanwhile went to a distant cousin who was slightly less impetuous, John Lindsay of the Byres (1598–1678), who was already Earl Lindsay and a keen ally of the Leslies. Back in 1633, he had already shown defiance against Charles I by standing up for the beleaguered Balmerino. With his properties at Struthers near Cupar and Wormiston near Crail, he, or possibly his predecessor Ludovic, chose the future archbishop James Sharp as parish minister of Crail. John was to be a prominent supporter of the war and his son William Lindsay (1645–98) was to become a fanatical Presbyterian, an active opponent of the Stuarts and significant supporter of William of Orange.

The third Fife branch of the Lindsays were the Earls of Balcarres, who had moved from Angus and built Balcarres House near Elie. Alexander Lindsay (1618–1659) was a strong supporter of the Covenant having been tutored at St Andrews by David Forret, who encouraged him. Alexander was also a close friend of the man who had married his sister Sophia, Sir Robert Moray of Craigie, a mercenary officer in French pay who later acted as an agent for arms supply. Their friend the Earl of Lauderdale was also a frequent visitor to Balcarres. Alexander's ties to the Leslies were close as he married the rich and glamorous ward of Rothes, Anna Mackenzie, who successfully grew bergamot pear trees from pips supplied from France by Robert Moray. Alexander fought with his cavalry regiment alongside David Leslie and Cromwell at Marston Moor, paying much of the cost out of his own pocket, though he was eventually almost bankrupt, despite selling his wife's jewels. Initially quite wealthy as his lands included coalmines and saltpans, the leading export commodities of the region, his outlays in keeping his tenants and their horses equipped for battle were considerable. He continued fighting for the Covenant when the Covenanters became Royalists in 1649 and died disillusioned in exile in Holland at the age of forty-one, having fallen out with both the extreme Covenanters and Charles II. His cousin Patrick Lindsay of Wormiston fought for the Covenanting Royalists at Worcester and was captured by Cromwell's troops. It was Alexander and Anna's feisty daughter Sophia Lindsay who, in 1682, organised the dramatic escape of her stepfather the Earl of Argyll from Edinburgh Castle.

A third strongly Presbyterian family with castles in or close to Fife were the Balfours. Robert Arnot (1600–1663) changed his name to Balfour when he married the heiress of Burleigh and as a key ally of Rothes was chosen president of the Scottish Estates in 1640. He helped negotiate the Treaty of Ripon and twice fought unsuccessfully against Montrose as a Covenanter general. He later had a massive row with his son John (d. 1688) who had become something of a rake and without permission married a distant cousin, the daughter of Sir William Balfour of Pitcullo who as an ex-mercenary in the Dutch army had risen to be a general in the English royal army. Balfour was to be governor of the Tower of London in 1640 when his fellow Presbyterian Campbell of Loudoun was sent there to be executed. As we shall see he prevented the execution and changed sides to fight for the Parliamentarians at Edgehill. Sir James Balfour of Kinnaird (1600–58) the poet and antiquarian helped write the ballad *Stoneyfield Day* commemorating the Jenny Geddes affair; he had been knighted by King Charles in 1633. The other most notorious Balfour was John Balfour of Kinloch near Cupar, one of the team that murdered Archbishop Sharp and fought for the Covenanters at both Drumclog and Bothwell Bridge.

A fourth group of anti-episcopal families in Fife included the Colvilles of Wemyss, recently made Earls of Culross, and their near neighbours the Wemyss family, whose head John Wemyss (1586–1649) had been promoted to Earl of Elcho. Significantly it was in his lodgings in Edinburgh that one of the key meetings of protesters took place in 1637, led by Earls Rothes, Balmerino, Lindsay and Loudoun, a more comfortable setting than some of the earlier meetings which had been near the 'stinking styll'. Significantly, the Earl of Loudoun's mother was a Colville and though now based in Ayrshire, he thus had strong Fife connections – his daughter married Balmerino's son – and with Rothes he was to be one of the two prime organisers of the armed rebellion. As Rothes himself put it of the 1637 meetings 'there were a great many gentlemen, especially out of Fife.'

Two of Scotland's great landowners of this time stand out because in different ways they exploited the problems of Charles I to flirt with the idea of themselves becoming kings of Scotland in his place. The less likely of the two was James Hamilton (1606–49), Marquis (later 1st Duke) of Hamilton; the other was Archibald Campbell, currently as Lord Lorn heir to the earldom of Argyll but shortly to inherit that title on the death of his disgraced father and later still to be promoted to Marquis. Having chosen widely different routes to power, both of them paid for their ambition when years later they were to be executed as traitors.

James Hamilton's rather tenuous claim to the throne was based on the fact that so many of the Stuart dynasty had died young over the past three generations; this meant that as a descendant of James II's daughter Mary, he was one of the only cousins left of Charles I. In fact, until 1628, he was third in line to the throne of Britain. Born in Hamilton Castle (later Palace), he had a strongly Presbyterian mother who later threatened to shoot him when he supported the policies of Archbishop Laud. Meanwhile he spent much of his early career cultivating the London court, but in 1631, surprisingly given his total lack of military experience, he enlisted some 6,000 men from the Scottish Lowlands to go and fight for the Protestant side in the Thirty Years War. The Swedish king Gustavus Adolphus immediately allocated one of his favourite Scottish mercenaries Field Marshal Alexander Leslie to be his mentor and a Lieutenant General or Colonel Archibald Douglas to run his artillery alongside his distant cousin Alexander 'Sandy' Hamilton. This Scottish force saw little real fighting though they held the River Oder whilst the main army fought the Battle of Breitenfeld. Allegedly under-armed and underfed, they were cast adrift during the siege of Magdeburg, so Gustavus Adolphus and Hamilton parted company on poor terms. Back in London, Hamilton was made a Privy Counsellor and five years later became chief adviser to Charles I on all Scottish affairs. It was in this role that he dealt with the aftermath of the Jenny Geddes incident and vainly tried to achieve a peaceful solution. He was later to be rewarded with a dukedom, which as he only had daughters was, after his execution, to pass to this brother William, another noted Royalist despite being later imprisoned for two years by the king (1644–46).

Hamilton's perceived rival as potential king of Scotland was Archibald Campbell (1598–1661), at this time still known as Lord Lorn for he only became Earl of Argyll in 1639 on the death of his father. His even more tenuous claim to the crown was based on his descent three centuries earlier from the sister of Robert the Bruce. To help matters, Thomas the Rhymer had produced a handy little prophesy suggesting 'that of the Bruce's blood shall come' a new king eight generations later. If this was a flimsy recommendation, far more impressive was the fact that Campbell was the largest landowner in Scotland and could raise a personal army of 5,000 men from his own clan, far more than any other individual clan except for the Gordons. The family's huge landholdings had increased during the regime of his father who had conducted a series of ethnic cleansing operations on the west coast, mainly aimed at Macdonalds and Catholics.

Due to the expense of his military and building activities, his father had somewhat overstretched his current assets, had come close to bankruptcy and twenty years earlier had absconded with his new Catholic wife to join the Spanish army. The ginger-haired Lord Lorn had thus, after a spell at St Andrews, devoted his abilities to straightening out the Campbell finances and overcoming the disgrace when his father was declared a traitor. However, it was excellent experience and by 1637 he was recognised as one of the ablest as well richest men in Scotland, a Privy Counsellor, an apparently sincere and loyal Presbyterian, who had become a great admirer of Alexander Henderson. He had conveniently gathered in more former Church property than most, and imported lowland ministers to anglicise the Argyll parishes. The huge disruption following the Jenny Geddes affair simply created an ideal opportunity for him to play a national role, which was sufficiently blatant for him soon to be referred to as King Campbell.

If his hopes of a crown were fairly distant he still could fall back on the continued expansion of his vast estates in the west as the crisis was a useful excuse for driving out more of the Macdonalds, Macleans and their kindred to northern Ireland. He was highly mobile, with his private fortresses straddling Scotland from Castle Campbell at Dollar, to Rosneath on the Clyde, and Inveraray on Loch Fyne, the last two of which he could travel to on his personal forty-oared birlinn. Dollar was just a few miles from Fife so he was in close touch with the Fife conspirators, aided by the fact that he had studied at St Andrews and as a youngster shared foster parents with the future Field Marshal Leslie, albeit with a gap of two decades.

Other Campbells feature in this period but without question the most articulate and politically adroit was John Campbell (1598–1662), a distant cousin of the clan chief and recently in 1633 promoted by King Charles to be the Earl of Loudoun. Born a highlander on the slopes of Ben Lawers by Loch Tay, John Campbell had been brought up a near neighbour of Lord Lorn and Alexander Leslie's foster parents. He had probably also had a brief spell at St Andrews, had done some travelling abroad and was very well read. What is more his mother Jean Colville came from Wemyss in Fife and her father had been made Earl of Culross. John Campbell had, in 1622, made a brilliant marriage to the heiress of another Campbell branch based in lowland Ayrshire at Loudoun. He was spotted as a natural leader at the time of Charles I's coronation but he was shocked by the treatment of Balmerino, with whom he established another Fife connection for his daughter married Balmerino's son. So Loudoun was, by 1637, already opposed to the king's religious policies and soon after the Jenny Geddes incident became one of the main spokesmen for the Presbyterian cause. He was perhaps encouraged by his local minister the fanatical John Neaves or Nevoy who was the recently appointed minister at Loudoun and Newmilns east of Kilmarnock, an area that later became renowned for extreme Covenanters and lace weaving. In due course Campbell of Loudoun was to turn out in the wars with his own regiment and undertook a dangerous mission to London, which ended with a spell in the Tower, only just escaping execution. He continued as a major power in Scottish politics and fought in several of the main battles, including Marston Moor.

The third Campbell to be involved was Duncan Campbell of Auchinbreck, a small, now-vanished castle north of Dunoon. Something of a thug, he was employed as Argyll's chief hatchet man and rewarded with two large extra castles at Carnasserie and on Loch Sween. Almost at the start of the crisis, Argyll was to make use of him as an ethnic cleanser in Kintyre, later to be sent on a genocidal mission to Ulster and finally to meet his nemesis at Inverlochy in 1645.

Since we have introduced three Campbells who exploited the prayer book crisis it seems only reasonable to bring in the two most relevant Macdonalds, though they had adapted their surname to the Irish spelling

Macdonnell. Randal Macdonnell (1609–82), based in the dramatic Ulster castle of Dunluce, was the grandson of the famous Sorley Boy Macdonnell who had built up his power with the help of shipwrecked Armada cannons. Brought up in the London court, Ranald had dutifully married the widow of the late Duke of Buckingham and was made Earl of Antrim in 1636, groomed for a starring Royalist role in northern Ireland, now seen as a potential source of angry Catholic warriors desperate to claw back their heritage in Scotland. As it turned out there was more talk than action from Antrim himself, but the mere threat of an attack by him on the Scottish coast was to motivate strong defensive measures by the Scots.

His distant cousin Alastair McColla Macdonnell (1610–47) was another matter. A tall man of immense strength, he had been born on the island of Colonsay off the west coast of Argyll, which had been the base of his father – known by his nickname of Kolkitto or Left-handed. Like many Macdonalds who had been forced out of the better lands on the west coast, Alastair inherited a long-term thirst for revenge and meanwhile Kolkitto had made ends meet by a spot of piracy. His son, also sometimes referred to as Kolkitto, was about thirty when the Campbells launched their raids on Ulster and he was to lead the amazing counterattack with Montrose. A brilliant field commander, he was credited with inventing the so-called 'Highland charge', a throwback to a more old-fashioned style of fighting that for some years was extremely successful in intimidating the slow-loading musketeers who were the backbone of most armies at this time.

Thus the rivalries and disputed territories of the Campbells and Macdonalds dictated the fact that the Campbells would for the next ten years be anti-Royalist whilst the Macdonalds, both in Ireland and Scotland, would support the king. The vast majority of the families north of the Highland line shared the Macdonald strategy.

One other Scottish landowner with Fife connections who stands out as an immediate champion of the church-inspired rebellion was young James Graham (1612–50), Earl of Montrose, whose main base was Kincardine Castle by Auchterarder, where he patronised the local Presbyterian church just a few miles west of Fife. He had also studied briefly at St Andrews where he was a medal-winning archer and a fine horseman. He had married as a teenager and had two children before heading to France for a year, where he appears to have attended the military college at Angers. Having returned in 1637, via London, looking for some post at court, he felt snubbed by both Hamilton and the king, so he was still looking for some outlet for his talents at the time of the Jenny Geddes incident. He immediately joined forces with Leslie and the two Campbells, played a prominent role in the Glasgow Assembly and quickly sought the limelight during the first three wars. Despite lack of formal military experience, he soon showed exceptional flare as a strategist and charismatic leader, though in the process he also gained a reputation for devious plots and dubious allegiances that in the end were to cost him his head. For some years he seemed basically unsure of which side he supported or which side would win him the greater glory.

Amongst the small number of the king's relations still living in Scotland was John Stewart, Earl of Traquair (d. 1659) who had been Lord High Treasurer of Scotland since 1630. It was he who foresaw the dire consequences of executing Balmerino and persuaded the king to let him go. He was chief lay adviser to Charles I on the introduction of the new liturgy in 1637, basically suggesting great caution to avoid the considerable unrest that he was shrewd enough to foresee. He was, however, trapped between a very obstinate king and some very angry subjects.

The other prominent Stewart and one of the French cousins of the king was James Stuart, Duke of Lennox (1612–55), who fell foul of the new bishops when he lost a lot of tithe income round St Andrews and was far from a supporter of Laud. However his career was mainly in England as a Royalist and he played minor roles such as the defence of Oxford in 1643, before dying in his early forties. Three of his French-born brothers were killed fighting for the king, including the charismatic Bernard Stuart.

Numerous other lairds brought their troops and appeared themselves at the head of them during the two Bishops' Wars, many fought at Marston Moor, some at Preston, Dunbar and Worcester. John Kennedy (d. 1668), Earl of Cassilis, was an early supporter and patron of the radical minister George Gillespie. He came to the First Bishop's War at the head of his own troops and did so several times more including at Marston Moor, where he must have attracted Cromwell's attention for he was made a member of the new English House of Lords.

Most of the Douglas clan were Royalist, but the border laird William Douglas of Cavers (d. 1658), sheriff of Teviotdale, was an active Covenanter who played an important but dangerous role in the

1640 mission to London; seven of his sister's sons were killed fighting Montrose at Auldearn.

One of the other rare early Royalists from the southern half of Scotland was Robert Dalzell, Earl of Carnwath, who at his own expense took a regiment to fight for the king at Edgehill and allegedly employed his remarkable half-sister Francis as a captain of his cavalry.

Amongst the more cautious supporters of the Covenant was John Maitland, the future Earl of Lauderdale, (1616–82). Certainly he signed the Covenant in 1638 but at the age of twenty-two was perhaps too young to play a serious role in the events that followed. Five years later, he was a participant in the General Assembly and soon afterwards became one of the key negotiators of the alliance with the English Parliamentarians, meeting at the Westminster Assembly. Within a year he was made a Privy Counsellor in both England and Scotland. He was also in London in 1647 when Charles I surrendered and by that time perhaps no longer believed the English Parliament would keep its promise of spreading Presbyterianism south of the border. So at this point he changed sides, believing that the king would be a better ally than Parliament. He organised a daring attempt to rescue the king from English captivity but Charles refused his help. Later Lauderdale helped do the deal known as the Engagement, which committed the Scots to the disastrous Preston campaign. By this time a dedicated Royalist, he had a secret meeting with the king's son on the Downs and next played a key role in organising yet another disastrous campaign, which ended at Worcester where he was taken prisoner. However, of all the combatant lairds, he came out the winner for he was rewarded in 1660 with the position of Secretary of State for Scotland, and became the L in the notorious CABAL, an acronym for the names of the five Privy Counsellors – Clifford, Arlington, Buckingham, Ashley-Cooper and Lauderdale. The Cabal ministry also refers to the fact that for perhaps the first time in English history, effective power in a royal council was shared by a group of men, rather than the king's favourite. Lauderdale was made a Duke in 1672. He had no son, so the Dukedom did not survive him.

Most of these noble dynasties were linked with each other by marriage, which sometimes helped cement their political and religious leanings, but not always. The same was true of the clergymen who frequently married daughters of the manse or even the spare daughters of lairds.

Of the main Scottish lairds who joined in the Wars of the Three Kingdoms none were killed in battle except the 2nd Duke of Hamilton who died of his wounds at Worcester. Four were executed: James, Marquis of Montrose; James, 1st Duke of Hamilton; Archibald, Marquis of Argyll, and George Gordon, Earl of Huntly, (1592–1649). This last laird was different for his was an aristocratic family in Scotland whose attitude to the whole conflict was more obscure; the Gordons with their massive estates in north east Scotland provided nearly as much manpower as the Campbells. Though many of his clan were Catholic, Huntly had been brought up in the court in England as a Lutheran Protestant and as a supporter of bishops. He was thus one of the very few major figures in Scotland to be a Royalist right from the start, and turned down a massive bribe from the Covenanters, who offered to pay off his huge £100,000 debts if he would support them. Charles secretly appointed him his Lieutenant in Scotland and Huntly therefore represented a significant potential danger in the rear for the Covenanters throughout the various wars, so Aberdeen was to change hands several times and suffer severe damage. He had a number of allied families, notably the Ogilvys, but he also now had a number of anti-episcopal families on his own doorstep, such as the Frasers and Seaforths.

Many of these families were to endure the hardships of war and devastation over the next ten years, to fall in and out of favour. We shall see that their children often did not share their views, thus the Lindsays and Leslies, so prominent as supporters of the Covenant in this generation, were to produce sons with quite different loyalties. The huge influence wielded by the Covenanting ministers was a threat to their own positions as leaders of the community. It also became evident that the hereditary antipathies of neighbouring lairds often helped shape their attitudes to religion, as did the possibility of lucrative rewards for following one side or another. It is also clear that their attitudes were often strongly influenced by their wives.

Chapter 5

THE ROYALS

I would rather die than yield.

Letter from Charles I

It must be said of the last three Stuart kings that all of them were deeply committed to the idea of episcopacy, not perhaps so much for religious reasons as because the clergy of the established Church were a key element in the infrastructure of monarchy. They provided their own layer of aristocracy, which was often more reliable than their lay counterparts. They were also a key medium for propaganda, using the pulpit to spread the Royalist message. They were important cogs in the wheels that taught civil obedience and justified autocracy on the basis of the divine right of kings. On the other hand, if the Church became genuinely presbyterian instead of being part of the infrastructure for monarchy, it would be a breeding ground for democracy – the last thing the Stuarts wanted.

It is also a fact that of the four Stuart kings, three had a Catholic mother and three married Catholic wives, though in the case of James II his first wife was a Protestant. This inevitably influenced all three of them, not just to lean towards their wives' religious proclivities but also to the political atmosphere of the countries from which they came: France, Portugal and Italy.

Ironically Charles I (1600–49) was born in Dunfermline in Fife, just a few miles from his future tormentors, but he left Scotland as a small child and had very few Scottish genes in his system. His mother was a Danish/German princess, so he had two Germanic grandparents on that side, with a half-French grandmother, Mary Queen of Scots, on the other. The remaining genes were a mixture concocted by the

Stewart/Stuart dynasty's long-term habit of acquiring Continental wives. His childhood had been plagued by rickety legs, a severe stammer, so he was slow to talk, slow to walk, slow to read and on the short side, though he had a stubborn streak to overcome all difficulties. He also initially suffered from a feeling of neglect or inferiority since he was for many years the spare heir and his more loveable big brother Prince Henry was, until his early death, very much the favourite son. Henry died in 1612 and Charles became Prince of Wales in a court dominated by his father's favourite, the Duke of Buckingham, to whom he surprisingly looked up, despite the public nature of his father's obsession.

Thus when his father James VI & I died in 1625, Charles had more or less matured. He spent his time out hunting at Oatlands or elsewhere three or four days a week and at least another half-day a week on his artistic or theatrical interests, for to overcome his shyness he delighted in performing personally in court masques. Immaculate in his grooming with perfectly trimmed beard and moustache, he remained a little conscious of his height, allegedly 5 feet 4 inches or less, so he made sure that it was disguised as much as possible. He was to last as king for twenty-four years and though he seemed to change his mind on many things, one theme was absolutely consistent: he had been chosen by God to be the king of England, Scotland and Ireland. He would delegate the tiresome details to his favourite officers of state but accept advice or instruction from no one, unless it was what he wanted. This was in tune with his father's other great strategy, which was that given his distrust of most lay individuals, particularly members of parliament, the best way to run the country was by having a core of bishops chosen by himself and obedient to himself.

Unfortunately, his father had left him serious financial problems. Due to his failure to manage parliament there was no proper budget, the finances were on a knife-edge, there was only a very small army and the navy had been so neglected that the Channel and North Sea were thick with pirates. For various reasons, Charles's plan to marry a Spanish princess came to nothing and with ill grace he accepted a French one as a poor alternative. However, after a few years of mutual antipathy the husband and wife settled down to each other and Henrietta became a loyal and equally stubborn bastion of his power. He sent her huge French retinue back to France; the only remaining problem was that she was a devout Catholic, so he was inhibited from persecuting other British Catholics, a tendency that contributed to his unpopularity. It also made him more sympathetic to the high Anglican rituals favoured by Archbishop Laud.

Within three years of commencing his reign, Charles had fallen out with parliament, disgusted with their refusal to grant him additional taxes, and had clearly made up his mind to pursue every source of finance that did not require a parliamentary blessing. The most controversial of these was Ship Money, which he started to levy from the English ports semi-legitimately in 1634, but then much less legitimately from inland areas two years later.

Our concern here is not so much with the actions that made him unpopular in England as those which, one way or another, affected the Scots. Having chosen William Laud as Bishop of London in 1628, he promoted him to Canterbury in 1633 and gave him wholehearted support for the suppression of Puritan sects in England and Presbyterianism in Scotland, the policy that produced the Jenny Geddes crisis four years later. The other key promotion, which potentially affected Scotland, was that of the Earl of Strafford or Black Tom Wentworth who, like Laud, was earmarked to be an instrument of autocracy. Though Strafford's main work was in Ireland, there was the threat of his troops from Ireland, possibly even Catholic troops, being sent across to cow the Scots into submission. This fear was to be a major contributory factor in the Scots taking the initiative to attack first, in 1639. That Scottish attack was, in turn, to be the primary cause of the First English Civil War.

Meanwhile Charles had already been crowned King of England for eight years before he ventured north to be crowned King of Scotland, but when he did so he chose to make the ceremony in St Giles a big public demonstration of all the new trappings of Anglican style and ritual. This was a stark warning of what was to come four years later and an immediate affront to many who attended it, particularly Lord Balmerino, who only just avoided execution for voicing his complaints.

Whilst Charles was always short of money he was able to be remarkably generous with one form of bribery that cost him nothing. He could promote men up the honours list in a way that, even though the value of the titles was rather cheapened by overuse, they still carried significant weight amongst socially ambitious men. Thus barons were made earls, earls were made marquises, successful soldiers were made knights and earls and there was even a new Scottish dukedom, that of Hamilton. Patently this bribery did not always have much effect but certainly the Scottish promotions probably did contribute to the rash decisions before the campaign that ended disastrously at Preston.

Apart from his wife and children, Charles had very few surviving relations. His sister Elizabeth, the ex-Queen of Bohemia, had fallen out with him over his refusal to offer significant military assistance for her eldest son to regain his inheritance of the Palatinate. Her two younger sons did, of course, come to their uncle's aid in 1642. Prince Rupert (1619–82), half-Stuart and half-Wittelsbach, had, despite his youth, already had experience as a professional mercenary fighting in both the Dutch and Swedish armies and enduring a period as a prisoner of war. Thus at the age of only twenty-three he became commander of the Royalist cavalry, and was to become renowned for his impetuously dashing charges. These were almost always initially successful but he tended to neglect the mopping-up stages of the battle as he let his men pursue the enemy far from the battlefield. They chased after booty when what was needed was a disciplined regrouping to finish off the main battle. After Marston Moor, Rupert's position soon became untenable and he created a new one for himself as admiral of the Royalist Navy, which he used to harass the Parliamentary fleet as well as to prey on merchant shipping. After the Restoration, he was to become a dabbler in the slave trade, the expansion of the Hudson's Bay Company, an inventor of new gunpowder recipes and a novel form of mezzotint.

Rupert's brother Maurice (1629–52) was an equally versatile leader of cavalry who fought in numerous battles before he too joined the fleet and was eventually drowned during a hurricane in the Caribbean.

Of Charles's other relations James Hamilton, for some time officially the closest to the throne, as we have seen, proved ineffective as a negotiator during the prayer book crisis and as a commander, both on land and at sea, despite his year or so with Alexander Leslie and King Gustavus in Germany. Similarly his leadership of the Engagement campaign was to be disastrous and result in his own execution.

The four Stuart brothers from the French branch of the family included the Duke of Lennox who was loyal but of limited value, perhaps largely due to failing health – he died in his early forties. The other three all died in battle: George, Lord of Aubigny, leading his men at Edgehill; Bernard of Lichfield at Rowton Heath; and the youngest, John, as a general of horse at Alvesford. Charles Stuart, grandson of the notorious Frances Stuart, was killed fighting as an ordinary trooper at Worcester. Sir Robert Stewart, survivor of the infamous Orkney branch of the dynasty, outlasted the war, fighting mainly in Ireland where he captured Sligo and settled afterwards in Londonderry.

More important during the later period of the civil wars were Charles's two sons, Charles, Prince of Wales (1630–85), and James, Duke of York (1633–1701). It was after extracting a promise from young Charles that he would introduce Presbyterianism to England, Wales and Ireland that the Scottish minister, Robert Douglas, agreed to conduct his coronation as Charles II and to the plan for sending an army into England to restore him to the throne so that he could impose Presbyterianism on the English. That was the disastrous expedition that ended in Worcester, the fourth time that the Scots had invaded England in a dozen years. Nine years later in 1660 when Charles was in fact restored, he almost immediately undertook the abolition of Presbyterianism in Scotland, a sad reward for all the blood shed trying to spread it to England.

James, Duke of York, even before he took over as king from his brother in 1685, had already made a name for himself for the persecution of Covenanters and for currying favour with the highland chiefs by encouraging them to raid the estates of the Presbyterians. During his brief stay in Edinburgh as Duke of York he was nevertheless quite popular as he revived concerts and theatre performances, which had been taboo under the Covenanter regime and, as a keen golfer on Leith Links, was amongst the first to use the term caddie, which up to this time had been the nickname for Edinburgh street porters. From the religious point of view, he was further 'to the right' than either his father or brother. In 1688 he was to self-destruct his brief reign by trying to manage a revival of Catholicism, which made him far more unpopular than the two Charleses had ever been. Both his son James the Old Pretender and his grandson Bonnie Prince Charlie were to be staunch Catholics so that both their two main wars to regain the Stuart throne had religious connotations and owed much to the example set by the Scots Presbyterians between 1640 and 1651.

One other member of the Stuart dynasty was to play a short but important role in Scotland. This was James, Duke of Monmouth, eldest illegitimate son of Charles II, who was put in charge of Scotland for the Bothwell Bridge campaign and who advocated a more conciliatory policy until he was unfortunately replaced by his intolerant uncle, the future James II. With the Earl of Argyll, he was later to lead an ill-organised attack on James II in 1685, which ended with the execution of both Duke and Earl.

Chapter 6

THE PROFESSIONALS

... two Scottish officers, Leslie and King, turned the tables on his assailants

C.V. Wedgewood: *The Thirty Years War*

Perhaps never before or since has there been such a large number of highly experienced and successful army officers born in Scotland, particularly Fife. Driven abroad by lack of useful employment at home, many of them were younger sons of the landed class who had been attracted by the rewards of fighting in Germany and Holland during the two great Continental wars, the Dutch Eighty Years War and the German Thirty Years War. Most of them had preferred the Protestant side in both wars, many of them had risen to high ranks and won considerable prestige, and most were tempted to return to Britain when rebellion and civil war were on the horizon and there was considerable demand for experienced officers. The same was true of several English and Irish mercenary officers, whose experience made them excellent candidates for quick promotion.

It was John Leslie, Earl of Rothes, who in 1638 made contact with his two relations Alexander and David Leslie and they needed little encouragement to respond positively. Alexander Leslie (1580–1661), later Earl of Leven, was born in Blair Atholl as the illegitimate son of a Leslie, possibly George Leslie of Balgonie, who had a fling with a local 'Rannoch wench'. The boy had been fostered by Campbells of Glenorchy, by coincidence the same family that a few years later also fostered the future young Earl of Argyll when his father had absconded. He was thus also brought up close to the home of the

Campbells of Lawers, one of whom was to become the politically active and very able Earl of Loudoun. Alexander Leslie, after a few years learning his trade in the Dutch army, had by this time spent three decades fighting for the Swedes and though barely literate, had proven himself such a resourceful general in Sweden's attack on the imperial forces of Germany that he had been promoted to Field Marshal by King Gustavus Adolphus just before the king's death at Lützen in 1632. Badly wounded and threatened with retirement in 1635, Alexander nevertheless made a remarkable comeback and was given credit for a key victory over the German imperial forces at Wittstock, north of Berlin in 1636. With his earnings he had been able to purchase Balgonie Castle (possibly once the home of his father) in Fife in 1635 and as a middle-aged married man, he had a grown-up family including a son Alexander who had served under him as a colonel and in 1636 was married to Rothes' daughter Margaret. His son-in-law Hugh Fraser, who had been in charge of his dragoons, was still in Germany.

On his return to Scotland he had rapidly become friendly with his neighbour Rothes and having, as his correspondence shows, spent decades fighting in a holy war against the Austrians he was quite receptive to the idea of a holy war in his own country. It is clear that as the post-Geddes tension increased, Rothes and Balmerino were expecting a royal backlash so the presence of such an experienced soldier in their midst suggested that it made sense for the Covenanters to use Leslie's expertise to create a new army of their own. To give added encouragement Alexander Leslie had returned from Germany with his family via London and seems to have passed on his impression that half the English were by this time Calvinist and might be allies rather than enemies if it came to war. What he could not, of course, foresee was that within a few years many of those Calvinists would have shifted ground to become independent sectarians who disliked presbyteries nearly as much as they did bishops.

Meanwhile Leslie's task was therefore to take charge of an untrained force of volunteers, and others conscripted by their lairds, and turn them into a respectable fighting force in a remarkably short time. Such was the respect in which he was held that he was later made commander-in-chief of the parliamentary forces at Marston Moor, though his reputation was somewhat tarnished by his premature flight from the battlefield. Three years later, still campaigning in his late sixties, he accepted the surrender of Charles I.

Later still, he was to change sides after the king's execution and was made a prisoner of war after Worcester, only released in 1654 when approaching his mid-seventies. An imposing figure with his curly beard, strong features and immaculate lace collars, his severe injuries in 1635 turned him into 'a crooked little man', which made him a candidate for the figure in a nursery rhyme. He was a cautious, highly professional commander and a staunch Presbyterian, neither of which characteristics impressed Cromwell.

David Leslie (1601–82) was twenty years his junior, born in Pitcairlie, north Fife, to the Rothes of Lindores branch of the Leslies and he was in the middle of a family of twelve, with a spendthrift father. He also was a veteran of twenty years with the Swedish army, though he also, in 1632–3, had a spell fighting for the Tsar of Russia under another relation, Alexander Leslie of Auchinloch. On an annual salary of 9,000 merks, he was highly regarded by the Swedes. He fought with the other Alexander at Wittstock and was wounded before receiving the summons back to Scotland in 1640. He was so highly regarded by the Swedes that his retirement bonus included 200 muskets, 200 suits of armour and a fine gold chain. Thus he sailed from Hamburg in 1640 with his companion, another Fifer, Colonel James Lumsden, and two dozen Scottish mercenaries who had been released from their contracts in Sweden.

David Leslie was to prove an extremely competent cavalry general of the Scottish forces and play a leading role beside Cromwell at Marston Moor, was to be the victor against Montrose, but to fall foul of Cromwell both at Dunbar and Worcester. Like his colleague in 1649 he bought himself a castle in Fife at Newark on the coast within an easy ride of Balgonie and Leslie so that the two generals could easily keep in touch. Unlike his field marshal, up to this point David Leslie seems to have been a bachelor and was just approaching forty, but eventually he married a Yorkshire girl half his age called Anna or Jean Yorke. She came from Gouthwaite Hall in Nidderdale and perhaps he met her just before or after Marston Moor in 1644, for the army had camped at Wetherby just a few miles away. It is perhaps significant that when he was on the run after the Battle of Worcester, he was eventually captured in Yorkshire, possibly on his way to Gouthwaite. Whatever the case, he can have seen very little of her until 1654 as he was either fighting or a prisoner in the Tower of London, but eventually they did settle happily at Newark by St Monans. Coincidentally there were three Newarks in Leslie's life;

the siege of Newark in England, the massacre at Newark Castle in the
Borders after his victory at Philiphaugh, and his own Newark Castle in
Fife, where he died of a stroke in his eighties. David's brother Robert
also served in the Swedish army and it was probably another brother
Colonel Ludovic Leslie who was in charge of finances for the Scottish
army and bought an island on Lindores Loch with his earnings. Major
Patrick Leslie (d. 1649) and Colonel Sir John Leslie were also part of
the Leslie ex-mercenary clique of Covenanter officers.

Also based in Fife were the three Lumsden brothers, all successful
mercenary officers during the Thirty Years War and all of whom played
a part in the Scottish wars of religion. James Lumsden (1598–1660)
fought for the Swedes at Lützen and had been governor of Osnabruck
in 1634. He led the Scots infantry at Marston Moor and was given
credit for rallying the troops when they came close to a disastrous rout.
Later he led the Scots cavalry at Dunbar. His brother Robert Lumsden
of Balwhinnie fought in Germany with Lumsden's Musketeers and was
killed defending Dundee against General Monck. The third brother
William Lumsden of Rennyhill was also in Swedish pay and fought
as a colonel of the Strathearn Regiment at Marston Moor. All three
brothers used their Swedish earnings to buy themselves castles in Fife.

In addition to the eight Leslies and three Lumsdens from Fife was
another Fife professional soldier, John Browne of Fordel, a cousin
of the Covenanter Earl of Balcarres. Referred to as a rittmeister,
presumably therefore a cavalry specialist with German experience, he
seems to have been shipwrecked off Newcastle and made a prisoner
on his way home in 1640 but he was knighted by Charles I in 1641
in the same ceremony at which Alexander Leslie was made an earl,
suggesting that Leslie was his sponsor. He may have been the same
Colonel Brown who fought for the English Parliamentarians at
Powick Bridge. He seems to have missed Marston Moor but achieved
a victory against the northern Royalists at the Battle of Carlisle
Sands in 1645, was with the Scots army at the sieges of Hereford and
Newark and was later general in charge at the Battle of Inverkeithing.

Browne married the daughter of another Fife ex-mercenary James
Scott of Rossie who had served in the Venetian army and is referred
to as eccentric, but who fought throughout the Civil Wars despite
losing to Montrose at Tippermuir. He had bought Rossie with his
Venetian payoff.

Less well known were two other Fife ex-mercenary officers
Charles Arnot, from Arnot just over the Kinross border, and the

future general Colin Pitscottie, who held key posts at Marston Moor, Dunbar and Worcester.

Apart from the group of Fife ex-mercenaries there were two Munros. Sir Robert Munro (1598–1675) with several other members of his clan from Cromarty had joined the Bohemian army under General Mackay in 1626, then returned to Hamburg in 1628 with some more recruits. He was made a colonel in the Swedish army at the siege of Stralsund and fought in several battles for Gustavus Adolphus before answering the summons to return to Scotland in 1638. He was to prove extremely useful in the seizure of the Dalkeith Castle armoury in 1638, Edinburgh Castle a year later, the bishop's palace at Spynie, then Drum and Huntly Castles, before spending four years in Ireland fighting the Catholics and exacting reprisals for the earlier massacre of Protestants. He was made parliamentary commander of all troops in Ireland in 1644 till he was routed at Benburb in 1646, partly due to a number of his troops having been withdrawn to Scotland and others having dubious loyalties. Then after changing sides for the Engagement he was captured in 1648 and spent five years in the Tower of London. The other Munro was George, Robert's nephew (1602–93), who served in the Swedish army 1629–34, then in the Covenanting army in Ireland under his uncle 1642–48 before being sent home to join the disastrous campaign to Preston.

Interestingly, the mysterious Sir Robert Moray (1608–73) had been in the French service and was close to Cardinal Richelieu for whom at times he acted as an agent. He had also become a very close friend of Alexander Lindsay of Balcarres whose sister Sophia he married, so he was a regular visitor to Fife. It was suggested that it was Richelieu who actually sent him to Scotland in 1638 to provide engineering expertise for the Covenanters and perhaps help with the import of guns from the Continent. He was briefly Quartermaster General during the Second Bishops' War before returning to his former post in France in 1643. He had taken a special interest in coal mining techniques and their relevance to warfare. Meanwhile he had joined the Edinburgh Lodge of Freemasons in 1641, was friendly with the pioneering family of Bruces at Culross and Kinross, an amateur philosopher and scientist who, with Prince Rupert, later helped found the Royal Society in London in 1660. Back in France he became commander of the famous Garde Ecossaise but returned to Scotland in 1653 to fight against Cromwell. Most significantly he was instrumental in persuading Charles, Prince of Wales, to head for Scotland in 1649.

William Baillie (d. 1653), the illegitimate son of the Laird of Lamington in Lanarkshire had joined the Scots-Dutch Brigade at an early age and was with the Swedish army under Alexander 'Sandy' Hamilton in Germany until 1633. He served as a colonel in the Covenanting army during the First Bishops' War, commanded the Scottish infantry with modest success at Marston Moor but lost the Battle of Kilsyth to Montrose, mainly because he had been overruled by a committee of church ministers and the Earl of Lindsay. Like some others he became a Covenanter/Royalist in 1648 when he led the infantry at the disastrous Battle of Preston, though he organised a gallant rearguard action in the Winnick Pass. He had to surrender but asked in vain for his fellow officers to shoot him before doing so. On his return to Scotland he was made to do penance by the Kirk party and died in 1653.

Somewhat confusing are the three Livingston cousins who played a part in these wars, two of them called James. James Livingston (1590–1674), the third son of the Earl of Linlithgow, was known as Lord Almond and later Earl of Callendar. He had served in the Dutch army under his elder brother from 1616 and was a colonel in the Scots Brigade by 1629. He joined the Covenanter army in 1640 but was involved in two of Montrose's plots, the Cumbernauld Bond and the Incident, then was second in command to Leven during the 1643 invasion of England, led the siege of Newcastle, but fell out with Leven. He rejoined to fight for the Covenanter/Royalists at Preston in 1648 when he also fell out with his commander and took some of the blame for the defeat. Like Montrose he was probably a very lukewarm Covenanter and, at heart, really a Royalist.

The same might be said of the highly unpredictable Sir John Urry or Hurry (–1650) from Pitfichie near Monymusk who served in Germany as a mercenary before returning in 1641 to join the Scottish army as a colonel. Given his Aberdeenshire background he had no empathy with the Covenanters and shortly, like Montrose and Livingston, became involved in the anti-Argyll Incident, but even then betrayed his companions by turning informer. He next disappeared south to join the English Parliamentary army under Essex and impressed with his bravery at the Battle of Edgehill, then again in the defence of Brentford against Prince Rupert. In 1643, however, he became dissatisfied with his prospects and changed sides to join

Prince Rupert, taking with him useful intelligence about his former colleagues' troop movements. He did well for Rupert at Chalgrove Field and helped at the sack of West Wycombe but after Marston Moor, changed sides yet again to rejoin the Scottish army. Alexander Leslie then dispatched him north to Scotland as a Major General to help General Baillie deal with Montrose. In this role he was insubordinate and incompetent as he organised defeat at the Battle of Auldearn, but stayed with the Covenanter army till the ill-fated Battle of Preston, where he was wounded and taken prisoner. Shortly after this, he changed sides yet again to join Montrose's final campaign at Carbisdale where he was again taken prisoner and then, at long last, executed as a traitor. He had meanwhile fathered five children. His less well-known brother Sir William Urry (–1673) also served as a Royalist officer, though perhaps more consistently and followed Charles II into exile in Holland, commanding a regiment under Lord Newburgh at the Battle of the Dunes in 1658.

James Livingston of Kinnaird (1622–70), later Earl of Newburgh, was brought up in England and only became a mercenary after serving on the Royalist side until 1656 when he became a colonel in the Spanish cavalry. On his return, he commanded the Life Guards in Scotland. George Livingston (1616–90), Earl of Linlithgow, had no Continental experience but fought at Preston and was later the general in charge of suppressing the Covenanters under Charles II.

John Middleton (1608–74) from Caldhame in Kincardineshire had served in the French army. On the Covenanters side he aided David Leslie at Philiphaugh but became a Covenanting Royalist in 1648 and was captured at Preston. He was in command of the Royalist cavalry at Worcester, was captured again, this time sent to the Tower, from which he managed to escape. Described as being without any religious or moral principles and a heavy drinker, he was nevertheless an advocate of bishops and made commander-in-chief in Scotland after the Restoration until transferred as governor to Tangier, where he died aged sixty-six having fallen down the stairs of his house after a drinking session.

Little is known about a number of other experienced officers who played significant roles and came from prominent families. Hugh Fraser, a specialist with the dragoons, led them at Marston Moor and was perhaps the Hugh Fraser, Master of Lovat, who was married to Alexander Leslie's daughter whist serving in Germany. So he had been close to the Fife conspirators, but allegedly died in suspicious circumstances in 1643, a year before Marston Moor, so there is some confusion. Thus it may have been Hugh Fraser of Kinnyllie or Kynnerie or Kinnaird Head Castle, son of the entrepreneur, who rebuilt Fraserburgh harbour and turned it into a commercial success, but these Frasers were consistently Royalists. Either way, Hugh Fraser of the dragoons is regarded as having made a major contribution to the victory at Marston Moor, which, but for his intervention on the wings, was in the balance. It also seems clear that a large proportion of his dragoons had fought with him before in Germany.

Sir Alexander Hamilton, otherwise known as 'Dear Sandy', was a younger son of the Earl of Haddington and had been an innovative artillery general with the Swedes in Germany alongside his namesake, the marquis. 'Dear Sandy' brought back the idea of the light Swedish frame guns, of which he had 88 at Marston Moor, as well as himself allegedly inventing the new ultra-light 12 pounders, only 3 feet long and able to be carried by a single horse, also a strange multi-barrelled infantry-support gun mounted on a wheel barrow. He set up a cannon foundry in Potterrow, Edinburgh, turning out the partly leather cannons that worked well at the Battle of Newburn. His elder brother, Thomas, Earl of Haddington, was also briefly a Covenanter general but was killed early in the wars in 1640, when the huge ammunition depot at Dunglass Castle near the border was blown up by a resentful junior.

On the edge of the Fife clique of ex-mercenaries was Colonel James Holbourne, later a major general and a cavalry specialist, who with his German payoff bought Menstrie Castle, a few miles west of the Fife border. Before returning to Scotland he chose to fight in the English parliamentary army at the Battle of Newbury but as a strong Presbyterian he did not fancy the New Model Army and Cromwell. His main Scottish career was spent aiding David Leslie against Montrose, in fact it was he who took Montrose prisoner at Ardvreck. He seems, like the two Leslies, to have opted out of the ill-fated Preston campaign but was at the lost Battles of Dunbar and Inverkeithing.

Amongst other named mercenary officers was Colonel Crawford who appeared on several occasions, perhaps confused with General Lawrence Crawford (1611–75) a Glasgow-born mercenary and strong Presbyterian who led an infantry brigade at Marston Moor but fell out with Cromwell over the promotion of sectarian officers and was later shot by a sniper. Colonel 'Crowner' Johnstone (possibly Frances) was best remembered for his role in the First Bishops' War and Colonel James Somerville, later Lord Somerville of Drum (Drum House in Edinburgh), had fought in both the French and Venetian armies before joining the Covenanters. During Leven's second invasion of England he was appointed governor of Durham but still made it to Marston Moor, fell out with Leven and, due to lack of ammunition, failed to save Morpeth when it was attacked by Montrose.

There is no direct evidence to prove that Colonel Archibald Strachan from Musselburgh had served as a mercenary, but the fact that he first appears as a dragoon captain in the English parliamentary army in 1642 and was promoted to major in 1643 strongly suggest that he was a professional. A fanatical Calvinist, he was to have an erratic career transferring to the Scottish army in 1645, then deserting to Cromwell for the Preston campaign, then helping the Scots at Dunbar and against Montrose in 1650 before being finally excommunicated by the Scottish Church in 1651 for his opposition to Charles II and dying soon afterwards, apparently in misery because of such treatment.

Colonel James Turner (1615–86) was an ex-mercenary who fought for money rather than principle; in fact, he had tried to enlist with Charles I but failed. The rebellious son of a Dalkeith minister, he had reluctantly done an MA at Glasgow. Still in his early twenties, he had fought for the Swedes at Oldendorf in 1637. He then fought under the Munros in Ireland and left a bitter record of his disgust with Alexander Leslie for failing to send reinforcements. Then he joined David Leslie for the campaign against Montrose and was involved in capturing various Macdonald outposts such as Dunaverty where he regarded MacColla as 'nae sojer'. He fought at both Preston and Worcester and, after spells in the Polish and Danish armies plus a brief Royalist plot in 1654, he returned to Scotland at the Restoration. He became a royal general and notorious for his brutal treatment of Covenanters who gave him the nickname 'Bluidy biter the sheep'. They captured him in Dumfries and he died soon afterwards in disgrace.

There was also, of course, a fair scattering of Scots ex-mercenary officers on both sides in the English Civil War. The most prominent was Patrick Ruthven (1573–1651) Lord Forth, a hard drinker who had fought for the Swedes for more than twenty years and had acquired a German nickname which misspelled his name as Rot(h) wein, Red Wine. He famously took over at the last minute for the

Royalists at Edgehill after a disagreement over cavalry tactics but was himself replaced by Prince Rupert in 1644.

James King, or Lord Eythin, (1589–1652), born in the Orkneys and recruited to the Swedish army in 1615, had famously fought alongside Alexander Leslie for the Swedes in Germany, did well at Minden, was made a major general for Hildersheim, but lost the Battle of Vlotho, where Prince Rupert was captured and blamed King for his misfortunes. Their bad relationship reduced their co-operation in the prelude to Marston Moor and after the defeat, Eythin headed back to Sweden in disgust.

Among other Scots ex-mercenaries who took the Royalist side was Alexander Lindsay of Spynie, who was made general in charge of Scotland by King Charles in 1626, later raised 3,000 Scots troops to fight for the Danes at Stralsund, fought with Montrose, was captured in 1644 and died two years later.

William Balfour (1600–60) from Pitcullo in Fife had Dutch experience but was a strong Presbyterian and a hater of Catholicism who chose to fight for Parliament in England and led one wing of the cavalry on the winning side at Edgehill, before becoming part of Waller's force. It was he who, as governor of the Tower of London, stood up against the king with regard to the orders to execute Campbell of Loudoun.

Another Scot who chose to fight against the Royalists was Sir John Meldrum (d. 1645) a solid professional who had served in Ulster, Holland and Germany. He was a strong opponent of Charles's autocracy, had a division of cavalry at Edgehill, beat Rupert at Newark, and won Ormskirk. Specialising in siege work, he was killed apparently falling from a cliff during the siege of Scarborough.

A third more shadowy Scottish ex-mercenary was Sir James Ramsay, who led the Parliamentary cavalry on the left wing at Edgehill and does appear to have returned to Scotland to join Hamilton's ill-fated march south to Preston. But there was at least one other Sir James Ramsay around at this time and little evidence as to which one was which.

Thus we see that Scottish professional soldiers not only played a major role in the Scottish Covenanters' army but also on both sides in the three English Civil Wars and even in the Irish Confederate War. Particularly at Marston Moor, the Scots not only provided the commander-in-chief but also the majority of the divisional commanders and the majority of the troops. Without them it is very doubtful if the English parliamentarians would have won but, in its aftermath, for a number of reasons, the English wanted to discount their contribution and made plans to manage in future without them.

There is no doubt that the availability of so many capable officers made it much easier for all four combatant groups, the Scottish Calvinists, the English Parliamentarians, the Royalists and the Irish Confederates, to start their various wars. It also made it far more probable that these wars would be protracted. These officers were all used to both winning and losing battles but above all, to surviving to fight another day. This very professionalism meant it was more likely that the wars would drag on, just as they had in Holland and Germany. This meant there would be endless sieges and counter sieges, which would encourage looting, collateral damage, disease and death to add to the combat casualties. It also meant armies had more often to live off the land, so agricultural depredation led to civilian malnutrition that, in turn, added substantially to the death toll.

There is no doubt that with a tally of six generals, including the two most important ones, and half a dozen colonels, Fife punched well above its weight from a military point of view, just as it did from a political and clerical viewpoint. This tally is even greater if we add the dragoon specialist Hugh Fraser, who was probably Alexander Leslie's son-in-law. It is also clear that the Fife ex-mercenaries were deeply committed to each other and particularly to Alexander Leslie after years of fighting alongside each other in Germany.

The irony of the whole situation was that while the professionals were content to win and lose individual battles, ready to fight again, it was an amateur, Oliver Cromwell, who insisted on outright victories and in the end defeated all the professionals.

Apart from the early memoir by Rothes, there is no specific record of the meetings of the Fife Conspiracy until the conference in the Tailors Hall, but a glance at the map shows just how close together the main leaders of the succession of wars that followed were. If we take John Leslie, the Earl of Rothes based in Leslie Castle, as the prime mover, we find his main parliamentary supporters the Earl of Balmerino a mere 16 miles away and the two Lindsays, the Earl of Balcarres and the Earl of Lindsay, about the same. Even the Earls of Montrose and Argyll had homes within easy riding distance, at Auchterarder and Dollar. Of the most influential clergymen Alexander Henderson at Leuchars was 20 miles away and colleagues such as James Wilson at Dysart about 7 miles. But most significant of all was the short distance, just 3 miles, from Leslie to Balgonie Castle where the old Field Marshal Alexander Leslie had moved on his retirement, as had his son the colonel who was married to Rothes' daughter. Even General David Leslie's family home at Pitcairlie was only about 11 miles away, where he was a near neighbour of Balmerino. Also within a morning's ride were the other successful mercenaries, the three Lumsdens, Arnot, Browne and Holbourne. In addition, Sir Robert Moray of the Garde Ecossaise was a regular visitor to Balcarres, bringing direct encouragement for rebellion plus money and access to the arms market from Cardinal Richelieu.

So it was so easy for the rebellious lairds, the still ambitious military men and the fanatical ministers to meet as neighbours, thrash out their grievances, and work out the practicalities of raising a new army in Scotland.

It was also a fact that there was considerable traffic on the sea roads between Fife and northern Europe, which made it far more tempting for ambitious young men to try their luck in Continental armies and equally now made it much easier to make contact to entice them back to ply their trade in Scotland. There had been considerable interchange of populations as many Flemish weavers and other skilled workers had settled in Fife whilst numerous Scottish merchants worked in staple ports such as Vere. James Spens (d. 1632) of Wormiston near Crail had been a major recruiting agent, and transporting mercenaries to Denmark or North Germany benefited from the commercial infrastructure of the textile and other trades. Small ship-owning families such as the Cooks of Pittenweem, the Binnings of St Monans and the Alexanders of Burntisland, could average about 100 miles a day across the North Sea, though sometimes voyages took much longer. Cupar shipped wool regularly from the River Eden. Dairsie near St Andrews seems to have picked up its other name, Osnaburg, from weaving a coarse linen or cotton, originally imported from Onsabrück in Germany. Exports of salt and coal were also increasing from ports such as Dysart. Ludovic Leslie, then a mere captain, had organised the transport of 120 men to Denmark in 1627. Kikcaldy, Dysart and Burntisland were beginning to thrive as North Sea ports as they could take bigger ships than the East Neuk harbours. There were several ship-owners operating from Ely and Anstruther exporting salt and coal, as well as numerous Flemish fishing boats using Fife harbours as temporary bases. Overall, it was clearly quite easy for ambitious Fife men to take passage to and from Germany, so the number of Fife mercenaries was larger in proportion to those from other parts of Scotland, which in turn meant there was a larger pool of experienced officers from Fife available for fighting back home. In addition, there were plenty of younger Fife mercenaries who had fought in the ranks and were experienced musketeers.

It is reasonable to suggest, therefore, that though there were many groups of angry people throughout the British Isles at this time nowhere was there such an intimate concentration in a small area of so many disgruntled landowners, rebellious church ministers, well-educated and articulate ex-students of St Andrews and newly retired mercenaries all within half-a-day's gallop of each other and all close to a chain of harbours with good contacts for the supply of arms and men from the Continent.

If we were to choose one man who was responsible for the large number of experienced soldiers in Fife, and thus for the Fife Conspiracy that started nine wars, it must be the mysterious James Spens of Wormiston whose visit to Sweden in 1623 resulted in the recruitment of so many young men from Fife to go to fight in the German Wars. Two at least of the Leslies were already there but the Spens boatloads lifted the total to a critical level, unmatched in other parts of Britain.

Chapter 7

THE COVENANT

After long and due examination of our consciences in matters of true and false religion we are now thoroughly resolved of the truth.

National Covenant 1638

Remarkably, only twenty-two months elapsed between Jenny Geddes throwing her stool in July 1637 and the outbreak of the First Bishops' War in March 1639, yet this period was packed with activity. If the political lairds and the rebellious church ministers had not already been manipulating affairs from behind the scenes, they certainly rapidly now sprang into action. Two institutions that had recently been dormant, the General Assembly and the Scottish Parliament, were both resuscitated. At the same time the rioting continued, including numerous attacks on bishops or their favoured ministers who still used the hated new service book. The Bishop of Brechin, Walter Whitford, was a regular target. In October 1637 Bishop Sydserf of Galloway was seized in Edinburgh by a crowd of women who stripped him of his upper garments to see if he was really hiding a crucifix round his neck. The Earl of Traquair, still officially the king's chief negotiator, lost his staff in a scuffle and shortly conceded that the High Commission Courts should cease operations. Members of the Privy Council were trapped in their own meeting room.

In this frenzied atmosphere the Earl of Balmerino had great credibility because of his brush with the executioner in 1634 and, with Rothes, he called a meeting of twenty noblemen and a large contingent of ministers, mostly from Fife, in September 1637, followed by an even larger meeting in November. The cautious, timid Archbishop Spotiswood recommended compromise, but it was in vain. The fractious ministers were now preaching openly against Laud's 'five bastard sacraments'. The common chant was 'God confound the service book.' Moderates such as the future Earl of Argyll and the Earl of Lauderdale still sat on the fence, whereas Lords Hume and Lindsay backed Balmerino.

In December a letter referring to 'the foul indignity' arrived from the king who was in no mood for any concessions, totally unwilling for his commands to be flouted and clearly underestimating the strength of feeling at all levels.

At some point the young Edinburgh lawyer, Archibald Johnston, and Alexander Henderson, minister of Leuchars, came together to start drafting the new National Covenant. There was a careful reworking of the original Covenant of 1581, with a detailed argument asserting the freedom of the Church of Scotland and its differences of doctrine and liturgy compared with the now far more alien style being forced on the Scots by Canterbury. In particular it condemned Roman Catholicism and all features of the new Anglican liturgy that remotely reminded people of it: bishops, fancy vestments, bowing to altars, kneeling for communion, blessing baptismal water, wasting the elements of communion, wearing crucifixes, private confessions and so on. This document was vetted by the three earls – Balmerino, Loudoun and Rothes – before it was presented to an informal assembly of 300 ministers held in the Tailors' Hall Edinburgh on 27 February 1638, where it was duly acclaimed. Rothes was active in dealing with the supporters who disagreed with minor points and used his persuasive powers to achieve a united front. He was also clearly in regular contact with the Fife ex-mercenaries, particularly Field Marshal Leslie. This meeting was followed the next day by an even bigger one in Greyfriars churchyard where the huge vellum document was allegedly spread on a tombstone for signing. Many of those who signed it found it a highly emotional experience, Lord Erskine for example being reduced to tears of joy. Many signed in their own blood. At the same time an official General Assembly was planned to take place in Glasgow in November.

Meanwhile Traquair had been replaced as the king's envoy by Hamilton who shuttled between London and Edinburgh listening to Charles's diatribes against the rebels, persuading him to be less stringent, bringing back offers of conciliation that became increasingly ineffective as the Covenanters' confidence rose and their attitudes hardened. The prayer book had vanished and so had the bishops – but resentment still simmered.

Late in 1638 the Fife group and its allies who opposed the new service book came together to create a new decision-making body that would take in not just the members of the Scottish Parliament and the General Assembly but also a broader cross-section of the people. Taking the so-called four Tables made up of noblemen, junior lairds, church ministers and town burgesses they selected four men from all four to create a fifth table of sixteen that would help organise the resistance to the expected counterattack from London, plus an even more select group of one from each table with Archibald Johnston as its clerk.

Meanwhile there were two separate expeditions to try to win over the Scots in the north east where religion was more conservative, in some cases Catholic, to join the rebels. The fiery preacher Andrew Cant and the young Earl of Montrose led one such expedition to Aberdeen and Inverness, with limited success. Aberdeen itself was deluged with Covenanter pamphlets, to little effect. The other expedition was Colonel Robert Munro's effort to bring in the Gordons with a massive bribe offered to their near-bankrupt leader, the Marquis of Huntly. Later knighted, Munro was one of the first ex-mercenaries recruited by the Covenanters, perhaps because he had been at home in Cromarty and was readily available. He played a leading role in recruiting the new Scottish army and was also to prove his worth when it came to tackling the major royal fortresses. Clearly the rebellion in Scotland could not hold its head up while Royal troops held the main fortresses and ammunition stores of the central belt, the three castles of Edinburgh, Dalkeith and Dumbarton, all of them capable of withstanding a long siege, particularly against an army that as yet had no artillery. Luckily, due to lack of funds, the garrisons of all three were quite small, the governors hesitant in their loyalties and uncertain about what was happening or what if any reinforcements they might expect.

The Scots remarkably were at this point not short of funds because they had at least one extremely wealthy supporter, Sir William Dick (1580–1655), the Provost of Edinburgh, a successful merchant and banker who had previously made 'loans' to both James VI and Charles I. Thus in 1638 willingly or half-willingly he made a massive loan of £200,000 to pay for the new army, probably not expecting it to be repaid in full. He also let the army camp on his estate on the Braid Hills outside Edinburgh. As a result he later went bankrupt, was imprisoned in London and died a pauper.

Just how much intelligence the Scots had with regard to the threat of retaliation is hard to estimate but if they imagined that Charles had a powerful army behind him, they overestimated him but were very brave. They must, however, have been seriously worried about four potential threats. The most obvious was from Huntly and his Gordons in their rear, with the added prospect that London would support his attack from the north. Certainly there had been contact and Charles was aiming for a co-ordinated attack from Huntly territory and elsewhere. Two other attacks in particular were dreaded, both from Ireland. There had long been rumours of an attack by the revengeful Macdonnells of Antrim, led by their Royalist earl Randal Macdonnell of Dunluce, and primed to attack the Campbell heartlands in Argyll to reclaim their lost heritage. Even worse was the threat from Dublin, where Strafford planned to bring his English troops over for a landing in Ayrshire or Dumbarton. The fourth potential attack was by the king himself who at this point, unknown to the Scots, had bought 40 lightweight cannons or drakes to use as field artillery and was calling up his nobles for armed service as if he was still a feudal monarch. He was expected to head up the east coast whilst Hamilton, once his duties as an envoy were no longer useful, would be put in charge of the navy to sail up the east coast and land in the Firth of Forth.

At some point the Scots also made contact with the French, perhaps through Balmerino, who had contacts there, or perhaps even Montrose, who was not long back from his year at Angers. This may also have involved Robert Moray, the mysterious Scot serving in the French army and a close confidant, if not spy, working for Cardinal Richelieu. Richelieu had a grudge against Charles I for interfering with French expansion plans in the Netherlands so he seems to have welcomed what he thought was perhaps a minor rebellion in Scotland. Moray, a close friend of the Fife Lindsays, was seconded to Scotland for five years to help organise the logistics of the new army. At the same time, Richelieu seems to have provided a fund of 100,000 crowns to buy 6,000 muskets and other arms in Holland. The deal was negotiated by a merchant called Barnes and the cargoes shipped to Leith via France.

In November came the promised formal meeting of the General Assembly in Glasgow Cathedral, with Hamilton as High Commissioner vainly trying to restrict the debate. Such was the hostile atmosphere that the bishops hid away in the nearby castle. Allegedly there was a young woman protesting loudly in the street outside that she had been made pregnant by the unpopular Bishop of Brechin, Walter Whitford.

Any opponents were intimidated and kept quiet while Henderson's opening sermon set the tone attacking 'the innovations such as the superstitious service books, the tyrannous book of canons, loose and profane lives, excessive and extraordinary drinking, filthy dancings, common swearing, profaning the Sabbath, excessive gaming, bribery, simony, adultery and slander.' By the end of the meeting all the bishops and archbishops had been dismissed or suspended from office and most of them excommunicated. Use of the dreaded prayer book and liturgy instructions was forbidden. Hamilton tried to halt the proceedings but failed.

As the new year dawned, the newly recruited Scottish army was still undergoing intensive musket and pike drill in various depots across the central belt, ready for the expected conflict. Most of the mainly Fife-based mercenary officers were in post and organising the troops, as were the various lairds who had brought in their tenant farmers and personal servants. It was time to fight. But it was not a battle against the king or against the English, only against the king's evil advisers – most particularly Archbishop Laud and his followers. So far as the king was concerned, the assembly at Glasgow still referred to its members as 'your Majestie's humble and loyal subjects' whilst Charles referred to them disparagingly as 'Covenanting rabble'.

The other essential move before any armies could start campaigning was to take over the three main castles, Edinburgh, Dalkeith and Dumbarton. The royal chief envoy Traquair was resident in Dalkeith, which held a major arms depot and the crown jewels of Scotland – but only a small garrison. Traquair made only feeble efforts to defend it when the two Fife earls, Rothes and Balmerino, threatened bombardment, after which Munro broke in without great difficulty. In the case of Edinburgh, Alexander Leslie intimidated the small garrison and had the gates blown open with a petard, thus taking the castle with no bloodshed. Dumbarton was even easier, for the governor Captain Stuart was waylaid on his way home from church on a Sunday and persuaded to confess the password for entry. Thus a local laird, Campbell of Ardincaple, obtained entry for his men and assumed control, a key capture since Dumbarton with its armoury had been one of the possible landing places for Strafford's Irish troops. The two Royalist Douglas castles, Tantallon and Douglas, both fell. Caerlaverock was now the remaining most likely place for Strafford to disembark Irish troops.

One factor explaining the speed and efficiency of organisation in 1638 was the strong Fife connection amongst supporters of the Covenant, a point made by the Earl of Rothes in his short history of the events. He was himself based in Leslie within a short ride of his two military cousins Alexander at Balgonie and David Leslie's family at Pitcairlie or later St Monans. Nearby were the prominent Lindsay earls based at Balcarres near Elie, Cupar and Crail near which were also the three ex-mercenary Lumsden brothers. A little further north was the Earl of Balmerino, still smarting from his near brush with execution, together with several Balfours who played a key role, including the future governor of the Tower of London, and Balfour of Kinloch who later shared with several other Fife lairds in the murder of Archbishop Sharp. Add to this the future General Baillie and we see how many of the lairds and generals were based in Fife. Both the Earls of Argyll and Montrose had studied at St Andrews and Argyll had been fostered out as a child to the Campbells of Glenorchy, the same family that had helped bring up Field Marshal Alexander Leslie. This tally leaves out only one of the lairds prominent in starting the Bishops' Wars and that was the Campbell Earl of Loudoun whose mother came from East Wemyss and whose daughter had married the Balmerino heir. So he had strong Fife connections, had been brought up at Lawers close to the Glenorchy Campbells and, given his remarkable oratorical skills, was highly likely to have been at St Andrews.

Finally the most prominent minister in the first Covenant campaigns was Alexander Henderson, based in Leuchars just north of St Andrews. There were active supporting ministers in Kingsbarns, Cupar, Aberdour, Dysart, Markinch and numerous other Fife churches, many of them having studied at St Andrews and several having had fractious relationships with Archbishop Spotiswood.

At the centre of this Fife Conspiracy was the neighbourly relationship of the Earl Rothes with the newly retired Field Marshal Alexander Leslie, 3 miles away at Balgonie, with each of them in turn having a wider network of contacts – Rothes political and Leslie military – whilst both were also close to the group of local anti-episcopalian ministers. In addition Leslie had with him a secretary, Robert Meldrum, who was sent as his agent to Sweden. They thus between them had all the tools necessary to start a war, except perhaps money, for while the ex-mercenaries were certainly rich they were probably reluctant to sacrifice their hard-earned wealth. One at least of the Fife lairds did provide money: Balmerino lent a sum of 40,000 merks and had good contacts both at home and abroad. So he may well have been involved in approaching the two biggest lenders, Sir William Dick of Braids (*c* 1590–1655) and Mary, the widowed Countess of Home (1586–1645). Dick was reputed to be the wealthiest man in Scotland and came from a Danish immigrant family who made a fortune trading between the Orkneys and Denmark. William Dick himself extended the family business with a fleet trading from the Baltic to Scotland and to the Mediterranean, with an agent called William Colville in Holland. His companies won royal approval for helping to ship James VI's wife, Ann of Denmark, to Scotland with her companions and, by 1639, Dick had an estimated fortune of £226,000, much of which he lent to the Estates Committee. Walter Scott in *Heart of Midlothian* describes the scene in the Luckenbooth with 'sacks of dollars coming out of Provost Dick's windows into the carts that carried them to the army at Duns Law'. With his international connections it is highly likely he had dealt with the Field Marshal and as Lord Provost he would sit with Rothes on the Privy Council. He also had Fife connections with his subsidiaries trading across the North Sea from Pittenweem and Anstruther.

Where Mary, Countess of Home, acquired her huge wealth is unclear for her maverick husband had died in 1619, leaving very little, but her father had been the English Earl of Dudley so she must have inherited some funds from him. Certainly in 1618, the year before her husband's death, she had a lavish new home built in Edinburgh, at Moray House. The fact that the large complex of buildings, including the new Parliament House of 1632, cost £11,630 gives an idea of the significance of her loans to the Covenanters of £70,000, followed by another £7,000 for the Irish campaign. Though one of her castles at Dunglass was blown up whilst occupied by Covenanters she seems to have been repaid just before her death, whereas William Dick was less lucky and ended up bankrupt. We have no evidence of a contact between Mary and Rothes but she lived for some time at Falkland when her husband was in charge of the royal guard and where he was excommunicated as a suspected Catholic by the Fife Presbytery.

Other rich supporters probably included the Edinburgh merchant John Mean, whose wife was at one time put forward as the real Jenny Geddes, or as a fellow stool-thrower with two other women called Craig. Edinburgh merchants had become fairly prosperous at this period and a number of them were capable of offering loans. At this time, judging by their dress, all the participants – retired soldiers, parish ministers and local lairds – could all afford the latest fashions of lace collars produced by the bobbin lacemakers of Leith. In their portraits they all looked much alike with smart pointed beards, long hair and the ubiquitous fancy lace. And they were mostly painted by the fashionable Aberdeen-born portraitist George Jameson, referred to as the Scottish Van Dyck, who must have employed assistants to recreate the repetitively intricate lace.

Apart from the ease of contact in Fife this group also met regularly in Edinburgh, where they all tended to have lodgings close to the new Parliament. Balmerino and Rothes were amongst the most regular attenders at the Privy Council. The nobles were also regularly arranging wives and husbands for their children and this must have helped bind the group together: for example, Rothes' daughter married Leven's eldest son, and Balmerino's son married Loudoun's daughter.

There was another area where networking was becoming more evident. This was the fashionable new institution of Freemasonry, which had arrived in Edinburgh by 1599 and took firm root alongside the thriving merchant guilds in the city. Here the older but financially fragile aristocratic families could mix on equal terms with the middle-class but cash-rich families of the city, such as the Dicks and Means. It is perhaps significant that at least two of the professional generals, Sir 'Dear Sandy' Hamilton and Sir Robert Moray – Hamilton having soldiered in Germany and Moray in France – both enrolled as Masons. This may well have helped Hamilton set up his artillery workshop in Edinburgh's Potterrow. It is possible also that some of the other ex-mercenaries, including the Marquis of Hamilton, acquired the same interest whilst serving abroad.

To add to this fertile mixture, the Kirk does not seem to have objected to ministers becoming members of the Lodge: for example, in 1652 the Presbytery of Kelso agreed to let a minister called James Ainslie become a Mason. It is also significant that the both the Earls of Cassilis and Eglinton are known to have served as deacons of their Lodge at Kilwinning in the 1670s.

Chapter 8

THE FIRST BISHOPS' WAR

For Chryst's Crown and Covenant

Banner of Scots Army

By the providence of God we are joined in one island and under one king.

Earl of Dunfermline: letter, 1639

In some respects the First Bishops' War was more like a rehearsal for war than a real war. Neither side was yet fully trained or up to strength. Yet the first target was clear, to get rid of the menace in Scotland's rear due to the supposed 5,000 men under the Huntly banner in Aberdeenshire. So in March 1639 some 8,000 troops, including levies from Dundee, set off northwards under the nominal command of the Earl of Montrose, with Alexander Leslie as the authorised decision-maker. Montrose was young and totally inexperienced but socially outranked Leslie who, though he was a Swedish field marshal, was not an aristocrat or even a legitimate junior laird. It is possible that this situation added to the slight chip on his shoulder that Montrose had displayed on his earlier visit to the London court. For the time being, Montrose was an enthusiastic Covenanter but his allegiance was fragile.

The first objective was Turiff where the local Covenanters were to hold a meeting and it was expected that the Earl of Huntly would send troops to disrupt it. Montrose arrived nearby without half his troops and without Leslie, so he was not allowed to give battle. Huntly also made an appearance, but he too was restrained from attacking as he was supposedly waiting for help from King Charles. Besides, he knew that Montrose would soon have additional troops and he was facing rebellion from some of his own Gordon tenants who half sympathised with the Covenant.

On 30 March Montrose and Huntly confronted each other again at Aberdeen, this time Montrose's troops outnumbering Huntly's, so Huntly withdrew and then met Montrose to discuss the next move. Montrose had orders to kidnap Huntly and take him to Edinburgh. Huntly, to avoid the humiliation of such treatment, preferred to head south on a voluntary basis and was imprisoned in Edinburgh Castle.

Meanwhile in late March the king himself was heading north from London, with the Duke of Lennox, to join up with his armies at York. Berwick was strongly defended by General Astley, as was Carlisle. Charles was so disgusted by the failure of his negotiators to cow the Scottish rebels that he had both Traquair and his colleague the Earl of Roxburgh put in the cells of York. There was a mixture of arrogance and panic that began to characterise his behaviour and he still naively overestimated the commitment and determination of the scratch army he had summoned to join him. Apart from general lack of training and experience, there were absurd jealousies in the command structure, which was headed by the uninspiring Earl of Arundel.

Meanwhile the twin-pronged attack expected from Ireland seemed to be no longer likely. The capture of Dumbarton, the favoured landing place, had been followed by the local Ayrshire troops under the Earl of Cassilis sealing off most of the other likely landing places, including Caerlaverock, so Strafford's plan was nullified. So far as the expected attack by the Antrim Macdonnells went, this too was unlikely as the Campbells, led by Argyll's ruthless henchman Campbell of Auchinbreck, owner of Castle Sween in Knapdale, had been sent in April to devastate with fire and sword the areas of South Kintyre that were Antrim's most sensible landing place. Auchinbreck fortified the village of Lochhead, later named Campbelton, and, as a bonus, seized Brodick Castle on Arran. The Campbells were essentially using the excuse of the Covenanting cause to do their own thing. The earl had ordered his own private arms supply from a Flemish merchant based in Edinburgh, called David Jonking, and this included a fully equipped Dutch frigate.

The Tables had ordered better defences round the Firth of Forth to deter the Royalist troops on the Marquis of Hamilton's ships from landing there. The artillery mercenary known as 'Dear Sandy'

Hamilton had motivated squads of men, women and children to improve the coastal defences round Leith, whilst cannons had been shipped to all the Fife coastal villages on the north side of the Firth. Only the two islands Inchcolm and Inch Kenneth had been left undefended, and the Marquis of Hamilton made use of these as a recovery or training place for his on-board troops, many of whom were suffering from smallpox. Thus his orders to deal with the Scots 'with fire and sword' were, for the time being, unlikely to take effect. Edinburgh itself was defended by a force of nearly 20,000 so the Marquis's 5,000, including invalids, was totally inadequate. His proclamations of amnesty and surrender to the demands of the Scots were too little too late, even if they were for one moment really believed. This was the point when his own mother disowned him and threatened to shoot him if he landed. He stayed on board his flagship *Rainbow* and received a defiant letter from Alexander Leslie and the seven lairds: Argyll, Rothes, Loudoun, Balmerino, Mar, Napier and Cassilis, describing themselves as humble men. So Hamilton was soon afterwards summoned to rejoin the king as he headed north from the Tyne.

In early April Montrose with more than 8,000 men was confronting the Gordons again outside Aberdeen. They had a much smaller force. What is more, Montrose's men looked the part, as spectators such as the Aberdeen diarist John Spalding remarked, clad in buff coats with the blue ribbon that signified the cause for which they fought, smart with their carbines and at their musket drill, showing the influence of 'the excellent field marshal Leslie' who also made sure they had their proper rations. Montrose was shortly joined by another 500 men, mostly Campbells who set about plundering the local farms, making life difficult for the Gordons who needed local supplies. Thus both sides were now making life very miserable for the people of Aberdeenshire, particularly Aberdeen itself, which kept changing hands.

The main focus from this time onwards was on the Scottish borders where a confrontation was inevitable between the Royalist army heading northwards and Leslie's new army heading south. Theoretically Charles had a force of approximately 20,000 foot and 3,000 horse, plus a reasonable train of artillery, whereas Leslie's advance force was well short of its target of 20,000, though there were more on the way behind him. But whereas Leslie was very much in control of his highly motivated, psalm-singing troops, the Royalist army was riven with the disagreements of rival aristocrats at the top, and comprised men who were far from sure why they were fighting. The second-in-command, the Earl of Essex, for example, was a strong Presbyterian who, two years later, commanded the Parliamentary armies against Charles. Similarly, the other senior commander, the Earl of Newcastle, was angrily disputing the leadership of the Earl of Arundel.

Thus on the last day of May 1639 Charles's army made camp at the Birks, 3 miles from Berwick. Leslie's force was divided between his own divisions at Dunglass and Munro's at Kelso, where both agreed to the king's suggestion that they should remain at least 10 miles from the border, on the basis that Charles would also keep his distance. Charles was so astonished by this apparent obedience that he assumed that the Scots were in awe of his army and made a huge error of judgment by breaching his own rules and sending his cavalry to attack the Scottish division at Kelso. This force was led by the less-than-reliable Henry Rich, Earl of Holland, and brother of the strongly Presbyterian Earl of Warwick, who later became leader of the parliamentary navy. Alongside Holland were two commanders later to become prominent in the English Civil War, the dashing George Goring and the more experienced Astley. Despite this, Holland seems to have been overawed by Munro's force and retreated without firing a shot. The results of this debacle were threefold: firstly, the Scots now felt free to ignore their agreement to keep 10 miles away from the English border; secondly, their confidence was increased by the apparent reluctance of the Royalists to fight; and thirdly, Holland's humiliating performance added to the already demoralised state of Charles's whole army.

Freed from constraint, Leslie now moved his whole force to a strongly defended position on Duns Law where, like a true professional, he had his troops dig fresh entrenchments, the remains of which can still be traced. Thus the two opposing armies faced each other, one well-fed and with high morale, the other short of both motivation and supplies. The Earl of Dunfermline, the least likely of the Scots to fall out with the king, was sent across to negotiate. The king's response offering a free pardon to the rebels was little more than an insult and his suggestion of freedom of religion was patently dishonest for it was accompanied by sarcastic references to the 'pretended assembly' of Glasgow. A further embassy included Rothes, Loudoun, Dunfermline, William Douglas of Cavers, the minister Alexander Henderson and the lawyer Archibald Johnston, on this occasion also referred to not surprisingly as a preacher. Loudoun as the chief spokesman kept reiterating 'the humble desires of the Scots' for freedom of worship and Charles agreed half-heartedly, but in the background was being briefed against surrender by the two unyielding bishops, Ross and Aberdeen. Loudoun's conclusion was almost certainly correct, that it was all just a delaying tactic.

In mid-June the king's offer was for there to be a new General Assembly in August, immediately followed by a meeting of the Scottish Parliament to sort out everything. There would also be an Act of Oblivion, meaning no punishment for any acts of rebellion. But this was hedged by demands for the disbanding of the Tables and both armies, the return of all royal castles, no more new Scottish fortifications, and so on. In theory it was a reasonable offer and was signed by both sides but it was riddled with inconsistencies, which of course reflected the inconsistencies of the main person responsible for it, a king who believed that sooner or later he would have the necessary troops to deal properly with these rebels.

Meanwhile there had been further changes in the north east. In mid-May the ex-mercenary Colonel Crowner Johnstone had captured Towie Barclay Castle, which held a significant cache of arms. The capture resulted in one casualty, who has been described as the first fatality of the Wars of Three Kingdoms.

With the Marquis of Huntly still in prison, his son and heir Lord Aboyne had been allowed to return to Strathbogie to raise funds. Fighting broke out again between the Covenanter lords such as Fraser and Seaforth against the Gordons and Ogilvys. There was another Covenanter meeting at Turiff after which there was a skirmish between the two sides described as 'The Trot of Turiff' where the Gordons came out marginal victors. Thus inspired, Aboyne and his followers retook Aberdeen from the Covenanters and again plundered the citizens' homes. Montrose, however, returned north with reinforcements in late May and the Royalists moved out leaving their opponents who in turn plundered all the Royalist houses including the bishop's palace. This included stealing all the salmon caught by the watermen on the Dee and Don, Montrose having great difficulty in disciplining his own men, '... not a fowl, cock or hen was left unkilled.' There was even a puerile reprisal against the dogs of Aberdeen, all of whom were killed by the Covenanters because as a joke the Royalists had tied blue ribbons round their collars.

Soon Aboyne's Gordons were reinforced from the south with troops sent by Hamilton along with an English ex-mercenary officer called Gun. In early June with the help of the ubiquitous Crowner Johnstone, they retook the luckless city of Aberdeen and subjected it to more than two days of additional looting. After this, in mid-June 1639, Aboyne and his men headed south to start the promised attack on the Covenanters from their rear. However, just south of Stonehaven, they were met by a Covenanter force at Megray Hill. The Highlanders were blamed for the resultant panic as they had not previously faced an organised barrage of muskets and they turned and ran, followed by the Gordons, who all made their way back to Aberdeen. There they made a stand at Brig o' Dee against Montrose who came down on them from Kincorth Hill. They met some resistance from Johnstone's better musketeers and some Royalist culverins or medium weight cannons with a 20lb missile. But after 48 hours, he had battered down the town's defences and re-entered the now 'pitifully plundered' city on 19 June.

By this time the Treaty of Berwick had been signed and the First Bishops' War was over. The treaty was riddled with loopholes but the Glasgow theologian Robert Baillie described the bloodless victory of Duns as bestowed 'by a hand clearly divine'. God was on their side.

In considering the consequences of the First Bishops' War some features are obvious. Firstly, the Scots enjoyed a considerable increase in military self-esteem; Duns was the first of seven southward invasions of which the first three were to be apparently easy and successful, whereas the last four were to be totally disastrous. From the Royalist point of view, Charles rapidly recovered from any loss of confidence in his military and conveniently forgot his promises of reconciliation, for once back in London he was again under the spell of William Laud and Thomas Wentworth, neither of whom would countenance such weak behaviour. This was endorsed by the exiled Scottish bishops, who still wanted to regain their positions and wanted no truck with the Covenant.

Chapter 9

THE SECOND BISHOPS' WAR

... the gangrene be cut off before it spreads too far
Speech by Charles I

... walk with the tenderness which becometh dutiful subjects
Speech by John Campbell, Earl of Loudoun

The Byzantine clauses of the Treaty of Berwick soon began to unravel. Traquair was back in Scotland as the chief royal envoy and soon received orders from London that implied that the treaty was to be ignored. The Covenanters rapidly came to realise this and they too were less likely to fulfil their obligations such as the handing back of all royal castles, the disbandment of their army, the removal of fortifications and so on. A General Assembly was called as agreed and confirmed the same reforms as its predecessor but Charles refused to recognise its decisions. Similarly, when the Scottish Parliament was called, Charles tried to challenge its validity on the grounds that it no longer included the bishops. Traquair was pelted with stones in the street yet Wentworth reassured the king that he would both fund and put backbone in the royal army by using Irish money and Irish reinforcements. As a reward for this moral support, Charles promoted him to be the Earl of Strafford. So by the beginning of 1640 the situation was again heading for confrontation.

Thus in February the Scots sent a three-man team to London to explain their position. It was led by the very able John Campbell, Earl of Loudoun, accompanied by the Borders laird, William Douglas of Cavers, and, as a representative of the boroughs, the third man was the provost of Irvine. Loudoun delivered a long and carefully argued defence of the Covenanters' position, emphasising that there was no challenge to the Stuart dynasty, but claiming that the combined decisions of the General Assembly and the Scottish Parliament on matters of religion could not be overruled by the king. He larded his speech with Latin tags such as *salus populi est suprema lex*. Charles, prompted by Archbishop Laud, quibbled over the right of this delegation to convey such demands and the arguments dragged on without sign of compromise. It was at this point that Traquair drew attention for the first time to a letter written by the Scots leaders to the King of France at the height of the Duns campaign, a copy of which had fallen into his hands. Loudoun admitted that he was one of those who had signed the letter, but pointed out that it was not an act of treachery asking for military aid but simply a request for an unbiased mediator. What is more, the letter had never actually been sent to France, and even if it had been treasonous, any such behaviour had been officially pardoned by the Act of Oblivion promised in the Treaty of Berwick. However, for Charles it was an excuse to put the Scots delegation in the Tower, despite their guarantee of safe conduct.

Loudoun himself was condemned to be beheaded as a traitor but the governor of the Tower, who was another Fife-born ex-mercenary, Sir William Balfour, according to Oldmixon's graphic account, received the execution warrant whilst playing cards with his chief prisoner. Loudoun allegedly told Balfour just to do his duty and give him a few moments to write his will, but Balfour contacted the Marquis of Hamilton – who was outraged at the idea of Loudoun's execution. Balfour and Hamilton sought an immediate audience with the king, who had gone to bed, but as an extreme emergency they demanded that he should be wakened, burst into the bedroom, to the horror of the queen, and argued forcibly that if Charles insisted on this execution it would lead to his own downfall. Reluctantly, Charles finally agreed.

Despite this, Charles now used the letter to France as a major propaganda tool to demonstrate the treachery of the Scots and encouraged his English subjects to supply men and money to stop this 'trampling of our crown under their feet'.

Meanwhile the Scots were still paying Alexander Leslie to be their commander-in-chief and he in turn was recruiting more professional officers as well as importing more arms from the Continent. The Scottish Parliament raised a new war tax, collections were made at church doors and women handed in their jewellery. The parliament also voted for itself to meet at least once every three years.

Strafford had returned to Ireland to call a meeting of the Irish Parliament which was expected to be helpful for the royal war effort and set an example for the English Parliament to follow. Charles further broke the Treaty of Berwick by sending his navy up to blockade Scottish traders in the North Sea. When, however, the English Parliament did meet in April it was so cantankerous that Charles dismissed it after only three weeks (hence the Short Parliament) and thus failed to raise the money he needed to fight off the Scots.

To consolidate Covenanter control of Scotland, the Campbells were ordered to take on the central Highlands and the Earl of Argyll, now looking even more like King Campbell, led 5,000 of his men into Badenoch and Atholl. The Earl of Atholl was captured in Glen Lyon and sent as a prisoner to Edinburgh. Airlie Castle, the seat of the Royalist Ogilvys, had already withstood an attempted siege by Montrose and now Argyll took over, creating a legend by attacking the 'bonnie hoose o' Airlie' when its master was away and his wife was expecting a child.

> Lady Margaret looked o'er the castle wall
> And oh she sighed sarely
> She saw Argyll and all his men
> Come to plunder the bonnie hoose o' Airlie.

The Campbells then took the opportunity to loot numerous anti-Covenanter estates as far as Lochaber.

Similarly Munro, who was in command at Aberdeen, conducted a series of ruthless campaigns wiping out opposition areas, conscripting unwilling Aberdonians to join his force, devastating the Huntly heartland round Strathbogie, seizing Drum Castle whilst its master was away, then the Bishop of Moray's palace at Spynie.

If the Covenanters were now universally hard on Episcopalians, they were also almost equally intolerant of any other sects such as Brownists and Anabaptists who now appeared in various places including Stirling. They also indulged in bursts of iconoclasm, as at St Machar's Cathedral in Aberdeen where stained glass windows were smashed, tombs vandalised, crucifixes destroyed and marks such as 'IHS' were chiselled out. (The name Jesus, spelt in Greek capitals, had the abbreviation IHS; there were a considerable number of variants of 'Christograms' or monograms of Christ in use at this time.)

In August the reformed Scottish army met for a review at Duns Law, re-using the previous year's defence works. Under Leslie there was now a new command structure with Lord Almond (James Livingston, later Earl of Callendar) as his deputy; William Baillie, as Major General; Alexander (Sandy) Hamilton, general of artillery; John Leslie, Quartermaster; and Alexander Gibson, supply. All nobles who had not been professional soldiers were made colonels. With twenty-five per cent conscription, the force amounted to 23,000 foot and 3,000 cavalry. Hamilton had a supply of lightweight artillery, tin and leather cannons that could be borne on horseback. His elder brother, Thomas, Earl of Haddington, also a Covenanter general, was killed whilst in charge of the main Scottish ammunition depot at Dunglass Castle near the border when it was blown up by a disgruntled local. This might have been a major disaster for the Covenanters but, as it happened, it had little effect on the outcome of this campaign.

At Duns the army remained for three weeks until news arrived that the Royalists were moving north under Conway, so it was decided to take the initiative and move south to meet him. The first man to plunge his horse into the Tweed was Montrose, ever seeking hero status, perhaps resentful that he was now just a colonel whilst mere commoner professionals outranked the old noble families like his. Perhaps he also felt slightly guilty as he had already had a secret meeting with the king and signed a bond or band at Cumbernauld with some like-minded colleagues, including Lords Fleming (it was in his home) and Almond (James Livingston), Leslie's second in command, who felt the new Covenanter regime was challenging the primacy of the old elite or simply that Argyll and the Campbells were laying the foundations for an alternative royal dynasty. Whatever the reasons, Montrose was dissatisfied with his own role as a subsidiary commander in the Covenanter army and was waiting for the right moment to change sides.

As the Scots crossed the border on 28 August 1640, they issued pamphlets justifying their action, promising friendship for their English brethren who were not as such the enemy and welcoming any Englishmen who wished to join their army. The only enemy they said were 'the troublers of Israel'. By the same token they received warm letters of welcome from several of the future members of the Parliamentary forces such as the three earls, Essex, Warwick and Manchester.

On the same day as the Scots crossed the border Charles left London and headed to York where he found his army in an ill-tempered state, some of the men close to mutiny and the Earl of Northumberland refusing the post of commander-in-chief, which went to the boorishly confident new Earl of Strafford. Orders were sent to Conway to advance no further than Newburn outside Newcastle and wait there for the main army.

A week after crossing the Tweed, Leslie and his army reached Heddon Law and camped there above the two fords over the Tyne at Newburn, where Conway's men had dug themselves in with two long protective breastworks, one at each of the fords, which were passable only at low tide. Leslie hugely outnumbered Conway, but Conway had a reasonably strong position. At night Leslie's army looked even bigger than it was, as his men had found abundant supplies of coal and there were thousands of coal fires visible over a broad area.

Leslie now prepared his assault by putting cannons and musketeers on the tower of Newburn Church and elsewhere looking down across the river at the Royalists. Both Leslie's artillery and his musketeers were more effective than Conway's, who were newly conscripted and not yet trained. The result was a panic that coincided with low tide so, as a test-run, Leslie ordered his troop of two dozen Edinburgh lawyers to try out the ford. Once this was accomplished, the next over were Loudoun and his Ayrshire troops. The battle was won. Though the Royalists only had some sixty casualties, the Scots had even fewer. Conway abandoned Newcastle, which was captured by Douglas of Cavers, and Presbyterian Church services were held in gratitude. Conway meanwhile carried on southwards, deserting first Durham, then Darlington.

The Scots quickly occupied Shields, Durham and Tynemouth, so the Covenanter army was now in effective control of the four northern counties of England. This engendered a serious loss of confidence in the royal army still waiting uncertainly at York. There the king reviewed his forces; they appeared smart and ready enough, even apparently armed with 'Scotch pistols' (how this was noted is obscure, but Scottish gunsmiths had been making a new design of flintlock pistol since 1619 – there is a sample in a Berlin museum – the only one surviving in Edinburgh was apparently stolen) though the famous Doune pistols did not appear till 1646.

Leslie was deliberately generous in victory because he wanted his 'English brethren' on his side, so he promised to allow the coal ships to set sail for London, which depended on them for survival. He also made sure that his army paid for all the supplies they bought from English farmers and merchants. Leslie sent a letter to the king signed by himself and the four earls, Rothes, Montrose, Loudoun and Cassilis, offering to cease hostilities and negotiate. Meanwhile there were other successes for the Covenant forces. Dumbarton Castle was recaptured and some Royalist troops from Berwick were defeated at Haddington. Edinburgh Castle, whose commander Lord Ruthven (Old Rot Wein), the Scots mercenary general employed by Charles I, had been bombarding parts of the city, surrendered to Argyll in mid-September. Caerlaverock Castle was also captured.

The Covenanters' demands to the king were little different from those accepted in the Treaty of Berwick, except that all the details now had to be precise with no room for misunderstandings. The only punishment asked for was against the so-called 'common incendiaries', obviously Traquair and the bishops, who had caused the need for war. The king was referred to only with respect and indeed was encouraged to make regular visits to Scotland once the war was over. The one significant addition was that now the Covenanters felt sufficiently strong to look beyond Scotland, to bring in complaints about the persecution of Presbyterians in Ireland and look for solidarity with co-religionists in England. This was, in effect, the start of the somewhat naïve dream of a Presbyterian Church for the whole British Isles that was to lead Scotland into three more disastrous wars.

It appeared to start with the idea that the English would welcome the abolition of bishops and instead have assemblies to control the church but, as it turned out, once the rigid control of bishops was removed, many were to find the idea of strict management by an assembly just as irksome, so the idea of independence was evolved. Each congregation could do its own thing without interference, a formula that specially suited the new sects such as the Brownists and Anabaptists or even the basic English Puritans such as Cromwell himself. Even in Scotland, there were hints that if bishops were abolished why not also assemblies? Significantly two of the main ministers who had led the rebellion of 1638, Andrew Cant and David Dickson, were both suspected of being independents. The next wars were not destined to be between Lutherans and Calvinists so much as between alternative versions of

Calvinism, some Lutherans, and other assorted sects ranging from the Baptists, Brownists, Ranters and later Fifth Monarchists to Diggers and Shakers. None of these would want to be managed by assemblies, particularly ones such as those in Scotland, which were closely linked to the secular state and insisted on universal obedience together with zero tolerance of any rival sects.

In addition to the considerable loss of life due to these wars there were also huge financial strains on the Scots. The Covenanters had to reorganise the taxation system three times, in 1639, 1643, and 1649, to cope with the military expenditure, imposing new excise duties and other fiscal tricks, yet despite this the national debt escalated. The personal costs to some of the great lairds were crippling. For example the Earl of Argyll, who was also himself involved in tax collection from recalcitrant lairds, had a £72,000 outlay for his Kintyre campaign in 1639, but had less than a third of that sum reimbursed by the Tables. Many other lairds, such as the Earl of Balcarres, paid their troops out of their own pockets instead of investing in land improvements or economic development. The determination of the ministers to defend and spread Presbyterianism throughout the British Isles was to come at a high cost in terms of blood and money, which held back Scotland's economic development for years to come.

Meanwhile the success of the Scottish invasion of northern England was such that Charles had no choice but to call another parliament as he was now desperate for money to buy off the Scots. Up to this point, as Trevelyan put it, 'the general temper of England had found no means of expression.' There was no single area like Fife with such a concentration of local rebels and top quality mercenaries. The Scots' initiative had forced Charles to recall parliament in November 1640 (the Long Parliament) and so exposed the weakness of the Stuart monarchy that the English now saw that rebellion was a perfectly practicable option. The Fife Conspiracy with its successful model of a largely amateur army led by ex-mercenaries had demonstrated how to start and possibly win a civil war.

Chapter 10

THE TREATIES AND
THE INCIDENT

God mixes our proceedings with success.

General Alexander Leslie, Earl of Leven

Now that hostilities had ceased, negotiations began in earnest; but the Scottish army still held northern England and the king had very little hope of driving it out by force. The two Hamilton brothers featured in the negotiations; James, the Marquis who had saved Loudoun's life, now did the same for two English generals whom Strafford wanted to have executed for cowardice, while Lanark, the younger brother, acted as go-between for the king and the Scottish army.

For a while the continuing occupation of northern England by the Scots was welcomed by the parliamentarians for they used it as leverage against the king and to help their own recruitment process as they began to prepare for war. The king, on the other hand, wanted rid of the Scots as soon as possible as they had made it clear that their upkeep had to be paid for at the rate of £850 per day, which was meanwhile extracted from Newcastle and the other towns. There was also considerable lawlessness due to English brigands pretending to be Scots soldiers and Scots soldiers acting as bandits without fear of punishment. Then the Scottish army began to suffer from desertions and disease, so Leslie was anxious to get things settled. Also at this point the scandal of Montrose's plan to change sides came to light, so he was arrested and sent back to Edinburgh as a prisoner. The army did, however, get reinforcements as Argyll and the Campbells had finished their season of ethnic cleansing in the north and came to join the main army.

At last a conference at Ripon was agreed on for the beginning of October. The Scots' team included the two earls Loudoun and Dunfermline, the borderer Douglas of Cavers, the ubiquitous lawyer Archibald Johnston, Wedderburn and Alexander Henderson. They immediately requested £40,000 per month for the army's upkeep and refused to have any dealings with Traquair. Charles reluctantly accepted the idea of the Scottish Parliament having a say in executive appointments, providing advice to the king and receiving regular visits from him, but the question of having a uniform Presbyterian Church throughout Britain was avoided. Three weeks later the Treaty of Ripon was signed. Significantly the commissioners now moved to London with another three ministers who started to do propaganda work for the cause – Robert Blair, the firebrand preacher recently returned from his exile in northern Ireland, George Gillespie from Wemyss and the Glasgow don, Robert Baillie – their objective the further spread of Presbyterianism. They were given St Antholin's Church, Budge Row, London, as their base and soon had it packed every Sunday as they preached against bishops to very sympathetic crowds.

At the beginning of November came the first meeting of the Long Parliament in London with the king behaving as if nothing had changed. He still wanted the 'shocking rebellion' put down by force, complaining that 'so great a sedition should be raised on so little a ground', a perception totally alien in his own time but one that might seem reasonable today. The Scots in London joined with the opposition ranks, demanding as they did the impeachment of Strafford who had treated the Scots settlers in Ireland so badly and, even worse, threatened to invade Scotland. And naturally they also joined in the cries for the impeachment of Laud. Their numbers increased with the arrival of Rothes, who seems to have enjoyed London society to the full and was no Puritan.

Charles was, as usual, adopting delaying tactics but gradually came to accept the Ripon proposals as inevitable unless he could find himself a new army. He tried to win over Rothes with the offer of a rich wife and high position; Rothes was wavering but died of a fever in Wimbledon without accepting the bait. In February 1641 Leslie's army was at last persuaded to return home with an advance of £300,000 and the promise of further instalments to follow. The new Act of Oblivion was passed, wiping out all guilt except for the Scottish bishops, the unpopular Traquair, the hated propagandist Walter Balcanquhal and Sir Robert

Spotiswood, who was unpopular in his own right but also had the ill luck to be the son of the late Archbishop – he was captured and later executed in 1646. His nephew John Spotiswood was to suffer the same fate in 1650.

Meanwhile the secret of Montrose's plans to change sides had been leaked by the minister of Methven Church, after which one of the Stewarts of Atholl claimed that Montrose's actions had been provoked by the Earl of Argyll's empire-building maraudings and the widespread belief that he was planning to take over from Charles as King of Scotland. Traquair and others joined in the effort to disgrace Argyll, but the wily Campbell survived and caused his luckless Stewart accuser to be executed.

The king arrived at Holyrood and though he attended church on the Sunday morning, was reprimanded by Alexander Henderson for failing to go to the afternoon service. Charles was clearly still nursing hopes of suppression by force but astutely disguised them. He recommended that the Scots should send an army of 10,000 men on a crusade to Germany to rescue his Calvinist nephew the Prince Palatine, the son of his popular sister Elizabeth and brother of Prince Rupert. Initially the Scots took kindly to this idea but the more suspicious amongst them worried that once recruited, this army would be used for quite a different purpose. Meanwhile Charles also doled out appointments and promotions to flatter the decision-makers: Argyll was made a marquis; Loudoun, Lord Chancellor; Archibald Johnston was knighted and made Lord Warriston, whilst the unpopular Sir Robert Spotiswood was dismissed.

At this point in September 1641 when all was going quite smoothly for Charles the situation was suddenly disrupted by a new scandal, known subsequently as 'the Incident.' As a consequence of some drunken boasting it came to light that William Lockhart, Lord Carnwath, had been heard to say 'There are now three kings in Scotland but by God two of them shall lose their heads.' The three to whom he was allegedly referring were Charles I, Hamilton and Argyll, so as it turned out he was under-estimating the death toll, since all three eventually did lose their heads. This was initially hushed up but following another drunken brawl, the Earl of Lindsay accused Hamilton of starting a plot. This was denied but Montrose sent word from his prison cell that it was true, both Hamilton and Argyll were plotting a coup – which he volunteered to foil by murdering the two plotters as well as Hamilton's brother, Lord Lanark. This supposed counter-plot to save the king was discovered by a Captain Stuart who informed both the fickle cavalry commander Sir John Hurry (Urie) and his commander-in-chief General Alexander Leslie, who in turn told Hamilton and Argyll. The three potential victims now delved more deeply into the counter-plot and learned from Hurry that the king himself was involved along with Lords Crawford, Almond (James Livingston) and Ogilvy, as well as two army colonels, Cochrane and Alexander Stewart. Montrose's alleged role in the plot was to break out of his cell and take over the castle, but defenders of Montrose claim that he was innocent and that the whole affair was devised by Argyll to discredit the Royalists. There is no doubt, however, that the signatures on the Cumbernauld Bond/Band had revealed genuine fear of Argyll's huge ambitions and the Incident can be viewed in the same light.

Alexander Leslie now took the lead in yet again hushing up a scandal and calming tempers all round. He was made Earl of Leven as his reward and Argyll confirmed as Marquis. The king denied all involvement but things had already turned sour. His relationship with his English Parliament had reached breaking point and the Scottish invasion, with its financial consequences, had already provided the explosive situation that would provoke the First English Civil War. In October, whilst Charles was as usual playing golf on Leith Links, news came to Edinburgh of a rebellion in Ireland that later became known as the Eleven Years War or the Confederate War, a bitter confrontation that had political and economic grievances at its roots, but was also very much a war of religion between Catholics and Protestants. It was a war in which the Scottish Covenanters were to take a major role since there were so many Scots-born Presbyterians recently settled in Ulster who would be a prime target for the dispossessed native Irish.

Thus the third war undertaken by the Covenanters was to be fought in Ireland. The Scots immediately volunteered to help the king and of course their own kin by sending an army of 10,000 at his expense to defend the Protestant cause against the Irish Catholics. Charles headed back to London immediately to deal with this new crisis on top of the ones he was already facing. It was to be his last visit to Scotland.

Chapter 11

THE SCOTS' WAR IN IRELAND

... it is no sin to kill a Protestant

Alleged remark by an Irish priest.

The Irish rebellion of 1641 that later developed to be part of the Eleven Years or Confederate War led to an estimated 400,000 deaths due to both fighting and consequential devastation, malnutrition and disease. It was only partly a religious war and Scotland was only partly to blame, though that blame could be traced back over many years.

Over several centuries Ulster had provided an asylum for warriors who had been on the losing side in Scottish wars, including for a while Robert the Bruce himself, then many of the MacSweens, MacDougalls and MacDonalds who had opposed him. Many of these Scots ended up as wandering mercenaries or gallowglass who survived in Ireland as useful aids in any rebellion. More recently they had been joined by more Macdonalds driven out of Scotland by the Campbells and the Stuart kings. They remained stubbornly Catholic but partly by marriage now had reasonable tracts of land and a grudge against any who tried to interfere with them or stop them from trying to recover their lost homelands in Scotland.

Even more recently when James VI had moved to London in 1603 he had inherited a problem in Ulster which the English, having concentrated their efforts on Dublin and the Pale, had failed to solve for many years. All efforts to settle Ulster with English Protestants had failed. Thus in his new role as King of England and Ireland as well as Scotland James decided to take an active role in encouraging new settlers in what became known as the Plantations. He already had an agent in Ireland, James Hamilton, a Presbyterian don at Trinity College, Dublin, who had acted as a spy for him in Ireland for some years. Hamilton with Hugh Montgomery, also from Ayrshire, was instructed to develop a network of contacts, initially reasonably rich men known as Undertakers who would themselves move to Ulster and then recruit Protestant families to move across from Scotland to work the land, the 'Plantin' o' Ulster'. This did not always involve the eviction of the previous tenants, for the atrocities and depredations of the Nine Years War had left Ulster underpopulated, but as numbers increased many more of the native Irish occupants were driven westwards to less fertile land. By 1622 there were about 20,000 new Protestant male settlers, mostly Scots Presbyterians, in Antrim, so given the new losses inflicted on the gallowglass there was already a serious threat of violence due both to the economic disparity and the religious divide. Taking into account the bitterness that had also built up in the south between the old Irish land-owning families and the slightly less old Anglo-Norman barons of the Pale, the addition of new English settlers brought over by Strafford provided a toxic recipe for serious conflict.

Over the previous few years Black Tom Wentworth, later Earl of Strafford, as the Englishman in charge of Ireland had managed to keep the peace by sheer force, but had added to the general resentment by the threat of further plantations in Sligo and elsewhere, and by trying to impose a uniform religion as dictated by Canterbury, a policy even less welcome in largely Catholic Ireland than it had been in Scotland. This had meant the persecution of Presbyterians, mainly the newly arrived Scottish settlers, as well as the Catholics, mostly those landowners, tenant farmers and gallowglass who had been pushed out to make room for English and Scottish newcomers. It has been estimated that some half a million acres of good agricultural land had passed from Catholic to Protestant hands over the previous thirty years, the Catholics having to make do with the less fertile land and peat bogs further west, so it was little surprise that they were looking for reinstatement. The religious divide was a facet of huge economic and political resentment at both landowner and tenant farmer levels.

Meanwhile the religious side of the conflict had been further polarised by the number of Catholic missions sent to Ireland at this time on orders from Rome. In addition there was resentment against the Episcopalian Church of Ireland imposed by Laud and Strafford, as well as the number of aggressive Presbyterian preachers driven out of Scotland in the period before the Covenant. The Catholics had been very active with both Franciscan and Dominican missions well-supported from the Continent. The Capuchins had founded new Irish colleges in Lille and Antwerp for sending missions to Ireland, which was seen as a good training area for ambitious young Catholic priests.

Thus there was now a messy new alliance of interests between the older dispossessed Irish families and the Anglo-Irish Catholics who had by this time become long-term residents, both sides hating the Strafford/Laud oppression. So the Confederacy uniting these groups was formed with two main targets – the newest settlers in the Plantations, particularly the Scots Presbyterians in Ulster, and the remaining half-English army that had been Strafford's instrument of control.

Further encouragement for rebellion came from the fact that as in Scotland and England, there were a number of experienced Irish mercenary officers such as Colonel Thomas Preston and Owen Roe O'Neill, who had good fighting experience in the Imperial and Spanish armies.

Initially aloof from the rebellion was Randal Macdonnell, Earl of Antrim, shown in later portraits as beardless and bewigged, who was more interested in the long-proposed attack on Scotland to reclaim the ancestral lands of the Macdonnells/Macdonalds and their related clans. This he saw as not just the advancement of his kindred but as a contribution to the cause of Charles I, of whom he was an ardent supporter; he had been brought up in the English court and had even encouraged 300 Protestant families to settle on his land. Twice he had begun to gather together significant armies – 5,000 to 8,000 men – at Carrickfergus ready to invade Scotland for the king, but each time, just as he was ready to embark for Scotland in 1639 and 1640, he had been forestalled by Anglo-Scottish truces and had to disband his men.

Thus despite his Catholic background, Antrim disapproved of the Irish rebellion as being against the king and even sent food supplies to help the starving Protestants of Coleraine, a town of earthen walls, which was enduring a long siege by the Confederates. This action may account for the strange fact that the Catholic rebels totally destroyed the new village he had built near his castle at Dunluce, presumably to house the mainly Catholic Macdonalds who had recently been driven out of Kintyre and the islands by the Campbells, most particularly the

belligerent Macdonalds of Dunyveg on Islay, long-term opponents of
James VI & I. The site of this vanished community was uncovered
recently and the excavations revealed that Antrim was well ahead of his
time in providing his tenants with some of the earliest indoor toilets in
the whole of Europe.

If Antrim stood aloof, the same was not true of his cousins, the father
and son Coll Ciotach Macdonnell. The father, known by his anglicised
nickname of Kolkitto or the left-handed Macdonnell, had seized the
island of Colonsay back in 1623 by murdering its chieftain, a Macfie,
and used it as a base for piracy until he was driven back to Ireland. His
son was the more famous Alastair or Alexander MacColla Macdonnell
whose mother was a Macdonald of Sanda, another small sept of the
Macdonalds that was clinging to its tiny island off Kintyre. Young
Alastair, a large and accomplished fighter, was to win fame as the pioneer
of the so-called 'Highland Charge'. He later acted as general alongside
Montrose in a series of battles against the Covenanters and meanwhile
was present at the siege of Coleraine. He was quite badly wounded in the
attack on the Protestant town of Lurgan, 18 miles south west of Belfast,
one of the key plantation settlements. As we shall see both Alastair, his
father and his two brothers were all to die violently before the end of
the war.

Thus in response to the massacre of Scottish settlers in Antrim
Sir Robert Monro of Obsdale Ross-shire was in April 1642 promoted
to the rank of major general and dispatched from Ayr under the
overall command of the Earl of Leven to land with an advance
party at Carrickfergus Castle, a huge Anglo-Norman fortress almost
surrounded by water on the estuary east of Belfast. Also officially
commissioned by the king was the new Marquis of Argyll's Regiment
of Foot, which landed on Rathlin Island under the command of the
ruthless Campbell of Auchinbreck, laird of Castle Sween. Curiously
this regiment, which remained in Ireland till 1649, was by some
strange military genetics to be the ancestor of the Scots Guards,
recycled first in 1650 as HM Foot Regiment of Life Guards to serve
Charles II at Worcester and again in 1661 to fight the Covenanters
before at last taking root in London.

In different ways the two forces were in Ireland for the same reason,
the devastating campaign waged in Ulster since October 1641 by the
Irish leader Sir Felim MacShane O'Neill. From his point of view it
was a justifiable rebellion against the intolerant regime imposed by the
English Earl of Strafford, the confiscation of so many estates by English

Protestant settlers and, particularly in the north, the huge influx of Calvinist Scottish farmers to the Plantations that had caused the eviction of the local Catholic farming families. The combination of religious persecution from England and Scotland, the loss of good farming land and the miserable condition of many of the native Irish meant that their attitude right from the start of this war was exceptionally bitter. In addition, there were numerous bands of Macdonnells, Macleans and MacDougalls who had been driven out of Scotland by the Campbells over recent years.

Thus there were already numerous atrocity stories, some perhaps exaggerated, such as the massacre of Presbyterians at Portadown where the women had allegedly been tossed off the bridge over the River Bann. The total deaths were claimed to be 20,000, again perhaps much exaggerated, as some suggest the total was nearer to 4,000 killed outright with a further 12,000 that either died due to starvation or cold or, if they survived, were driven back to Scotland in penury. In November 1641 an Irish Confederate army under Rory O'More had scored a significant victory over the resident English troops at Julianstown near Drogheda, which they had been sent to defend. By this time the rebels had captured Mountjoy, Dungannon and Charlemont, but Dublin proved too strong for them.

Robert Monro, accompanied by his nephew George, another veteran of the German wars, immediately set about the recapture of Newry – which they then looted and began ruthless reprisals against the Catholic bands that had done so much damage the previous October. Left in charge by Leven, who returned to Scotland, General Monro continued mopping-up operations but there were no major battles for the time being as the main Irish armies avoided pitched battles. Instead they left behind groups of guerrilla fighters, who continued their molestations on a smaller scale and were thus more difficult to catch. Once Munro had driven the besiegers away from Coleraine, he established a new base there for himself and left one of his kindred, Major David Monro, in charge.

To help the retaliation against the Catholic rebels, two Stewart brothers, Sir William and Sir Robert, recruited volunteers to form what became known as the Lagan Army, or the Laganeers. These two Stewarts had come across from Wigton in Scotland thirty years earlier with the Plantations and had become major landowners in Donegal with a new castle at Ramelton, ruins of which survive. In June 1642 they achieved a decisive victory over Irish Confederate troops led by Felim O'Neill at Glenmaquin in Donegal, eliminating one of the senior Macdonnells in the process.

Meanwhile a month earlier, the Campbells had landed on Rathlin Island from Kintyre and under the command of Auchinbreck began a ruthless cull of the asylum-seeking Macdonalds, many of whom had been driven there by Auchinbreck's earlier campaign in Kintyre. Like Monro's force he was there on the orders of the Edinburgh estates, but in reality he was also pursuing the traditional Campbell agenda of ethnic cleansing, perhaps also of forestalling the promised invasion of Argyllshire by the Earl of Antrim, chief of the Macdonnells. Rathlin was devastated and allegedly some of the women were tossed off a cliff into the sea, the cliff in Church Bay being subsequently known as the Hill of Screaming.

At about the same time, Monro's troops achieved the surrender of Dunluce Castle, a large, inaccessible clifftop fortress on the Antrim coast. There they arrested the earl himself, both tasks made much easier by the fact that Antrim was a supporter of the king and at this time Monro was still fighting under orders from the king and his Scottish Parliament. Antrim was imprisoned in Carrickfergus but remarkably escaped to join the queen at York, only then to be recaptured, sent back to Carrickfergus and escape a second time as he gradually achieved his long-term ambition of an Irish Royalist invasion of Scotland.

The three Monros were to fight on in Ulster for another four years, having changed seamlessly from a royal army sent by the Scottish Parliament to a purely parliamentary one, until Sir Robert was eventually routed by the Confederates at Benburb in 1646. One of the most fanatical and probably violent officers serving with Monro was the strange Major Weir, who later became a religious recluse in Edinburgh, much admired for his devotion until in old age he confessed to numerous brutal crimes and deviant practices. (See Chapter 22.)

The Scots had not started this war but they had certainly entered it of their own volition to protect their own Presbyterian enclaves, which had been created by the policies of a Scottish Protestant king. They carried on long after their initial objective was achieved and by aping the violence of their enemies they exacerbated the long-term antipathies of two rival communities struggling in a shared landscape.

Chapter 12

THE SOLEMN LEAGUE AND COVENANT

The help that we give to His blessed church shall not want a reward.
Solemn League and Covenant 1643

When in November 1641 King Charles had raced back to London from Edinburgh following the news of the Irish rebellion, he left behind him greatly divided opinion. For most of his visit he had appeared to be totally amiable, attending Presbyterian services every Sunday, golfing on Leith Links several times a week, apparently agreeing to the requests of his Scottish Parliament and avoiding any criticism of the belligerent church ministers who had fomented the rebellion against him. So many of the Scots elite, both lay and ecclesiastical, had begun to take him at his word – but others suspected, no doubt rightly, that it was all an act whilst he searched desperately for some way of raising an army to put them all in their place.

Certainly the Scots had welcomed his idea of a Scottish army going to Germany to fight for his Protestant nephew there. Similarly, they had welcomed his sponsorship of a Scottish army going to Ulster to defend their countrymen in Ireland. Equally there was no sign in Scotland of any desire to depose Charles for, after all, he belonged to a Scottish dynasty. All they wanted was for him to get rid of unpopular advisers like Laud and Strafford. However, there was perhaps now one subtle difference between the attitudes of the Scottish and English Parliaments. The Scots had got rid of bishops from their upper house but were now very much under the influence of their fanatical and middle-class clergy who dictated policy by ranting Calvinism from their pulpits and threatening excommunication for all who disagreed.

Buoyed up by the success of two little wars, they were now also obsessed with the idea of spreading Presbyterianism to England and Ireland, a far more serious and potentially dangerous proposition.

The English Parliament on the other hand was dominated by upper middle-class squires, many of them Presbyterian or at least Puritan, but more concerned about money, free enterprise and civil liberties than religion. Quite a few of them had suffered imprisonment in the Tower for objecting to semi-legal taxes such as Ship Money. Many of them in addition to being landowners, who resented unorthodox forms of taxation, had interests in trade and the colonies. In particular the three most articulate members of the opposition, Hampden, Pym and the Earl of Warwick, were amongst others investors in the Providence Island Company, a project that entailed stealing territory in the West Indies from Spain. Such men were entrepreneurs and empire-builders in a way that was still quite alien to most of the Scots and were far more materialistic.

Thus Charles had his final quarrel with the House of Commons, his botched attempt in January 1642 to arrest the five main opposition leaders. The Scots' attitude to this was in some ways hesitant, whether to believe the king's promises to them or to support their angry 'brethren' south of the border in what was mainly a political rather than a religious affair.

So for the first months of 1642 the Scots kept up negotiations with Charles, constantly looking for a firm commitment to enforce Presbyterianism in all three of his kingdoms. The usual men were involved, the fanatical pair of Alexander Henderson and Archibald Johnston, now Lord Warriston, the Chancellor Campbell of Loudoun, and sometimes Lord Lindsay. This series of deputations continued even after Charles raised his standard at Nottingham on 22 August 1642, signalling the outbreak of the First English Civil War, one of whose prime causes had been the Scottish attacks in 1639 and 1640, which had bankrupted the king and forced him to call a very hostile parliament.

By October the Royalist armies had won a few skirmishes and with a Scottish commander-in-chief, the claret-loving Lord Ruthven, had come close to an outright victory at Edgehill. Had Prince Rupert's victorious cavalry not wasted time chasing booty and stragglers, they might well have finished off the still somewhat amateurish Parliamentary troops. Even after that, Rupert was confidently heading for London and it could all soon be over. Thus Charles was far more confident of victory and had little interest in making any concessions to the Scots. He would welcome their armed support, but only on his own terms.

Therefore when the English Parliament wrote on 7 November 1642 to ask for Scottish military support against the king, the Scots agreed to consider it, but at the same time sent a deputation to Oxford to negotiate new terms with Charles. As usual the main negotiators were Henderson, Warriston, Loudoun and Lindsay, with the Provost of Irvine. Rumours were being spread that Charles was bringing across a papist army from Ireland, his troops had been looting the outskirts of London at Brentford. The Royalist retort was that the parliamentary army was riddled with Brownists, Anabaptists and even some Papists. Loudoun was warned that he would lose his Chancellor's salary whilst the two Hamiltons, the marquis who was now made a duke and his brother Lord Lanark, kept playing for time until early 1643.

Meanwhile the queen had returned from France with supplies and renewed determination. In York she was greeted by the renegade Montrose, who allegedly proposed one of his usual secret plots – including the murder of the senior Scottish Covenanters, an invitation to Robert Monro in Ireland to change sides and an invasion of Scotland by the Earl of Antrim, whilst he himself would raise the Gordons and their allies to capture Edinburgh.

The Scottish negotiators still lingered in Oxford and there was yet another plot in which one of the Lindsays seems to have been involved, this time to murder his colleague John Campbell of Loudoun, the Chancellor. Then in June the Scottish Parliament met, complaining vigorously that the costs of Monro's army in Ulster had not been paid either by the king in Oxford or by the English parliament, but for the time being agreed to forward the money itself. The erratic Robert Dalzell (1611–54) Earl of Carnwath, was prosecuted for suggesting that it was time for the Scots to aid the king against the rebellion in England, and later went south to fight in the Royalist army at Naseby, for which the Scottish Parliament deprived him of his earldom and condemned him to death. The sentence was never carried out, for he later fought at Worcester with the Scots army and was sent to the Tower. This change of mood intensified when the General Assembly met in early August with Alexander Henderson again as Moderator.

The request for help from the English Parliament was taken seriously and the Assembly approved 'the endeavours of this kirk for the reformation of the kirk of the English,' belligerent as ever and tantamount to another declaration of holy war against King

Charles. Having blessed its 'pious intentions' the Assembly group led by Henderson drew up a document entitled the Solemn League and Covenant, which amounted to an offer of military aid to England in return for England becoming Presbyterian. The draft was shown to the English commissioners and they cunningly altered the wording to endorse the abolition of bishops but not their replacement with organised assemblies. This might seem a modest difference but in the end it was to cause two further wars. For the scandals spread by the king were based on fact as the English Parliamentary army did now include increasing numbers of soldiers who disliked conformity imposed by an assembly just as much as they disliked conformity imposed by bishops. These were the Brownists, Anabaptists, Congregationalist Puritans and increasing numbers of new sects who objected to all forms of central supervision of their faiths.

Ignoring any misgivings, a deputation was sent to London made up of two church ministers, Henderson and Gillespie (both from Fife), with John Maitland, the future Earl of Lauderdale, as a kirk elder. The document of the Solemn League was signed by the English and Scottish delegations at a ceremony at St Margaret's Church, Westminster, and subject to the right financial arrangements the Scots were committing themselves to another war of religion. Whereas the aim of the English Parliament was to force the king to abandon his authoritarian stance and his unlawful taxes, the objective of Scotland's entry alongside it was simply to spread Presbyterianism, though the financial arrangement was undoubtedly an additional incentive.

Thus the Scottish entry into the English Civil War was embarked on for religious reasons, not to help topple the monarchy or help the English Parliament. Whilst as a military venture it was supposed to be self-liquidating, it was naïve of the Scots to assume that in its current chaotic state the English Parliament would hand over the wages promptly, if at all. Thus to support such a large army the Scots would almost inevitably have cash flow problems in the short, if not longer, term. The strain on the fragile Scottish economy would thus be extreme, a fact the fanatical churchmen in charge of policy chose to ignore, just as they did the possibility of a large number of casualties. In fact the war was to cause serious inflation at home; considerable exports of bullion resulted in the Scots being unable from 1639 to mint any gold coins and a currency that was one of the most debased and unreliable in Europe. This was particularly painful as at this time there were periodic famines due to a rising population and woefully inefficient agriculture, so the Scots needed gold to buy additional wheat from the Baltic ports. On top of this, owing to war disruption, Scotland's limited export trade in iron, coal, salt, glass (the new glass industry had been founded by George Hay of Kinnoul with a Venetian patent in 1610), soap, altar pieces and feather beds, was being seriously impeded.

Chapter 13

THE SCOTS HEAD
SOUTH AGAIN

... due to the ambitions of prelacy (bishops) it has been necessary to
take up arms in defence of religion and liberty

Part of Covenanter tract, 1644

From the Scottish point of view there are three important questions
to be asked about the Battle of Marston Moor, the biggest battle ever
fought on British soil and the by far largest ever fought by the Scots
on English soil.

The first is whether the English Parliamentarians would have won
if the Scots had not provided so many extra troops. The answer to
that is almost certainly no, and it might have been a shattering defeat
that would have ended the Civil War in favour of King Charles.
On the other hand if the Scots had not been there, the English
Parliamentarians might have avoided battle altogether.

The second question is just how much the Scots did contribute
to this hugely important victory. The answer at the time was much
obscured by the reluctance of Cromwell to share his glory and the
general denigration both of the Scottish commander-in-chief, the Earl
of Leven, and some of the Scots infantry.

Thirdly there is the question about the extent to which for the Scots
this was a war of religion to promote Presbyterianism whilst many in
the English army, particularly its rising star Oliver Cromwell, were
strongly opposed to such an outcome and regretted very much that their
Parliament had ever signed up to an alliance on that basis.

Meanwhile, however, the Scots took the English Parliament's
acceptance of the Solemn League and Covenant at face value and

went to war on that basis. By December 1643, Leven was in the Borders gathering some 20,000 troops. David Leslie joined him as major general of cavalry and had to break a promise he had made never to fight against the king again, but in their propaganda sheets the Covenanters claimed that they were in fact rescuing the king, not attacking him. The so-called 'purity of their intentions' was well publicised. Dutch propaganda artists such as Wenceslaus Hollar were paid to produce pro-Covenant leaflets.

Thus on 13 January the main Scottish army met by the River Tweed, some 18,000 foot and 3,500 horse along with committee members from both England and Scotland, as previously agreed, as well as a large contingent of church ministers, mainly from Fife. Six days later they crossed the border and Royalist tracts appeared saying any individuals who joined the Scots were 'traitors and vipers'. The following week Leven's second-in-command William Baillie also brought his six regiments over from Kelso to Wooler, despite deep snow followed by floods when it melted. The Royalist commander at Alnwick retreated to Morpeth and failed to demolish Felton Bridge, as he had been ordered. Meanwhile Argyll and his Campbells captured Coquet Island.

Leven and the main army rested for five days at Morpeth then reached Newcastle at the beginning of February. The Royalists had burned the suburbs to deprive the Scots of food and shelter. They now sent out a sortie under Marmaduke Langdale that picked off the cavalry detachment led by Leven's son Lord Balgonie. Another sortie led by a Colonel Bradley attacked the Scots rearguard but in the skirmish that followed he was himself captured by a Lieutenant Elliot. So his troops retreated back to the city.

After a fortnight beside Newcastle, the siege seemed likely to be protracted so Leven headed south with the bulk of his troops, leaving six regiments behind under General Lumsden to continue the siege. By March he had reached Sunderland in harsh snowy weather after fording first the Tyne at Ovingham, then the Derwent and finally the Wear, driving any Royalists troops in the area before him. Their leader in the north, the Marquis of Newcastle, had escaped from Newcastle and collected an army of approximately 18,000 men. Thus the two armies faced each other at Hylton for three days without either side showing any eagerness to start a battle, though Montrose, who was passing at the time, tried to encourage Newcastle to attack.

The Scots were reluctant because they were short of supplies, particularly fodder for their horses. Five ships with supplies had been sent south but three were sunk in a storm and the other two were driven into the Tyne where they were captured, so with hungry horses Leven could not use his cavalry or risk a battle. He headed for Durham but turned back to attempt a storming of the great fort at South Shields, thus preventing Royalist reinforcements or supplies arriving by sea. His troops were reluctant, so he punished them the following day with a 'solemn fast'. Then on the third day, under Colonel William Stewart, they successfully stormed the fort and captured its stores of ammunition. At the same time Colonel Ballantyne ambushed some Royalist cavalry at Chester-le-Street and took forty prisoners. Leven avoided battle again when Newcastle's army came close as shortage of fodder was still a problem until he found plenty at Easington.

On 25 March there were the beginnings of a major battle between the Scots at Cleadon and the Royalists at Boldon Hill, but the weather was atrocious and it was almost dark. Seven wagon-loads of English bodies were mentioned, but otherwise it ended as no more than a skirmish with a modest advantage to the Scots. So Leven allowed the army to rest till early April.

Meanwhile the joint Anglo-Scottish committee in London had sent orders to their northern army, which had just won a skirmish at Selby under father and son Fairfax; they were to join up with the Scots for an attack on York. This resulted in Newcastle's Royalists hastening back to defend York, the king sending orders to Rupert to go to his aid, and the London Parliamentarians sending their Eastern Association army also towards York. Thus there was about to be the largest gathering of troops from both sides in the entire course of English civil wars.

In this process the Scots met the Fairfax regiments at Wetherby and agreed to join the various contingents together at Tadcaster, but even this united force was still too small to risk a full siege of York, for the city's circumference was so large that the troops would be too thinly spread and therefore vulnerable to attacks by Newcastle's 5,000 cavalry. So the decision was made to wait for the Eastern Association army under the Earl of Manchester. A bridge of boats at Gainsborough helped the junction of the three armies in early June and at last the siege began. The garrison came out to burn the city suburbs to make life less comfortable for the besiegers, the Scots attacked Micklegate Bar to get booty and cattle for food, and most of the garrison's sallies were easily beaten back.

Help for the beleaguered garrison was now on the way as Prince Rupert made his roundabout way towards York, raising the siege at Lathom House in mid-May, looting Bolton a week later, and plundering Liverpool for men and materials. Meanwhile the garrison at Newcastle had offered to talk about surrender and Leven sent Lord Lindsay as negotiator, though it turned out that the Royalists were just playing for time and were far from desperate at this stage.

The news reached the triple army of besiegers that Rupert was getting nearer with some 20,000 men – so, at the beginning of July, the siege was abandoned and all the Parliamentary forces mustered on Marston Moor south of the Ouse, 5 miles from the city, intending to get between Rupert and York. Leven had now been appointed commander-in-chief of all three armies, as he was by far the most experienced general and had also provided the majority of the troops. Rupert, meanwhile, surprised everyone by choosing a different route and slipped into York without hindrance.

Inside the city Rupert met with an unexpected obstacle. He wanted Newcastle's army to join with his for a joint attack on the three enemy forces, since that way the difference in numbers would not be too great. He claimed to have had orders from the king to force a battle. The Marquis of Newcastle felt this was foolhardy and he was backed up by his second-in-command, the seventy-year-old Scots mercenary general Lord Ruthven (Rot Wein) and Lord Eythin, against whom Rupert had a long-term grudge. He had been his commander when Rupert was captured at the Battle of Vlotho and Rupert blamed Eythin for his misfortune. So in the end it was with great reluctance that Newcastle and Eythin eventually agreed to join Rupert's attack.

Meanwhile the Scots, after a night at Marston, decided to move to Tadcaster to try to trap Rupert in York and cut off his supplies, but Rupert again did the unexpected and took his joint army to Marston Moor, forcing Leven and his men to double back and find that Rupert had now occupied the best part of the Moor.

Chapter 14

THE BATTLE OF
MARSTON MOOR

Wae's us, we are all undone

Alleged cry of retreating Scottish soldiers

The precise numbers involved in this battle are uncertain but the Parliamentary forces are usually reckoned as 24,000, of whom 7,000 were cavalry, and the Royalists approximately 17,000, of whom 6,000 were cavalry. The Scots contingent had left behind a force led by Lord Callendar to besiege Newcastle but still had approximately 13,500 men, more than half of the combined Parliamentary army and a third of the cavalry. Callendar, previously James Livingston, Lord Almond, was an experienced officer from the Dutch wars and was a siege specialist but was not a zealous Covenanter. He had even joined Montrose in the Cumbernauld Band and was involved in the so-called Incident, but still trusted by Leven to do a professional job. Others had been left behind for garrison duty in the northern counties, whilst the Marquis of Argyll and the Campbells had returned to Scotland to deal with the threat from Ireland.

To make it harder to apportion credit and blame for the various stages of the battle, the Scots and English troops were mixed together across the entire front. While it may seem pedantic to detail every single regiment, this does demonstrate the way in which almost the entire Lowland aristocracy of Scotland, particularly the Fife families, turned out in force with their levies, many of them never having been in a serious battle before, many of them with only rudimentary training, though nearly every regiment had at least one ex-mercenary officer to advise their amateur commanders. It was therefore still unlikely that they would match up to the rigid standards of Cromwell's troops, shortly to be nicknamed the Ironsides, but then in Cromwell's eyes the same could be said of all the rest of the English Parliamentary army. If Cromwell subsequently found fault with the Scots on the basis that some of them lacked determination on the field, he had the same complaint about many of the English – and in both cases his disapproval was linked to their Presbyterianism.

On the right wing were Leven's own eight troops of horse, led by his son Alexander Leslie, Lord Balgonie, who had fought with his father in Germany. Beside him were the eight Dalhousie troops under their new earl, the seventy-year-old William Ramsay, a strong Covenanter, who later fought against Montrose. Then came the seven Eglinton troops under their earl, Alexander Montgomery. Beside these twenty-two troops were English cavalry regiments under Thomas Fairfax. Overall this wing was to have a difficult battle due to the much rougher ground in their part of the battlefield and they had to face the dashing Royalist cavalry commander George Goring.

On the left wing was Scotland's Lieutenant General of Horse, the experienced David Leslie, who shared this position with Oliver Cromwell, and 3,000 of what became known as his Ironsides after a quip by Prince Rupert. Leslie had a thousand men, twenty-four troops including his own eight and eight troops each under young Alexander Lindsay, Lord Balcarres, who was in his mid-twenties, and Thomas Maclellan, Lord Kirkcudbright, who was known always to keep a barrel of brandy on the front line for his own and others' refreshment. On the whole, the left wing was to have a much better battle than the right, for though faced by the experienced Royalist Lord Byron and Prince Rupert himself, Cromwell was to play a major part in the victory, well supported by Leslie who took over command while Cromwell was off the field having a wound dressed. With a contribution of sixteen of the twenty-four troops, Fife also thus played a major part in this section of the battle.

To the left of the left wing were the Scottish dragoons, under the able Hugh Fraser who made a major contribution to the battle and had strong Fife connections as he was not only the Earl of Leven's son-in-law but his battle-hardened dragoons were mainly recruited from the Scottish mercenaries in Germany, many with a Fife connection. He had personally advanced 2,000 merks for firelocks and pikes. It was these dragoons who played the vital role of breaking up the pike formation of the Newcastle Whitecoats who had withstood the other cavalry.

The Scottish infantry on the right of the centre were under the control of William Baillie, with Sergeant Major General James Lumsden, another experienced Fife mercenary, at his elbow. They shared the centre with the English foot under the Earl of Manchester and the elder Fairfax. They were facing Newcastle's famous veterans known as the Whitecoats, or the Lambs. In the van was the Earl of Crawford and Lindsay's Brigade including his own Fife regiment and the Midlothian regiment, sponsored by the Maitland family but with the future Earl Lauderdale (his father was close to death at the time) back on duty in Parliament, it was led by Colonel Pitscottie. Then came the Alexander 'Sandy' Hamilton's Brigade with his own Clydesdale regiment, and the Edinburgh regiment led by James Rae. Finally there were the Teviotdale and East Lothian Regiments under Patrick Hepburn.

Behind was the Chancellor, John Campbell of Loudoun's Brigade, including his own Loudoun and Glasgow regiment; the Tweeddale regiment under the teenage Francis Scott, Earl of Buccleugh, son-in-law of the prominent but now deceased Covenanter Earl Rothes; and Lord Gordon's Regiment, the only one from north of Dundee. Next was John Kennedy, Lord Cassillis' Brigade with his own Kyle and Carrick regiment, plus the Nithsdale and Annandale regiment, led by William Douglas of Kilhead. The Earl of Dunfermline, Charles Seton's Brigade included his own Fife Regiment and the Strathearn Regiment under John Elphinstone, Lord Cupar, Balmerino's heir. Seton was later to turn half-Royalist in 1649, if not before. Lord Livingston's Brigade had the Stirlingshire regiment, under Lord Livingston himself, and the Linlithgow and Tweeddale regiment, under the Master of Yet. Finally there was Viscount Dudhope's Brigade, with the Angus regiment led briefly by himself, until he was made a prisoner, and the so-called Ministers' Regiment, the Levied Regiment, led by Lord Sinclair, and the Galloway Regiment under William Stewart.

The performance of some of these troops was to be called into question but they did face very strong opposition from Newcastle's Whitecoats or the Lambs, amongst the very few troops in this war who fought to the last man. Amongst those who did well, however, was Lindsay's Fife regiment.

In charge of the artillery was General 'Dear Sandy' Hamilton. Doing two jobs on the day, he had around fifty culverins (primitive field guns with a roughly 5-inch bore) and twenty assorted cannons.

Leven positioned himself in the centre whilst in the rear was the Ministers' regiment commanded by Arthur Erskine. Ministers acting as chaplains included the fire-eating Robert Traill, Robert Blair and Robert Douglas, who had been a chaplain with the Scottish troops in Germany, plus several of the Fife diehard Covenanters. Adam Hepburn was in charge of money and Ludovic Leslie, David's brother, quartermaster general.

Amongst the Scots serving with the English Parliamentary army was the strongly Presbyterian Lawrence Crawford, an experienced ex-mercenary stationed on the left wing with his musketeers beside Cromwell, and Crawford was to do well. John Meldrum was absent, fighting in the south. Of the three main Scots on the Royalist side, two were in the centre – the Orcadian ex-mercenary John King, Lord Eythin, who had been so reluctant to obey Rupert due to their on-going personal feud; as was the bibulous Patrick Ruthven, Earl of Forth, the commander at Edgehill who refused to serve under Rupert at Marston Moor. The third was the enigmatic Sir John Hurry, back in England since the Incident, who was to do well with Byron in the Royalist cavalry but was perhaps already considering changing sides. Colonel Robert Napier was also to acquit himself well in this section of the battle under Byron. The main Scottish Royalist not present at the battle was of course Montrose who passed by the next day on his way north to start a new war in Scotland.

On the day of the battle it was 4pm before the troops had all reached their positions on the moor, particularly the dilatory Lord Ruthven's garrison troops. So Prince Rupert decided that it was too late to start the battle; he went for his supper and the Scots could be heard singing their psalms. There was an artillery barrage but it did little damage. It was soon after this that the commander-in-chief Alexander Leslie, Lord Leven, stout, elderly, plagued with rheumatics and old injuries, consulted his committee and made the most important decision of the entire Civil War. There had been a thunderstorm and he used this as cover to order a surprise attack on the unsuspecting Royalists. It was a bold move and assumed that the battle would be over by nightfall, in a couple of hours.

Initially on the left Crawford's infantry made good headway against Napier on the opposite side, while in the same area Cromwell's horse going forward at his trademark disciplined fast trot overcame Byron, his opposite number. Byron however managed to counterattack with some success and at this point Cromwell was injured so he left the field briefly to have his neck-wound bandaged. David Leslie took over command, driving Byron back again with his cavalry and musketeers until Cromwell came back in time to meet the next big charge by Rupert's reserve. So between them Cromwell and Leslie achieved victory on the left wing.

The right wing meanwhile under Tom Fairfax was faring much worse after suffering a full gallop charge by Goring's cavalry, but from a Royalist point of view this success was wasted for Goring's men just like Rupert's at Edgehill galloped off to chase the fugitives and plunder instead of regrouping to finish off the battle.

Whereas the overconfident Goring thus failed to regroup until it was all too late, Cromwell and Leslie having won their battle on the left wing were disciplined enough to regroup and go to the aid of the right wing and centre, where many of the Scots and English infantry had been put to flight by the Royalists. Sandy Hamilton's regiment was badly mauled, as were Lindsay's and Maitland's, but they held their ground. Eglinton's cavalry on the right wing was also in severe trouble; his own son was killed as were two other Montgomery family officers. Similarly struggling were Loudoun's and Buccleugh's infantry in the centre. Many had started to retreat, if not flee away altogether.

The elder Fairfax and the Earl of Leven had in their part of the battle despaired of success and fled after their men, Leven himself riding all the way to Leeds before he heard that in the end his men had won a total victory, so he shamefacedly hastened back. But above all things Leven was a survivor, a veteran of nearly seventy who had been a professional soldier for four decades and was well used to losing as well as winning. After all, it was not a custom of war at this time to fight to the death, but to survive and fight again; the only troops which did so in this battle or any other in the First English Civil War were Newcastle's home regiment, the Whitecoats or the Lambs, who did just that and made up a high proportion of the overall Royalist casualties, approximately 4,000 with 1,500 prisoners of war. By contrast, the Parliamentarians allegedly only had 300 casualties, which it is hard to believe, Cromwell had a habit of downplaying his casualty figures.

Leven was far from the only senior officer to make a premature escape, but it was just very unfortunate that he had given Cromwell the chance to denigrate his and the other Scots' contribution to the victory. Apart from Leslie's cavalry and Fraser's dragoons other Scottish contingents that had fought well included Cassilis' Ayrshire troops, the Kennedys, as did Lindsay's and Maitland's regiments of pikemen and Eglinton's light cavalry, who distinguished themselves on the right wing against Goring. As Stuart Reid in his analysis of Marston Moor sums up the Scottish contribution to the victory, 'there can be no doubt the victory was really down to the Scots for without their invasion and without Leven's ruthless pursuit from the Tyne to the gates of York the battle would never have been fought in the first place, far less won.' He also gives considerable credit to David Leslie's able support of Cromwell. Thus two of the original Fife conspirators played a crucial role in the victory, Leven by choosing the right moment to attack and David Leslie by his brilliant handling of the cavalry during Cromwell's absence from the field. In addition, three of the other Fife earls with their regiments had played an important part: Balcarres, Lindsay and Dunfermline.

Certainly some of the other Scottish regiments did perform poorly, as did some of Ferdinando Fairfax's men and the Earl of Manchester's. However, it was now part of Cromwell's overall career strategy to play up his own role and downgrade that of the Scots – partly because their presence implied a commitment to the Covenant and Cromwell certainly did not want the imposition of Presbyterianism on England, which had been promised in the Solemn League. Secondly, he was now perfecting the Ironsides and planning to form the New Model Army as a highly professional force made up of 'godly men', with most of the Presbyterian officers weeded out. Thirdly, the Scottish army was now not only apparently unnecessary but it was expensive, so he wanted rid of it as soon as possible. For the time being, it was sent back to finish the siege of Newcastle. While he marched northwards Leven caught up with some of his own deserters and hanged a number of them to enforce discipline.

The English Parliamentarians now set about mopping-up operations in the south, but did it so ineffectively under their current commanders that it further angered Cromwell, whose main objective was to get rid of most of them. Of the Royalists, Prince Rupert's pride was dented and he was mortified at the death in battle of his pet dog. The Marquis of Newcastle had lost all his Lambs and all his money so he resigned and headed for the Continent, as did Lords Eythin and Forth.

The First English Civil War may have been started by a group who were mainly Presbyterian but it was to be finished by an army made up mainly of Independents, men who wanted neither bishops nor assemblies. So despite fulfilling their side of the bargain made at Westminster, making it possible for the English Parliamentarians to inflict a major defeat on the Royalists, the Scots were not to win their promised reward, nationwide Presbyterianism and adoption of the Westminster Confession. Thus disillusionment began to set in and if the English Parliamentarians would not keep their promise, perhaps there was an alternative. So the next major battle between English and Scots would be between Presbyterians and Independent Puritans.

Marston Moor was the apparently triumphant climax of the great Fife Conspiracy to confirm Presbyterianism throughout Scotland and spread it to the rest of the British Isles, but in reality it was the beginning of the end. For in fact by helping Cromwell's Independents to defeat the Anglican Royalists, they had turned a short-term victory into a long-term defeat. The final throw of the dice regarding the Solemn League and Covenant came when the so-called Treaty of Uxbridge was offered to the king in November 1644. Largely drafted by the Scots lawyer Archibald Johnston, Lord Warriston, its basic demands were for England to be made Presbyterian and Charles to hand over control of the army to Westminster. As usual, Charles prevaricated, playing for time.

Chapter 15

THE SCOTTISH CIVIL WAR

For the True Protestant Religion and His majesty's Sacred Authority
Banner slogan of Montrose

It is extremely hard to assess the career of James Graham, Marquis of Montrose, without bias in one direction or the other. He was certainly a brave, charismatic and heroic figure who had the appeal of a constant underdog and made good against incredible odds, a fine swordsman and rider who could also write poetry. But even before Marston Moor he had been involved in a number of controversial if not hare-brained plots, was desperate for personal glory and something of an exhibitionist, as for example in his crossing of the Tweed at the start of the Second Bishops' War. Sir Walter Scott, John Buchan and others have portrayed him as an iconic Scottish hero and martyr, but it is worth remembering that all his most famous battles were fought against fellow Scots. They were also almost entirely against Presbyterians, though he was one himself, an elder and patron of Auchterarder Church.

Back in Oxford in the period prior to Marston Moor, Montrose had been threatened with punishment for refusing to sign the Covenant, though he had signed it willingly enough in 1638. However, the king had fallen out with his two other favourites, the Hamilton brothers, and the marquis had been imprisoned in St Michael's Mount. So Charles now began to listen again to the idea of a joint Royalist attack in Scotland with Antrim supplying his Irish troops and Montrose raising the Gordons in the north east.

Montrose had already tried out some of his plans in 1643 with a series of skirmishes in northern England where, with a small troop of followers, he had briefly captured Carlisle from its Scots Covenanter garrison and plundered Morpeth. In March 1644 there had also been a promising rising in Aberdeenshire by the Gordon lairds of Haddo and Drum, who had plundered Aberdeen. George Gordon, Earl of Huntly, despite the opposition of one of his own sons, had also joined in 'Haddo's Raid' before retreating as he always did when faced with serious opposition to Auchindoun. Argyll and his Campbells came to the rescue of Aberdeen, plundering Drum, Kellie and Geich castles. Huntly was excommunicated by the Church of Scotland and fled to Strathnaver. The Laird of Haddo was captured and executed in Edinburgh. So the north-eastern part of Montrose's plan had failed before he even arrived on the scene. Two of his main supporters, Lords Crawford and Maxwell, had also been captured in the siege of Newcastle. Thus when he passed the site of Marston Moor in July 1644, all he had with him were two companions, William Rollock and his servant Sibbald. Even his close associate Lord Ogilvy was left behind as he journeyed northwards in great secrecy.

As it happened his timing on this occasion was perfect for on 8 July, some 1,600 Irish/Scots warriors had landed in Ardnamurchan under the command of Alastair/Alexander MacColla Macdonnell acting on behalf of the Earl of Antrim. He had already conducted a trial expedition to Scotland in 1641 when 150 of his men were trapped and killed on Islay by Campbell of Ardkinglass. MacColla now began moving rapidly round Skye and Kintail, encouraging the local Keppoch Macdonalds, Farquharsons and Macphersons to join him and sending round the fiery cross as a symbol of rebellion. He captured two Campbell-held castles, Mingary and Kinlochaline. Argyll and the Campbells were in pursuit but failed to catch him, though they did manage to burn all his ships, thus cutting off his escape back to Ireland. Donald Macranald of Glengarry, a veteran of the Thirty Years War, retaliated with wholesale killings of Campbells, aided by John Macdonald of Moidart (d. 1670) and his alcoholic son Donald Dhu (d. 1686), later to be obsessed by an apparently giant toad that lived in the dungeons of his castle on the remote island of Canna. His unfortunate wife was lucky to escape his clutches by abseiling down the castle cliff using a rope of knotted sheets.

Despite huge secrecy MacColla and Montrose did eventually manage to exchange messages and arranged to meet in Badenoch. Thus in the end Montrose arrived dressed as a simple highlander at Blair Atholl with a single companion, Patrick Graham, and raised his standard on the hill. MacColla arrived with some 1,500 men and Montrose recruited 800 from Atholl with another 500 under John Graham, Lord Kilpont, and Sir John Drummond, who was supposed to be fighting for the Covenanters. Montrose was also at some point joined by his nephew the Master of Napier and his brother-in-law Lord Napier (son of the famous mathematician and inventor of logarithms), one of his closest advisers. With this force he headed southwards beyond Perth. It was a pioneering example of what became a pattern in Scottish history for the next century, the harnessing of the restless, impoverished clans of the north to intimidate opposition in the south, the lure of booty to provide a self-liquidating military force to achieve the objectives of the Stewart/Stuart dynasty as it struggled to maintain or recover power in the south. For the same ends, Montrose was also exploiting the age-old hatred of the Macdonalds for the Campbells of Argyll, who had been eroding their lands for so long.

After bypassing Perth, Montrose was confronted by a Covenanter force twice the size of his own, 6,000 men under Lords Elcho, Tulliebardine and James Drummond, with Sir James Scott. Despite his lack of numbers and complete absence of cavalry, Montrose deployed his troops three deep instead of the more usual five deep over the fields of Tippermuir, with his front rank musketeers ordered to fire first, followed by the second stepping forward, then the third. This was more or less standard practice when there was no panic and would be followed by a charge with swords or pikes. However, with the relatively untrained Irish, some without muskets, the charge was faster, the first example of what became known as the Highland Charge, a tactic often successful over the next century. On this occasion it worked well for the Covenanter cavalry, under James Drummond, unexpectedly fled the field, perhaps because his brother Sir John with his family levies had already decided to change sides. The cavalry were soon followed in retreat by Elcho's foot, who were barely trained raw recruits. James Drummond (1615–75) was certainly not an enthusiastic Covenanter and did eventually join Montrose after the Battle of Kilsyth. He later became Earl of Perth and his son was a prominent persecutor of the Covenanters in the 1680s, a Catholic and a staunch Jacobite.

It was a devastating victory against the odds with very few casualties on Montrose's side, except for his newly joined supporter Lord Kilpont, and he was now joined by more local lairds, three Ogilvys, Lords Dupplin and Kinnoul. He captured Perth where he collected a sufficient number of horses to form his first cavalry units and headed for Dundee, then Aberdeen.

At the Bridge of Dee there were 2,400 Covenanter troops waiting to prevent his entry, but he by-passed them and sent in a party under flag of truce to negotiate the city's surrender. Sadly, and probably by accident, the Aberdonians shot the drummer boy escorting the deputation and Montrose seems to have lost his temper. He ordered an immediate attack without quarter and a two-hour battle was followed by slaughter, rape and looting. As Spalding put it 'nothing was heard but pitiful howling, crying, weeping and mourning through all the streets.' Unfortunately it was one of the preconditions of having Irish and Highland troops that they were always anxious for booty. Meanwhile all the Aberdeen clergy had withdrawn to the safety of Dunnottar Castle.

Despite his two victories Montrose was still far from safe, for Argyll was still pursuing him with some 4,000 Covenanter troops. So he soon abandoned Aberdeen for the mountains where cavalry could do him little harm, burning Dun and picking up arms on the way whilst his Gordon allies captured Fyvie Castle.

There was now a reward of £20,000 for Montrose's head but he maintained his characteristic carelessness about scouting. So on 28 October his force was caught unawares by Argyll and escaped with difficulty, helped by his usual trick of leaving the camp fires burning and a forced overnight march to safety. As he made these tactical retreats, morale amongst his troops declined and he suffered a number of desertions, including several of the nobles who disliked the hardship of constant retreats and the Highlanders who wanted to go home for the winter. Even his trusty servant Sibbald absconded. Yet he nearly caught Argyll's army by surprise at Dunkeld. The frustrated Argyll resigned his command.

Meanwhile there was other work for Argyll as the Scottish Parliament had met and appointed him, with his namesake Loudoun, Lords Balmerino and Warriston, plus three town provosts – Edinburgh, Ayr and Irvine – to join English parliamentarians in talks with the king, planned to take place in Uxbridge early in 1645. Lauderdale as a London-based commissioner was also involved and at this time gave his first hints of a change of attitude. Superficially King Charles appeared to be on the verge of surrender and open to negotiation but, as ever, he had no intention of making concessions and he was clinging to hope now that Montrose showed some signs of success.

Charles also sensed that the growing rift between Presbyterians and Independents in England would help his case.

Montrose spent the winter of 1644–45 laying waste Glenorchy and other Campbell territories, always on the move in what was now a war of revenge and attrition between two great clans, the Macdonalds and Campbells. It was in December 1644 that the MacIain Macdonalds of Glencoe came to join Montrose's army at Inveraray. Argyll had to escape by boat from his winter quarters in the town whilst Montrose swept through Lorn and Lochaber.

In response Argyll gathered a force of 3,000, about half of them Campbells, plus another 1,000 sent from Edinburgh, to defend his clan's territories and headed for Inverlochy (near what later became Fort William) at the end of January to wait for reinforcements from Inverness led by Mackenzie of Seaforth. Montrose aimed to attack him before these reinforcements could arrive, so he headed up Glencoe, perhaps guided over the Devil's Staircase by one of the local Macdonalds, then took 1,500 men on an epic winter 36-mile march through the Corrieyairack Pass, over Glens Roy and Spean, to emerge at nightfall unexpectedly on the Campbells' more vulnerable flank. It was 2 February 1645.

After a short rest and despite being seriously outnumbered, Montrose attacked at dawn on a broad front, his lowland musketeers in the centre, the Irish on the wings. Argyll himself had suffered a fall and was resting offshore on his birlinn, so his force was led by Duncan Campbell of Auchinbreck, the hate-figure who had ethnically cleansed Kintyre and massacred the people of Rathlin. Thus the Antrim Macdonnells and their Macdonald cousins from Keppoch, Glencoe and Glengarry were highly motivated and charged with such violence that many of the Covenanters and Campbells panicked and fled, only to be chased and slaughtered by Ogilvy's cavalry. For the Ogilvys and the Gordons who were present it was sweet revenge, though Sir Thomas Ogilvy was one of the few Royalist casualties. No quarter was given to any of the Campbells, some 1,500 – or half the force – were killed and Auchinbreck either died in the fighting or according to an alternative record was executed afterwards.

As Ian Lom, the resident Macdonald bard, wrote (in Gaelic, so translated here):

> On the day they thought all would go well
> The heroes chased them over the frozen ground.

John Buchan's narrative gives a vivid picture of the green Campbell kilts contrasting with their blood.

Montrose still had enemies to face and though he moved on to Inverness the town was too well defended for him to storm, so he went on a recruitment and plundering expedition along the Moray and Buchan coast. In April, he suffered a devastating personal blow when his eldest son John, aged sixteen, died at Bog of Gight Castle after a short illness, his health doubtless damaged as he had accompanied his father through the tough winter campaign. Montrose extracted blackmail in return for sparing Elgin, let the Farquharsons plunder Cullen, took Craigievar Castle, and stopped at Dunnottar where sixteen kirk ministers were hiding – including Andrew Cant and William Douglas. The castle would not surrender so he carried on south where the latest army of Covenanters was gathering under William Baillie, with Sir John Hurry, plus Lords Cassilis, Balmerino, Kirkcudbright and Lothian, some of them part of the Estates Committee sent to supervise the unfortunate General Baillie. With an additional 1,500 so-called redcoats from Monro's force in Ireland, plus the cavalry of Lord Balcarres and Sir William Hacket, Baillie's force far outnumbered Montrose's total of 3,000 men.

Argyll refused categorically to serve under Baillie, so he headed home. The two armies came within sight of each other near Brechin, but Montrose headed away to plunder Dundee. He then again carelessly neglected to send out scouts and was nearly caught by Baillie, who wanted to attack. For some reason his rebellious colleague John Hurry (he had changed sides after Marston Moor) refused to co-operate and Montrose did one of his overnight disappearances, marching off 20 miles to Glenesk. Meanwhile with nothing happening, the members of both the Parliament and the Assembly were arguing and blaming the bad state of the country on the sins and selfishness of the people, so the army received orders to be sober and righteous; they also complained to the king about the 'horrible cruelties' of the Irish and told him to 'repent or face the consequences.' Finally they imposed extra taxes and ordered further conscription of soldiers before retiring to study the new Westminster Confession, which had just arrived from London.

As Baillie continued trailing Montrose, he had problems. Army morale was poor due to delays in wages, he had the parliamentary committee looking over his shoulder and his cavalry commander, the former Royalist John Hurry, was regularly obstreperous. So for relaxation he took his troops to plunder the enemy territories of Atholl and the Gordons.

At last, however, in early May, the two armies confronted each other at Auldearn near Nairn – though Baillie and some of the Covenanter troops had not yet caught up. Meanwhile, Hurry was in charge and snatched the chance of a personal victory. Montrose had time to place MacColla and his Irishmen on a hill out of reach of the cavalry whilst he put up a decoy standard and hid his main troops in the village. Hurry fell into the trap, attacked the decoy standard and exposed his flank to cannon fire from the village. MacColla charged too soon and suffered from Hurry's remaining cavalry. The troops of Loudoun and Lothian held their own against the Royalists until they were scattered by their own locally raised Moray cavalry, led by a Major or Colonel Drummond, who either deliberately or accidentally turned the wrong way. It was almost a repeat of the incident at Tippermuir and this time Drummond was court-martialled and shot at Inverness. The battle was finished off when the Gordons attacked the Covenanters' rear, though their chief was killed in the action. Also killed with many of his regiment was Sir Mungo Campbell of Lawers, Loudoun's nephew, who had formed the Argyll Regiment of Foot back in 1639 and had led them in both Ireland and Scotland for six eventful years. Famously, the seven nephews of Douglas of Cavers were among the dead.

Montrose was now able to resume his raids along the north-east coast with impunity, recruiting more Highlanders to his army and heading down to Cupar, which he burned, then again plundering Campbell lands. The Keppoch and Glencoe Macdonalds joined the Macnabs and Macgregors in a savage killing and plundering spree through the Glenorchy Campbell heartland on Loch Tay. At the same time, Baillie was ordered by the Committees to head north but to leave behind some of his best troops to defend Edinburgh. He joined up with Hurry and the remnants of his force before taking Montrose by surprise again near Coklaroquhy, but Montrose pretended to dig in when in fact he was doing one of his quick escapes. The wasting of crops had been so thorough that Baillie was running out of food for his troops, so more of his men were taken away from him to defend Argyll. He resigned at this point and was briefly replaced by Lord Lindsay with orders to attack Montrose, but Montrose kept out of his way at Keith.

The next opportunity for battle was at Alford when Baillie, once more in command, caught up with Montrose on the Don. Lord Balcarres for the Committee ordered Baillie to attack against his own judgment as Montrose was in a good position and for once had the larger of the two armies. Thus Montrose formed up with his cavalry under the Gordons to the rear and his infantry line six deep, whereas Baillie could only manage three.

Balcarres leading the Covenanter cavalry was the first to charge, but about a third of his men refused to join him while the Royalist cavalry were able to attack the opposing infantry from the rear, Gordon himself one of the casualties. Yet again the micromanagement by committee impaired the Covenanters' war effort. What is more, the Fife contingent had done more harm than good.

Montrose now had another raiding spree and his troops were let loose on Cupar and neighbouring Campbell lands, but Baillie was still in pursuit. He nearly caught Montrose again, fording the Almond, but this time it was Hurry who was too slow arriving, so Montrose carried on with his depredations, burning Muckhart, Dollar and Alloa as he passed. Baillie was ordered to establish his force above Kilsyth and chose a good position to await the arrival of Montrose. However, his committee were not happy and ordered him to change his position at the last minute. Thus he was exposed to a flank attack by Montrose while making the awkward move from one side of the hill to the other. It was another rout with some 6,000 Covenanter casualties, survivors chased up to 14 miles away and given no quarter. Fought on 15 August, it was the most costly battle of the Scottish Civil War and left Montrose for a short time the virtual master of Scotland. In reality, however, it was utterly pointless because news had now arrived of the crushing defeat of the English Royalists by Cromwell at Naseby in early June. The Scottish Civil War had been no more than a side-show to the much larger drama in England and Montrose's tiny army would soon be at the mercy of the big battalions.

In the meantime, he made his new headquarters at Bothwell – then proceeded to extract money from Glasgow in return for not setting it on fire and for only executing a few of its malcontents. As official Viceroy of Scotland he was joined by even more of the Scottish aristocracy: the Marquis of Douglas, the Earls of Linlithgow, Annandale and Hartfield, Lords Seton, Drummond (his former opponent at Tippermuir), Erskine, Fleming, Carnegie, Madertie (another Drummond) and Johnston, whilst in the opposite direction flew all the top Covenanters, heading for England and Ireland. He sent his nephew Napier to take over Edinburgh, where there had been an outbreak of plague and there he obtained the release of prisoners such as Crawford and Ogilvy, both of whom were able to rejoin Montrose for his next campaign. In his new role he knighted his colleague MacColla and summoned the Scottish Parliament to meet in October.

But his moment of glory was short, for a month before the parliament was due to meet, he was faced by an enemy stronger than any he had previously come across. He had set a dangerous precedent by mobilising the Highland Host and had achieved remarkable success but it was unsustainable.

> He either fears his fate too much
> Or his desires are small
> Who does not put it to the touch
> To win or lose it all.
>
> From a poem by Montrose

Chapter 16

THE FOUR SIEGES

Not only were their hopes of establishing Presbyterianism dashed but it became increasingly plain that now the Scots had served their purpose the English wanted rid of them.

Stuart Reid: *Crown, Covenant and Cromwell*

Whereas the Scots had played a decisive role in the Battle of Marston Moor they played absolutely none in the even more crushing victory of Naseby. The Scottish army in England, under Leven and Leslie, had been given only minor roles for twelve whole months between the two battles whilst Cromwell purged the parliamentarian army of Presbyterians and focused on his professional New Model Army. He now only had Thomas Fairfax above him in the rankings and dominated the arguments, so he had little use for the expensive and demanding Scots. He had no desire to acknowledge the Solemn League and Covenant, which meant England becoming Presbyterian, so he wanted to finish off the war without any help from the Scots, but was not yet quite ready to have them paid off and sent home.

In the meantime, Leven had completed the capture of Newcastle in late June 1645 whilst half his army went westwards to prevent any effort by the king to join Montrose in Scotland. The Scottish commissioners in London ordered Leven to join up with the New Model Army, but he moved southwards slowly, during July, stopping at Nottingham and Birmingham and headed for Hereford to prevent Charles from recruiting in the West Midlands and Wales. Thus began his siege of Hereford at the end of July and whilst there he was visited by Sir William Fleming, a relation of Lord Callendar, with a suggestion that he and Leslie should change sides. Leven was disgusted and reported the affair to the parliament commissioners who rewarded him with plate valued at £500. David Leslie was in pursuit of the king who had moved to Litchfield, where rumour had it that he was gathering a new army of up to 6,000 men. Once Leslie had prevented this from happening he was sent with a considerable force back to Scotland to deal with Montrose.

While Leven had headed off down to Hereford, some of his troops had been diverted to complete the capture of Carlisle and this success was consolidated when a Scottish cavalry force under Colonel Sir John Browne of Fordel routed the north east Royalists at the Battle of Carlisle Sands in late 1645, with an estimated 600 captured or wounded. Browne's career is sketchily recorded and to make matters worse there was also a Parliamentary general referred to as John Brown. Browne however definitely appears to have been part of the Fife/Leslie/German connection.

Leven was now becoming increasingly impatient because of delays in the payment of his army and lack of supplies for the siege of Hereford. In his mid-July letter he complained that his troops were 'constrained to eat fruit and the corns that were growing on the ground' and 'they have never received but a farthing.' Nearly half his force was back in Scotland with Leslie and one of his ablest generals Lord Callendar, who was quite close to Montrose (both the Cumbernauld Bond/Band and the Incident), had resigned. The siege had been plagued with floods so that eight of his fifty miners digging tunnels under the town walls had been drowned. He thus asked the dual nation committee for permission to abandon the siege. He now received orders to besiege Newark, the last remaining major Royalist stronghold. In return he would get £1,400 per week from the Eastern Association, a lump sum of £30,000 from London and supplies for the new siege. Leven, however, was increasingly distrustful and was himself increasingly unpopular with Cromwell and the Independents, particularly when he chose to court-martial an Englishman called Case.

In this mood Leven and his army dallied through Yorkshire instead of going straight to Newark, suggesting he would not start the siege until the money and supplies were delivered to his troops. In fact it was to be November before he actually began the siege.

Meanwhile David Leslie on his route to Scotland with Balmerino had chased a Royalist force in Cumberland which, as we have seen, was subsequently eliminated by John Browne, the Scottish governor of Carlisle. Then in early September 1645 Leslie crossed the Tweed with 6,000 cavalry and 800 infantry. Montrose was still at Bothwell but MacColla had taken most of his Irish away to pursue booty, whilst some of the Highlanders had headed home for the harvest. Montrose himself with his remaining small army of 800 men headed for the Borders but with his usual lack of scouting, failed to get information on Leslie's movements and set up camp at Philiphaugh on the Ettrick Water near Selkirk. This time it was Leslie who did a surprise night march, one of Montrose's favourite manoeuvres, and he caught the little Royalist force completely off guard on 13 September.

Montrose had by this time only about 700 men, 100 of them cavalry led by Ludovic Lindsay, the ex-earl of Crawford who had been condemned to death but not executed by the Scottish Parliament a year earlier. The battle lasted only an hour, with about 300 casualties. The cavalry fled or absconded; they were almost all Gordons from Lord Aboyne's troop and objected strongly to Lindsay being given command instead of James Gordon (1620–49) Viscount Aboyne. Aboyne had been fighting with the English Royalists in 1644 before he returned to help Montrose. Ironically his first war experience as a teenager had been fighting for the mainly Catholic Gordons against Montrose at Megray Hill and Brig o' Dee. In his absence his fiancée was expropriated by his younger brother Louis, named after Louis XIV as he was born in Paris when his father Huntly was commanding the Garde Ecossaise. The son of this slightly incestuous marriage was George Gordon (1643–1716) 1st Duke of Gordon and prominent Jacobite.

As the battle fizzled out, some of the surviving Irish surrendered after an offer of quarter from Leslie. However, Leslie's army included the usual committee of politicians and clergy who overruled him and, near Newark Castle, ordered the slaughter of some 300 prisoners, including women and children camp followers. One of the ministers demanding such a breach of trust and ruthless killing may well have been John Nevoy of Loudoun, who certainly adopted this stance two years later with Leslie at Dunaverty. Such was the Presbyterian concept of divine punishment.

Montrose himself escaped, as did Lords Douglas and Napier along with ex-Lord Crawford, who died in exile in Holland after a spell in the Spanish army. Lords Drummond, Hartfield and Ogilvy were captured, as were Napier's son, William Rollock, Nathaniel Gordon and Robert Spotiswood.

A hundred more Irish stragglers were shot at the stake but MacColla was still at large with his main force, cut off from Ireland though still able to live off the land in the north. Also at large was the Marquis of Douglas, who had escaped with Lords Napier, Erskine and Fleming.

Montrose at once started recruiting a new force but, for the time being, his efforts were insignificant and it was to be another five years before he met his end. In the meantime, since Leslie and most of his army had headed back to England to join the siege of Newark, there was limited follow-up by the Covenanters after Philiphaugh. This meant Montrose was able to continue his efforts, the only problem being that this encouraged the Edinburgh committee to execute more of the Royalist prisoners. Those who met this fate included Sir Robert Spotiswood (1596–1646), the son of the late archbishop, but himself a non-combatant lawyer and Secretary of State. He was decapitated by the Maiden at St Andrews. The others were William Murray, Colonel Nathaniel Gordon and Andrew Guthrie. The hard-drinking General John Middleton (1608–74), who had been Leslie's deputy at Philiphaugh, now led a Covenanter force to attack Montrose's old allies and besieged his castle of Kincardine by Auchterarder, which he then burned after executing twelve of the garrison who had surrendered. It was to be a foretaste of his trademark ruthlessness when he later converted to be a dedicated Royalist after 1648.

Montrose, meanwhile, with a small remaining force, attacked Inverness but received orders from the king to abandon his campaign. Somehow he arranged an indemnity for himself and a few followers so he actually spent a brief period at home in Montrose, presumably with his much neglected wife Magdalen whom he had barely seen for the past ten years. Then, in early 1646, he headed into exile in Norway and was to be still abroad when she died in 1648 in her mid-thirties.

Montrose's campaign of 1644–45 had probably cost around 15,000 deaths in battle – most of them Scottish – and perhaps the same again due to looting that resulted in malnutrition and homelessness. And it was not finished yet. The major Campbell estates in Argyll and Perthshire had been systematically devastated for two years by MacColla's men and in revenge, the Campbells did the same to Kintyre and Islay, both sides indulging in what amounted to small-scale ethnic cleansing of a style which those who had served in the 30 Years War would have witnessed in Germany. Looting, murdering and crop destruction were also accompanied by the collateral spread of bubonic plague, which so reduced the population that many of these areas had to be recolonised from further south. In 2018, numerous bodies of plague victims were dug up during road improvements in Leith.

Even the lairds suffered, for the Campbell chiefs could collect no rent for years on end and were often close to bankruptcy, as were many others.

It was to be another year before the last of the Irish troops were either killed or driven back to Ireland, and another three years before Montrose made his last and fatal attempted comeback.

God has expressed his displeasure against Scotland by sending a lying spirit into the mouths of the prophets.

Pre-execution words of Sir Robert Spotiswood

Chapter 17

THE LUCK OF THE IRISH

...not only like a desert, like hell.
Comment on Ulster border lands by Owen Roe O'Neill

Whilst the Irish had been fighting in Scotland, most of the Scottish Covenanter force under Sir Robert Monro had carried on fighting in Ireland. Still in his mid-forties, he had published a diary of his service in the Thirty Years War as 'one of the Mackeys'. Since his first campaign in Ulster in 1642, when he had captured Newry and rescued Coleraine for the Presbyterian cause, he had made little further progress other than clearing northern Ulster of Catholics and preventing further attacks on the Scots Presbyterian farmers in the Plantations. The Irish Confederate Army under Felim O'Neill avoided any pitched battles and preferred to undertake guerrilla missions, whilst Monro responded by systematically destroying castles, farms and villages belonging to Catholic families. However, the Edinburgh committee always kept him short of supplies and money, so to the disgust of the future General Turner he never felt strong enough at this stage to fight his way down to the south. Thus the ambition of the Scots to conquer all Ireland and convert all the Irish to Presbyterianism was making little headway.

Monro's tactics, and those of his allies the Laganeers under Sir Robert Stewart in Derry, were consistently ruthless so that the death toll was higher than in the English Civil War owing both to the rarity of taking prisoners and the collateral damage to crops, leading to starvation and disease.

In 1644, however, the picture changed somewhat as the English Royalists in Ireland under Ormond received orders from the king to make peace with the Irish Confederates, so it now became a two-sided war instead of three-sided. Monro, as part of the Scottish army, was bound by the Solemn League and Covenant; this made him an ally of the English Parliamentarians and in April 1644, he was appointed commander of the English as well as the Scottish troops in Ireland. With this backing he was able to capture Belfast then headed south towards the Pale, attempting, without success, to capture Drogheda and Dundalk. He had been ordered to send home many of his original Scottish soldiers to combat Montrose, so his army was now about 6,000 strong with sixty per cent Scots and forty per cent English, but he also had with him the Laganeers together with a small troop of Ulster cavalry.

With all this new activity Monro gave the impression that his target was Kilkenny, the capital of the Confederate Irish, but this turned out to be much harder than expected. The Confederates had just received a large new delivery of arms and money organised by the Papal nuncio Giovanni Battista Rinuccini, who had been drafted in from La Rochelle. So their able ex-mercenary general, Owen Roe O'Neill, was able to raise an army of 5,000, smaller than Monro's force and devoid of artillery, but capable of doing at least some damage.

Thus in June 1646 Monro was heading towards Benburb on the Blackwater in Tyrone, not expecting any serious opposition. His troops had just done a tiring 15-mile march when they found O'Neill had arrived at Benburb ahead of them. Monro's small cavalry force was sent into the attack but was badly mauled by the Irish musketeers and pikemen who then, by push of pike, inflicted a rout on the Anglo-Scots Parliamentary army. Some of the success was attributed to the extra-long pikes of the Irish. Munro lost 2,500 men, a huge reduction in his fighting capacity. He had no choice but to drag the survivors back to Carrickfergus and hold out there for as long as he could.

As it turned out, he lasted two years until Cromwell's General Monck captured the castle. This was mainly due to the fact that Monro had sent most of his troops, under his nephew George, back to fight for the now Covenanter/Royalist regime in Scotland, which was opposing Cromwell in the disastrous Preston Campaign. And in addition, some of Monro's remaining troops at Carrickfergus were opposed to his new Royalist leanings and preferred Monck. Cromwell had Monro spend five years in the Tower of London before he eventually allowed him to return to his wife, an Irish widow whom he had married before his capture.

The Irish and Scottish Highland troops who had fought with Montrose had still been staging their long retreat back to Ireland. Sir Alastair MacColla spent most of his remaining two years in Scotland ravaging Campbell territory. Starting with Loudoun in Ayrshire, he then defeated a Campbell force under Ardkinglass in Perthshire, burned down Castle Sween – the home of his dead but still hated adversary Campbell of Auchinbreck – and burned a barn (the Barn of Bones) containing some two dozen Lochnell Campbells at Lagganmore in Glen Euchar. The Campbells responded with a massacre of the Lamonts of Cowal at Asgog, who had been supporters of MacColla. As he retreated down Kintyre, burning everything in his way, MacColla fought a rearguard action at Rhunahaorine Point opposite Gigha to gain time, and then got his father and brothers to make a last stand at Dunaverty Castle, a rock-top fortress on the Mull of Kintyre, which was almost impregnable but had a poor supply of drinking water. The garrison, mostly MacDougalls and Macdonalds, surrendered to General Leslie on the promise of mercy. However, the devout John Nevoy as an army chaplain overruled Leslie and insisted that all should be executed. Leslie's deputy, Colonel and later General Turner, commented in his diaries that MacColla was 'nae sojer' if he paid so little attention to water supply.

There were similar last stands at another remote Macdonald castle at Dunyveg on Islay and on the tiny island in nearby Loch Gorm. MacColla's two brothers were both killed and his father, the old pirate Kolkitto, was hung from the mast of his own ship. Many other prisoners of war were impressed for service in the French army.

The Irish and Scottish survivors of MacColla's campaign were immediately re-employed in the Irish Confederate Army and almost all were killed; MacColla himself was executed after being made prisoner at the Battle of Knocknanus in 1647. He was still only thirty-eight.

Have you had enough of it now, Master John?
Alleged question addressed to John Nevoy by a disgusted David
Leslie, when he noticed the minister's shoes were spattered with
blood after the execution of Macdonalds at Dunaverty.

Chapter 18

THE KING SURRENDERS

Then I am bought and sold.

Charles I, January 1647

The third siege of Newark, begun by the Earl of Leven's army in November 1645, was a protracted affair but Newark had already survived two sieges. The first, ironically, was when the Royalist governor of the town was a Scottish mercenary, Sir John Henderson, and he beat off a small Parliamentary army without difficulty in February 1643. The second, equally ironically, was in March 1644 when the Parliamentary force was commanded by another Scottish mercenary, the wily Sir John Meldrum. He had a much bigger force but a big area to cover and was driven away by one of Prince Rupert's lightning cavalry strikes. On both these occasions Newark's defences had proved hard to overcome, for as the River Trent split in two it meant that part of the town was effectively an island. However, Newark was such an important base for the Royalists, given its control of the north-south road, that it was given additional artillery and fortifications after the second siege. A huge 300-foot square earthwork, named the King's Sconce, was built covering 3 acres with bastions and cannons at each corner and surrounded by a ditch 30 feet wide and 15 feet deep. A similar fort, the Queen's Sconce, which still survives, was built on the southern approach to the town.

King Charles had visited the town just before the third siege in October after his defeat at Rowton Heath and it was at nearby Welbeck Abbey that he heard the bad news about Montrose's defeat at Philiphaugh. It was also at Newark that he had his biggest quarrel with his nephew Rupert whom he had rather unfairly dismissed after his surrender of Bristol. He also caused offense by sacking the governor of Newark, one of Rupert's friends. Charles then left for Oxford again on 3 November and Rupert retired to Belvoir nearby.

The new town governor Lord Belasyse made preparations for the expected siege by laying in provisions and having an additional defensive ditch dug round the whole town. He also demolished all buildings outside the town walls to deny cover to the besiegers.

On 26 November 1645 Leven arrived with his troops and met the Parliamentarian General Poyntz, who had been storming nearby Royalist outposts and killing off the garrisons. It was his role to attack the southern defences of Newark, while the Scots would cover the north. The two forces now comprised about 16,000 men, compared with a garrison of 2,000 Royalists. Leven's men stormed the Muskham Bridge, just as John Meldrum's men had in 1644, to keep control of the island area in the Trent, west of Newark. Poyntz's men also began digging a chain of earthen forts and ramparts on the south and east, while the Scots appropriately built 'Fort Edinburgh' on the island. So by March 1646, Newark was completely surrounded. Poyntz even tried to dam the river to stop the watermills from grinding the garrison's corn. Meanwhile Leven, who at sixty-five was getting a bit old for winter sieges, had moved his quarters to Newcastle and David Leslie, back from Philiphaugh, took over command of the force besieging Newark.

Meanwhile developments were in hand on the diplomatic front. Back in July 1645, the mysterious Jean de Montereul (*c.*1614–51) had appeared in London volunteering to act as a negotiator between the two sides. A church-trained diplomat in his early thirties and **protégé** of the Bourbon Contis, he had already been to Edinburgh but made no headway with his negotiations there. Specifically his brief came from his master, Cardinal Mazarin, for French policy was as usual to divide and rule, to weaken Great Britain by getting the Scots to do a separate deal with the king. Montereul therefore dealt secretly with the Scottish commissioners in London, including Lauderdale, and with the king, to organise a separate treaty, though little was put on paper.

Charles was in an awkward position: Generals Fairfax and Ireton were closing in on York, so there was real risk that he would be captured by the New Model Army. However, he still clung to hopes of raising a new army from Ireland or Wales and, perhaps thanks to Montereul, began to appreciate the growing divide between the Scots Covenanters and the English Independents, the two alternative styles of Calvinism. Neither wanted bishops, but the Scots wanted assemblies whilst the English majority, at least in the New Model Army, wanted churches free from all central control.

So on 27 April 1646, the king shaved off his beard, donned simple clothes and escaped at night from York. He also sent off several decoys dressed to look like him and travelling in various directions to confuse his enemies. He himself headed apparently for London as if undecided as to where he was going to surrender, but then he turned back towards Newark and presented himself after eight days travelling to General David Leslie at his quarters in Southwell, Kelham. Despite Charles's understanding that Montereul had informed the Scots in advance, his arrival came as a complete surprise, 'a strange providence', but it was to turn out to provide the Scots with the temptation to start another two wars.

David Leslie was embarrassed by the fact that Charles hinted at some secret deal behind the backs of the New Model Army and immediately insisted that Charles should order the governor of Newark to surrender the town, so the king sent the order a day later, on 6 May. Two days after accepting the surrender, Leslie and his army headed back north with the king to the greater safety of Newcastle. The English Parliamentarians, convinced that Charles had done some deal with the Scots, ordered that the king should be sent to Warwick, but the Scottish commissioners in London wrote back saying any suggestion that there had been any secret 'agreement between the king and the kingdom of Scotland is a most damnable untruth.'

In Newcastle Leslie could share the responsibility of dealing with the king with the Earl of Leven. Charles appeared to be willing to repeat the kind of conciliation that he had offered at Uxbridge and Leven refused to hand him over to the New Model Army on the basis that it would be a breach of the Solemn League and Covenant. At the same time he insisted that Charles sign the Covenant. Basically the Scots wanted three things; Presbyterianism throughout the British Isles, all other sects to be forbidden, and the monarchy to continue with a repentant Presbyterian King Charles at its head. The English Parliamentarians perhaps wanted much the same but the New Model Army was beginning to show signs of adopting many of the rival new sects, resenting the strictures of Presbyterianism just as much as it did those of the high Anglicans. It was also demanding toleration for all Christian sects except Catholicism and a king who would have to surrender most of his powers.

The Scots now used the opportunity to pin Charles down by insisting that he sign the Covenant. This he refused to do on two grounds; that for him episcopacy was a divine institution, and that he felt bound by his coronation oath to uphold the Church of England. So the senior church minister present in Newcastle, the veteran Fife conspirator and co-author of the Covenant, Alexander Henderson, was put to work to argue with him whilst Montereul lurked in the background. Henderson, who was by this time seriously ill, made little progress and his fellow minister Robert Baillie commented shrewdly about the king 'Though he should swear it, no man will believe it,' adding: 'If that man so now to stickle on bishops and delinquents and such foolish toys it seems he is mad. If men will not be saved who can help it?' He was probably right, for Charles was still sending letters to Ireland and Wales looking for support. The exhausted Henderson died soon afterwards without having persuaded Charles to change his mind.

In Edinburgh meanwhile, the Marquis of Argyll made an able speech to the combined committee proposing a settlement based on the Uxbridge formula, together with control of the militia passing from king to parliament for the next twenty years. Lords Lanark, Balmerino and Lindsay (now having taken over the Crawford earldom forfeited by his cousin Ludovic) joined the negotiating committee with Argyll and went on a mission to London, then back to Newcastle with the commissioners. Charles delayed replying for ten days and old Leven begged him to accept. Loudoun told him 'they desire not you nor any of your race longer to reign over them' and told him that he must accept. The two Campbells pointed out 'if your majesty lose England by your wilfulness you will not be permitted to come to reign in Scotland.' But at the beginning of August, Charles still refused to sign.

By this time Leven was becoming preoccupied with the financial state of the Scottish army in England, for the costings had long since become confused and the Scots wanted to go home just as much as the English now wanted rid of them. The English Parliament offered an advance of £100,000 and the total claim was assessed at £2 million, less £700,000 already received in kind. After considerable haggling, a settlement was eventually reached and £200,000 was actually handed over in late November. It arrived in thirty-six carts and took nine days for the Scots in York to count. The Scottish Royalists looked on this as a Judas-like act of selling the king to his enemies.

Meanwhile the Marquis of Hamilton had reappeared from his prison cell on St Michael's Mount and took over the role of chief Royalist negotiator, the beginning of what turned out to be an ambivalent relationship that later led the Scots into yet another war of religion. At the same time the various parties were indulging in a propaganda battle about the rights and wrongs of both sides. Hamilton with his brother Lanark went to London to argue the case for modified monarchy but the Church of Scotland was still arguing for the Covenant and nothing but the Covenant, overruling the Scottish Parliament committee.

On 14 January 1647 the king again refused to sign and once the Scots were sure of their money, they agreed to leave England and hand over Charles to the English Parliamentarians at Holmby or Holdenby House in Northamptonshire.

This was the end of Scotland's involvement in the First English Civil War from which it had gained nothing but money and fighting practice. If anything, as most of the soldiers of the New Model Army were anti-Presbyterian, the Scots' desire to have Presbyterianism throughout Britain now looked much harder to fulfil than it had in 1642. So this just marked an interval before the next outbreak of fighting and the Scots who had started it all had apparently helped the wrong side to win.

Chapter 19

PLOTS AND COUNTERPLOTS

The abominable heresies and horrid blasphemies now being professed in England under the name of religion.

> John Campbell, Earl of Loudoun

Charles I remained as a prisoner of the English Parliament at Holdenby House for four months until June 1647, when he was seized by a New Model Army squad under Cornet George Joyce. He was then taken to the headquarters of General Thomas Fairfax, who had doubtless instigated the kidnap. This marked a drastic change in the negotiating style of the four main parties, the Royalists, the Covenanters, the English Presbyterians in parliament, and the New Model Army, not to mention the numerous people who were not really sure which of these groups they really wanted to join.

On its return home the Scottish army was reduced to 6,000 men. With part of it, David Leslie was sent to subdue the Royalist Gordons and their kin in the north east. In March 1647 General Middleton had captured Strathbogie/Huntly Castle with its medieval keep, after starving out the garrison. Subsequently he had them all executed, though the still indestructible marquis escaped yet again. It was the third time this castle had been captured since 1640 and the troops further destroyed the already badly damaged interior. Auchindoun Castle near Dufftown was also captured, as was Aboyne, which had been taken earlier by Argyll.

In his various lodgings after Holdenby House the king renewed his compulsive plotting of new alliances, for he had noticed the increasing divide between the Presbyterians who dominated the

English Parliament and the Independents who now dominated the army. So his latest idea was to use the Presbyterians, both Scots and English, to challenge the New Model Army. There were encouraging signs when the English ex-mercenary and respected former defender of Gloucester, Edward Massey, himself a strong Presbyterian, started organising anti-Independent activity in London after which large crowds of apprentices, water-men and other 'Reformadoes' staged a major demonstration in the city in favour of the king and Covenant. At the same time the English parliament, still mostly Presbyterian, was trying to disband large sections of the New Model Army, whilst the army was in retaliation driving prominent Presbyterians into exile. While at Newmarket on 8 June, Charles received a letter from Argyll offering military help if Charles would make concessions on the Covenant, but Charles refused. At about the same time the Scottish committee sent the Earl of Dunfermline to France to meet Queen Henrietta Maria and ask her to send over the Prince of Wales to lead an invasion of England.

In his plotting Charles once more employed the newly promoted Duke of Hamilton as his negotiator in Scotland. The new Earl of Lauderdale, the able John Maitland, was perhaps already veering towards a similar point of view and he was sent by the Scottish parliament to London to protest about the snatching of the king by Cornet Joyce. Then on 22 July, he had a secret meeting with the king making much the same offer as Argyll who was by this time becoming again disillusioned by the king's insincerity. A week later Lauderdale attempted to have another secret meeting with the king at Woburn Abbey but his presence now excited suspicion and he was prevented from entering.

With the two Hamilton brothers Lauderdale joined the Scottish commissioners in London. Then Lord Lanark, Hamilton's younger brother, together with John Campbell of Loudoun and Lauderdale were briefed by the Scottish Parliament to consult the king to see if he would be any more receptive to the Covenant if the nationwide plan for Presbyterianism was initially limited to three years. But meanwhile Charles was experimenting with a lukewarm offer to the English Parliament for reducing the power of bishops and allowing the English Presbyterians freedom of worship.

So the negotiations dragged on, with both the Scots and the king apparently ever more desperate for a solution – but neither actually ready to give way. By a small majority the Scottish Parliament decided not to disband its army but remain ready for war.

Thus when the king was moved to Hampton Court Palace in October 1647, he was still only under house arrest, provided with plenty of his servants, his best furniture and many of his favourite paintings were moved from Whitehall. It perhaps gave him a feeling of enhanced security while the New Model Army may have been allowing him so much freedom in the hope that he would provide a good excuse for his elimination. Again, on 22 October, the three negotiators Lanark, Loudoun and Lauderdale offered military help if he would accept the Covenant. A day later they told him to escape from Hampton Court and head north to Berwick. On 5 November they offered him full support and six days later he locked his bedroom door and made his escape through the gardens. Lauderdale had secretly also organised a small troop of horsemen to persuade Charles to escape while out hunting near Nonsuch Palace, but he had refused.

Despite all this encouragement from the Scots Charles perversely ignored their plan, for he had an alternative one up his sleeve and he headed to Titchfield Abbey in Hampshire. There he met his chaplain's brother, Colonel Robert Hammond, whom he thought would be sympathetic. Hammond was the Parliamentarian governor of the Isle of Wight but, predictably, was not as sympathetic as Charles had expected. Charles did, however, get permission to continue his negotiations from the governor's headquarters at Carisbrooke Castle, where he arrived on 22 November. Having found no encouragement from Hammond, he now resumed his negotiations with the Scots.

It is perhaps extraordinary that three intelligent negotiators who had been thwarted so frequently should still be willing to try to coax the king to accept their offer. In the background was Hamilton, who was certainly no Covenanter, and simply wanted to save the monarchy, whatever promises had to be made to do so. His brother Lanark was much the same. Loudoun, on the other hand, had been a strong Covenanter right from the start but, equally, was no republican and perhaps believed that any token acknowledgment of the Covenant was better than having the chaos of Brownists, Anabaptists and Levellers undermining the Scottish establishment. This view was probably shared by the level-headed Lauderdale, who had never been all that happy with the Scottish Parliament being bullied by fanatical middle-class clergymen. This standpoint appeared for the time being to be true of the majority in the Scottish Parliament though not in the General Assembly. For the time being politics was more important than religion, although for appearance and propaganda's sake the Covenant must be signed.

So on 7 December the Stewart Earl of Traquair was sent to Carisbrooke to beg Charles to accept the terms; two weeks later he was followed by the three earls to help convince him. At long last, on Boxing Day 1647, Charles signed the so-called Engagement and the following day so did the three earls.

For Hamilton and the other Royalists it must have seemed like an amazing political victory, to have made their Covenanter colleagues believe that the king was at least partly sincere and to have persuaded them to fight a war on behalf of a man who had so often let them down. Even now under duress he had only given his half-hearted promise to impose a uniform bishop-less church system for three trial years on a half-unwilling England, and an even less willing Wales and Ireland, a task utterly against his principles. He had also sworn to make efforts to suppress 'Arians, Socinians, Anabaptists, Independents, Separatists and Seekers or any others destructive to the peace of the church' – a slightly less disagreeable prospect. However also in this so-called Engagement were some interesting offers of improved trading conditions for the Scots, perhaps a hint that there was now a streak of mercantile materialism affecting the Scottish aristocracy who had so much recent evidence of just how rich were their English counterparts.

Thus Scotland was committed to start its sixth holy war since 1639 and its third invasion of England; this time religion was still the excuse, but saving the establishment and the Stuart dynasty were closer to the real reason and for once the scepticism of most of the Covenanting clergy had been overruled or ignored. To make it worse the commitment was to fight against one of the best armies in Europe. Ironically the Scots had played a major part in the downfall of the Stuart dynasty, both by provoking the Civil War and then by providing an army to help win it, yet now that Charles I was essentially a lost cause they were going to war again to save him, just because in his dire straits he had at last agreed to become a champion of Presbyterianism. For religious reasons they had switched from Roundheads to Royalists. Meanwhile the Engagement Treaty was enclosed in a lead casket and buried in the garden of Carisbrooke.

Chapter 20

SCOTLAND ENTERS THE SECOND CIVIL WAR

... the war is an ungodly one which will bring on them the displeasure of heaven.

Instructions from Church commissioners to ministers with regard to sermons

... increasing numbers, particularly noblemen, had doubts about the soldiers' divine mission.

David Stevenson: *Revolution and Counter Revolution*

In the previous eight years the Scottish army had twice crossed the border into England and never been defeated, so perhaps the Scots had excessive confidence in their ability to repeat the process. However, this time it was much harder to raise a new army. Their two best generals the Earl of Leven and David Leslie, later to become Earl of Newark, refused to serve, as did a number of the hard-line Covenanter earls: Argyll, Eglinton, Lothian, Cassilis and Balcarres, for they could not yet accept the idea of fighting for Charles I instead of against him. Of the original Fife earls, Rothes and old Balmerino had both died, as had the most active of the Fife ministers Alexander Henderson, so this time it was not a Fife conspiracy. Hamilton and Traquair organised propaganda to exaggerate the ill-treatment of the king by the New Model Army and had the support of Lauderdale and Callendar who were both probably secret Royalists. Also in support were those of the clergy who were most enthusiastic for the suppression of heretical sects and Independents: Guthrie, Ramsay, Colville and Fairfield. In the background was the manipulative French envoy Jean de Montereul, enjoying the prospect of anyone causing problems for the aggressive Oliver Cromwell who, once freed from military demands at home, could turn his attention to damaging French interests in Europe and its colonies.

Thus in February the Scottish Commissioners in London, who had supervised the wars of the Solemn League and Covenant, came back to Edinburgh. They were followed by some English commissioners whose aim was to keep an eye on Scotland, and to encourage the main opposition leader to the new war, the Marquis of Argyll and his fellow-clansman Loudoun who was beginning to waver, but who, as Lord Chancellor, had rashly authorised a further £100,000 of the army debt.

Hamilton now formed a 'Committee of Danger' to back his war preparations and forged a secret plan to occupy Berwick and Carlisle, an action in breach of the Solemn League and Covenant. It was to be undertaken with the help of the Northumberland die-hard Royalists under Marmaduke Langdale, so it potentially confirmed the impression for many that Hamilton's war was no more than a revival of the Royalists, nothing to do with religion.

To boost his credibility as a champion of Presbyterianism Hamilton, for whom this pose was utterly alien, put up a show of ranting against the New Model Army as 'underminers and destroyers of religion and the Covenant'. For appearances' sake he demanded that the English Parliament sign the Covenant, approve the new Westminster Confession, disband the New Model Army and agree 'to extirpate heresies ... Socinians, Brownists, Anabaptists.' This demand, made on 3 May 1648, gave the English two weeks to reply, after which he would pursue 'the pious work of the Solemn League and Covenant'. But naturally he was already convinced the answer would be negative, which was exactly what he wanted to provide a popular camouflage for his real objective, to restore Charles I to his throne. As window-dressing for his war it was impressive enough, but in real terms it was preposterous for by this time it was the New Model Army and not the Parliament that was running English affairs and England was fast becoming a military dictatorship with no affection for Presbyterians. So the Covenant south of the border looked like a lost cause.

By the beginning of June 1648 the newly promoted Duke of Hamilton had been appointed commander-in-chief in place of the unwilling Leven and his second-in-command instead of David Leslie was James Livingston of Callendar. The only other senior professionals were John Middleton and William Baillie, both men who earned their living by war and found changing sides quite easy. Recruitment was still poor, particularly in the west, and Glasgow was punished for lack of volunteers by having six regiments garrisoned in the city, a penalty that cost some £50,000 due to provisions and plunder.

Callendar and Middleton mustered around 10,000 foot and 1,600 horse at Stewarton. Two thousand Clydesdale Covenanters and eight ministers staged a protest against the war on Mauchline Moor and after refusing an appeal they were charged by John Middleton's troops with the result that forty of them were killed. There were more protests but most of the opposition was intimidated. There was clearly now a deepening rift between the hard-line Covenanters who distrusted the king and the Hamiltonians whose prime interest was to preserve the monarchy and use the Covenant as an excuse.

There had been a plan for what was now the Second English Civil War to co-ordinate the Scottish attack on England with other Royalist risings in the North, the Home Counties and Wales. However, these started prematurely and were easily put down by the New Model Army, so the Scots were left to bear the full brunt. Marmaduke Langdale with his men survived the attacks of a small force led by Lambert but in Wales Cromwell was close to finishing his siege of Pembroke Castle, Fairfax was doing the same at Colchester, Charles, Prince of Wales with a small navy was cruising ineffectively off the Essex coast and the Yorkshire Royalists were busy defending Pontefract.

On 13 July 1648 the Duke of Hamilton crossed the border with an army of 15,000 men including 4,000 cavalry, to which were added another 3,000 brought over from the Scottish army that had been fighting in Ireland under Robert Monro. He sent his nephew George in charge of them but these troops became rebellious and refused to fight under either Baillie or Callendar. To this number was joined for a while the 4,000 Cumberland levies led by the veteran Royalist, Marmaduke Langdale.

Hamilton himself strutted ahead of his army with trumpeters in scarlet cloaks and his aristocratic lifeguards, but he took little interest in strategy. Nor was his army well trained or well equipped; many were raw recruits as many of the Marston Moor veterans had refused to re-enlist. In addition whereas Leven was a consummate professional in terms of organising provisions and pay, Hamilton was a relative amateur, quite happy to let his men live off the land and plunder at will; both traits contributed to the dislike for them felt by the English.

There were divided opinions as to whether the army should head straight south to join the Cheshire Royalists under Byron or go east to relieve Pontefract. Baillie said Pontefract and Callendar with a louder voice preferred Chester. Lambert was waiting to pounce from Penrith; he had too small a force to tackle the whole Scottish army, but was mobile enough to inflict damage on isolated units.

Cromwell, meanwhile, having captured Pembroke and punished its garrison in early July, made it as far as Doncaster by early August, topping up with men, supplies and ammunition from Hull and Pontefract. He joined up with Lambert making his total force up to 8,600 and headed westwards down the River Ribble to Hodden Bridge on 6 August. At the same time the Covenanter/Royalist army was now reduced to about 15,000 men, two-thirds of them Scots, so in total still larger than the New Model Army force.

With its weak command structure the Covenanter/Royalist army was now heading south in a disorderly fashion, Monro's Scots from Ireland lagging far behind, Baillie's infantry nearly as bad, and Marmaduke Langdale's English force so far ahead that it was out of touch. Thus Langdale either failed to report that Cromwell's army was approaching or did so and Hamilton paid no heed to the warning.

Hamilton was persuaded by Callendar to send Baillie and his infantry over the Ribble whilst Langdale with his 3,000 men separated from the rest of the army, was attacked by Cromwell at Preston Moor. Cromwell's men were tired after a long march and in his own words 'we lay close to the enemy very dirty when we had some skirmishing.' After four hours hard fighting, the Covenanter/Royalists were driven into the river.

Baillie tried but failed to hold the two bridges over the Ribble at Darwin and Wigan Road, so in one day the Scots lost 1,000 killed and 4,000 prisoners of war. The remaining Scots retreated towards Wigan, with Cromwell in pursuit on 18 August. The next day they made a stand at Winnick for a couple of hours and sustained more heavy losses, but when they got to Warrington Bridge even Baillie was ready to surrender. A thousand more Scots had been killed and another 4,000 taken prisoner. Total losses were therefore 2,000 dead, mainly Scots and 8–9,000 prisoners. Monro's men mostly missed the battle and regrouped near Lancaster to make an orderly retreat back to Scotland. Hamilton with 3,000 men had carried on to

Uttoxeter losing on the way about 500 stragglers who were mostly massacred by angry locals whose lives had been disrupted by their earlier plunderings. At Uttoxeter he too surrendered. Some 1,500 of Callendar's cavalry did however break out and escape.

It was a humiliating and costly defeat, which, since the new war had been started with Charles's blessing, meant that he would have to pay the penalty for it ending in failure, as eventually would the Duke of Hamilton who had initiated the war and mismanaged it so woefully. But for the time being he had escaped. Worse in many respects was the fate of about 9,000 prisoners, of whom all the troops identified as volunteers were sent as indentured labourers, virtual slaves, to the West Indies, Carolina or New England or to the Venetian galleys. Colonel Archibald Strachan from Musselburgh, having opposed the Engagement, had chosen to fight for Cromwell against his fellow Scots and was thus probably the only Scot on the winning side.

Chapter 21

THE BIRTH OF THE WHIGS

> Theirs was the religion of the Old Testament run amok and for the first time in Scottish history massive cruelties were inflicted in the name of God.
>
> T.C. Smout: *A History of the Scottish People*

The news of the massive defeat at Preston caused a huge shock in Scotland which had recently become accustomed to winning battles in England. However the Kirk party, which had opposed the Engagement with the king, derived some satisfaction from this proof that they had been right to oppose the war. Nevertheless, thanks to the king's execution it did not prove that Charles had made a false promise to uphold the Covenant, for he never had the chance either to keep or break his promise. On 30 January 1649, six months after the battle, he was executed at Whitehall. So the barely credible idea that a Stuart king would support Presbyterianism was not put to the test but allowed to survive the debacle at Preston, with disastrous consequences.

Before news of the defeat arrived in Edinburgh the General Assembly had met in July. The Hamilton supporters made an attempt to gag their main opponents, the two Campbells, Argyll and Loudoun, plus the lawyer Lord Warriston. Despite this the Assembly led by George Gillespie condemned the Engagers as 'unlawful, popish, prelatical and malignant', this last adjective becoming one of their favourite words. It proclaimed that no Engagers should any longer be allowed positions of power. The Engagers responded by accusing the Assembly of interfering in politics but back came the answer that the war had been 'unlawful and sinful'. Then came the news of the unexpected defeat.

The opposition now had an even stronger case. The two Campbells supported by the two Ayrshire earls, Cassilis and Alexander Montgomery of Eglinton, began to organise resistance from the west coast and recruited David Leslie to command their militia. In the absence of any official army in September this force was able to invade Edinburgh in what became known as the Whiggamore Raid. The name apparently came from the Ayrshire dialect in which horse drovers supposedly yelled 'Whiggam' to get their charges to move and were themselves therefore called Whiggamores. The name stuck and in abbreviated form became the new nickname of the Kirk party, later adopted in England for the party that dominated the country during much of the 18th century. Coincidentally the nickname Tory also emerged about the same time, originally the old Irish word for robber (tóraidhe), which was at this time used to describe the Irish Confederate Royalists.

The Committee of Estates still briefly dominated by the Hamiltonians began to recruit a new army and put the duke's brother Lord Lanark in charge with orders to march south to meet George Monro who was coming back from Preston with his surviving regiments. The two groups met at Gladsmuir near Haddington with a combined force of 3,000 and began planning an attack on the rebels in the west, effectively a new Scottish civil war between Engagers and the opposition, on the one side a mixture of hard-bitten Royalists and credulous Covenanters or Hamiltonians who had accepted the word of Charles I, on the other the sceptical Kirk Party Covenanters who had rejected it but were in due course to accept it from his son.

Happily the Engager generals Lanark and Monro were overruled by the Estates Committee, so they restricted themselves to trying to cut off Argyll from the others. Monro very nearly captured Argyll at Stirling but the marquis with his usual skill as an escapologist managed to dash across the bridge, leaving Monro's force to capture Stirling and massacre its small garrison. Monro's success, however, was short-lived for his request for more volunteers was met with a very poor response whilst the new Covenanters from the west now had the old Earl of Leven as well as David Leslie as their chief generals. Argyll, acting as their spokesman, now wrote to Oliver Cromwell asking for his help in getting rid of the Engagers. Cromwell was delighted to have a legitimate excuse to invade Scotland and did so 'for the assistance of the faithful in Scotland'. So the Scots' strategy was very foolhardy.

The presence of Cromwell in Edinburgh allowed the Engagers to be ousted from all their official positions and the Committee to be purged, but none were punished any further. Monro and his troops were sent back to Ireland. The Scots handed back Berwick and Carlisle to the parliamentarians. Cromwell took up residence at Moray House in the Canongate and in the Great Hall of Edinburgh Castle attended a banquet with Argyll, Leven, Leslie and the rest of those who had opposed Scotland's entry into the Second English Civil War. A banner was put up with the slogan 'FOR AN OPPRESSED KIRK AND A BROKEN COVENANT', which cannot have pleased Cromwell. Meanwhile, the Scottish army under the two Leslies was reduced to 1,000 foot and 500 horse. Then Cromwell headed back to London leaving Lambert to maintain contact.

Whether the Scots had discussed the possible trial of Charles I with Cromwell before he left Edinburgh, let alone his alternative regime, is unclear. However, once he was back in London the Scottish Parliament began to protest about the threat to the monarchy, a threat that Loudoun, as once more the Kirk Party's mouthpiece, pronounced to be 'sinful and ungodly'. When even worse news came about the king's impending execution, the language became more heated, the Party did 'abominate and despise so horrid a design on His Majesty's person.' So Charles met his martyrish end in January 1649 and the Duke of Hamilton who had at last been captured in late August was executed soon afterwards, leaving Scotland's only dukedom, since he had no sons, to his brother Lanark. The witch who had allegedly promised that he would be king had been over-optimistic.

In Scotland the reaction to Preston persisted and rose almost to hysteria as the blame was placed by the clergy on the sinfulness of the Hamiltonians. The purge of Engagers from all positions of influence was pursued more aggressively and to the list were added any who had supported Montrose and even those who had failed to protest against the Engagement. This was in turn extended to 'all persons given to uncleanness, bribery, swearing, drunkenness or deceiving ... or openly profane and grossly scandalous.'

The result of this outburst of moral fervour was that many of the so-called Malignants such as the new Duke of Hamilton and the Earl of Lauderdale fled to Holland and the court of the king's eldest son.

On the whole the Covenanters, now purged of bad blood, were still in favour of the monarchy and could not conceive of any alternative, though the more radical such as Argyll and Warriston wanted its powers seriously reduced. So on 5 February 1649 the Committee for the first time approached the heir to the throne to see if he would accept the Covenant in return for being offered the crown of Great Britain and Ireland. Campbell of Loudoun as Chancellor led the cautious negotiations warning that 'it was our duty to desire no tolerance of idolatry, popery, prelacy, heresy, schism or profaneness.' To win his throne as Charles II, the Prince of Wales would have to sign the Solemn League and Covenant. Loudoun dressed in his black velvet robes of office read out the formal proclamation at the High Cross of Edinburgh. This meant that Prince Charles if he wanted to become king must promise to impose the Presbyterian form of church organisation on all of his three kingdoms and allow no other. In addition he was to bind both himself and his successors to the Covenant, to get rid of all his malignant advisers and leave all ecclesiastical matters in Scotland to the General Assembly.

To obtain the vital signature Sir Joseph Douglas of Pumpherston (later to be drowned at sea whilst sailing to collect the new king's brother the Duke of York) was now dispatched to The Hague to present the document to Prince Charles. Commissioners from the various estates followed including the Earl of Cassilis, a strong Covenanter, the Laird of Brodie, Alexander Jeffrey, a baillie from Aberdeen and Robert Barclay, Provost of Irvine; plus two church ministers, Robert Baillie and James Wood with a church elder, George Winram of Liberton. So it was a genuinely representative group, though with a significant proportion of churchmen.

They had an amicable meeting with the prospective king but like his father, Charles was playing a double game. His ally Ormond was doing well in Ireland and there was again hope of Royalist help from that quarter. Lauderdale and the new Duke of Hamilton, who were in The Hague already, argued that Charles should accept – but he delayed until an unexpected scandal broke out. On 3 May Dr Isaac Dorislaus, the English envoy to the Dutch, was murdered and amongst the suspects was the exiled Marquis of Montrose; in fact one of his associates, Colonel Whiteford, was much later pardoned for his share in the crime. Dorislaus, a Dutch-born lawyer, was a hate figure for the Royalists; he had been chief advocate for Cromwell's army, a legal persecutor of Royalists in England, and one of the counsels involved in the trial of Charles I, so he was a prime target.

Montrose was, like Ormond in Ireland, one of Charles's hopes for a military revival of his cause, so this was yet another reason for Charles to stall the commissioners from Edinburgh. Montrose had spent some months flirting with the ex-Queen of Bohemia, Rupert's mother Elizabeth, and gathering recruits for a new campaign whilst he trailed Charles from The Hague to Breda and Brussels, chatting up other Royalist exiles. By early September he was to be in Hamburg and Copenhagen looking for money, men and supplies, ready for a new invasion of Scotland.

Due to the Dorislaus scandal Charles was no longer welcome in Holland, nor was he in France, so he moved his court to Jersey, still without signing the Covenant, but as usual not without plenty of female company to distract him. However he now heard bad news from Ireland, where all hope of a Royalist revival there had been smothered by the victories of Oliver Cromwell. That left Montrose as the forlorn hope. To encourage him, Charles had been corresponding secretly with Royalists in north eastern Scotland, particularly the Mackays under Lord Rea and the Mackenzies under the Laird of Pluscarden, aided by General Middleton who had been sacked from the Scottish army as one of the Malignants. They had seized Inverness in February and held it till May when they were overcome by a force under Colonels Strachan and Hackett.

This incident had finally motivated the Estates in Edinburgh to order the beheading of that long-term opponent of the Covenant, George Gordon, Marquis of Huntly, who had been a prisoner since 1647. A childhood friend of Charles I, brought up in England as a Protestant, he had served as an officer in the Garde Ecossaise in Paris but never quite been at ease with his role as chief of the largely Catholic Gordon clan. Nor had he been successful as a leader of the Royalists in north eastern Scotland, first being attacked by Montrose, then becoming his ally. As his portrait by Van Dyck shows, his hair and beard exactly like the king's, he looked more like a London courtier than the master of Strathbogie. To add to his difficulties, he had the Campbell chief's sister as his wife and ten children with her. His eldest son had been killed at Alford, and his second, Montrose's friend Viscount Aboyne, died in exile very soon after him.

Again the General Assembly met and its pro-king group briefed the elder George Winram to return to Breda to negotiate. Once there, he was shocked by the number of frivolous and allegedly dissipated courtiers surrounding the would-be king. Charles, however, was more amenable than before and when urged to sign the treaty by Lauderdale, perhaps with fingers crossed behind his back, he agreed at last. The Breda treaty was then signed by the two earls, Cassilis and Lothian, no doubt with misgivings about the king's sincerity, but perhaps just desperate for a settlement.

Chapter 22

THE GREAT SCOTTISH WITCH HUNT

> There must have been many an old woman with a small knowledge
> of herbal cures and a good line in invective who in her widowhood
> found it profitable to be thought a witch.
>
> T.C. Smout: *A History of the Scottish People*

One of the less savoury new laws instituted by the Kirk Party in
1649 was the new Witchcraft Act. Not that witch hunting was new
in Scotland for James VI and I had given it plenty of encouragement,
but in the decade up to 1649 it had been in abeyance. Now with
the general purge of sinners that followed the disaster at Preston,
coupled with the onset of a mini-ice age, poor harvests, malnutrition
and plague, the clergy became obsessed with purging the ungodly.
Worship of false gods, blasphemy or beating of parents became
capital offences. Thus the General Assembly as part of its campaign
against immorality and false religion had passed motions on at least
four occasions, 1640, 1644, 1645 and 1649, ordering ministers
and local presbyteries to become more active in pursuing suspected
witches, anyone accused of dabbling in magic or other eccentricities
that did not meet with the approval of church elders. The suspects
were almost all women and mainly from the poorest class.

This programme encouraged the recruitment of professional witch
finders or prickers who earned money by obtaining confessions from
likely candidates. Pricking involved the use of a needle to find the
so-called witch's mark, an area of skin which when pierced by a needle
or sharp knife neither caused pain or bleeding. This was not regarded
as absolute proof of witchcraft but as a useful indicator, sufficient to

start a trial at which other evidence could be taken into account. Thus prickers such as John Kincaid at Dirleton Castle supposedly proved that a Patrick Watson and Manie Haliburton were witches. Similarly George Cathie in Lanark made a good living as did another Scottish pricker who earned 2 shillings per witch in Northumberland and was eventually executed for causing 220 deaths by cheating. The favourite trick was to use a knife with a hollow handle so that the blade could be retracted without anyone noticing, hence no pain or sign of blood. The subsequent witch trials were often then held locally with no professional lawyers involved so that many of the convictions were based on no more than local gossip.

Eventually the Chancellor John Campbell of Loudoun called a halt to amateur witch trials, but by that time some 300 perhaps gullible or eccentric people had been executed out of a total of about 800 who had been charged. The first after the Preston panic was probably at Inverkeithing in March 1649 when the local minister Walter Bruce started preaching against the devil, another aspect of the Fife Conspiracy. Thus the paranoid fantasy spread along the Fife coast to Burntisland, Aberdour and Dysart. A brewer in Dunfermline was one of the few victims who proved his innocence. In Inverkeithing itself Lady Pittadro (Margaret Henderson had married William Elchin of Pittadro in Fife) was driven to suicide or died in her cell, and five others were executed for allegedly having sex with the devil. However the purge got out of hand when some of the accusing elders discovered that their own wives were about to be charged.

Generally the witch hunting was confined to the Lowlands, mostly the east coast, particularly Fife and Lothian, where the ministers and their elders were most active in purging so-called Malignants. In Tranent, Jean Craig was condemned for allegedly driving another woman mad. In Cullen, the local presbytery excommunicated Marjorie Plumber for divination, which was regarded as a less serious form of witchcraft; she had used some old tradition of necromancy to find out if her sick child was likely to die and divination was regarded as a symptom of witchery.

Overall it was symptomatic of the way that after the abolition of bishops the local clergymen had become steadily more domineering in their own parishes, in the Assembly and in the Scottish Parliament. God had been on their side in warfare until Preston, which could be blamed on the Malignants. They themselves could use the threat of excommunication against people of all ranks, from kings downwards, and this together with their record of dominating and motivating most of the nation since 1637, had given them an excessive confidence in their own infallibility.

It was also symptomatic of the huge fear of the plague that swept through Scotland in 1644–48, particularly in 1645 after the Montrose campaigns when the usual consequence of civil war included constant troop movements, insanitary billeting conditions, trashed crops, middens out of control and blocked wells. Edinburgh itself was particularly vulnerable to outbreaks of the plague due to overcrowded tenement blocks, lack of sanitation and infestations of rats and fleas. Common symptoms of the disease were severe vomiting, breathlessness, swollen lymph glands, and puss-filled boils or 'buboes'. Plague doctors like John Paulitious and George Rae were in huge demand, especially Rae, who became an iconic celebrity protecting himself from germs with a beak-shaped mask made of leather and stuffed with herbs.

Whether the epidemic was bubonic or some other form of plague is not certain but deaths in Leith alone were up to 2,500, a third of its estimated population, some sources suggested 9,000, so the overall death toll must have been considerable and predictably it was sin that was to blame. The death toll meant a considerable loss of manpower both for warfare purposes and agricultural production. In Edinburgh it was said in 1645 that only 60 men were left who were capable of military service.

However, when Oliver Cromwell came to Scotland in 1650, the Kirk Party lost most of its power as it had now followed exactly the same policy it had so strongly condemned in the Engagers; it had placed its trust in a Stuart monarch. It had committed the country to another holy war to impose Presbyterianism throughout the British Isles, relying on a royal signature of dubious credibility.

After the fall of Cromwell's republican regime there was to be a renewed outbreak of witch hunts in Scotland in 1661. The restored Scottish Parliament cancelled the ban placed on them by the Commonwealth and over an eighteen-month period, some 660 suspects were charged and perhaps a third of that number were executed, though there is no accurate record. The hunts were mainly in the Lothians, where there were 206 trials in eight months during 1661. It came to a stop when several professional prickers were found to have been cheating and the main method of prosecution was totally discredited. Even after that, however, there were limited sporadic outbreaks into the following century, usually at times of plague, economic downturn or general malaise.

Amongst the more peculiar witch incidents in the later period was the tale of Archbishop Sharp's interrogation of a supposed witch called Janet. He asked what she had been doing on a certain Saturday night. Rather wittily she responded by asking him the same question and gave the answer for him, that he had been seen consorting with Satan. By contrast the Covenanter minister Alexander Peden went out of his way to confront the Devil when he had supposedly been pestering a weaver called Gilbert Campbell at his parish in New Luce. Peden was also said to have confronted a witch in Galloway. Meanwhile Satan, so it was claimed, paid a visit to Glasgow where he terrorised some of the population in 1684.

Another example of supposed witchcraft was the mysterious Major Thomas Weir (1599–1670) who had fought as a professional soldier under Monro in Ireland and later under Montrose. A fervent Covenanter he lived in retirement with his eccentric sister Grizel at the top of the Grassmarket and became known as the Bowhead Saint, but in old age began to confess, rightly or wrongly, to unmentionable sins. He was confined with Grizel to the leper colony on Calton Hill before being garrotted and his body burned at Gallowlee on the road down to Leith.

It is reasonable to suggest that in this period, when disagreements over religious belief were taken so seriously, and interpretation of the Bible was so literal, that irrational superstition was likely to be on the increase. Apart from the persecution of witches and heretics, this period was also notable for the attacks on gypsies who were regarded as almost a cross between the two. Thus there were executions of gypsies after they had an internal feud in 1677 at Romanno Bridge, known as the Gypsies Field of Blood.

The reformers though rejecting the miracles of the Roman Catholic Church still retained the belief in sorceresses ... and enforced the penalties against them.

Sir Walter Scott: *Tales of a Grandfather*

Chapter 23

MONTROSE'S LAST STAND

Montrose was as far off as ever from commending himself to that
Covenanting bourgeoisie which he never lost hope of converting.

John Buchan: *Montrose*

Despite the signing of the Treaty of Breda on 1 May 1650, Charles
II had already given secret orders to Montrose for his new expedition
to raise Scotland for the cause. He was still quibbling about the
right of the Committee of the Estates to negotiate with him when
Montrose landed on the Orkneys with a band of exiles and German
mercenaries. There he made vain efforts to get Orcadians to enlist in
his army before heading across the Pentland Firth to John o' Groats
in Caithness, where he raised his new banner with the words:

JUDGE AND REVENGE MY CAUSE O LORD

Meanwhile he had sent his second-in-command, the ambivalent but
courageous Sir John Hurry to Ord of Caithness. They then both
headed south past Dunrobin, which was too close to impregnable
for an attack. Leslie sent a small army against Montrose under two
colonels, Strachan and Holborne, who met the oddly assorted force at
Carbisdale on the River Shin in Sutherland. The raw Orcadian recruits
almost immediately fled and the German mercenaries surrendered, so
Montrose and his followers had to make an escape, which he did to
the west, eventually seeking shelter in the Macleod castle of Ardvreck
in Assynt. Unfortunately for him, the Macleod laird decided to claim
the reward that had been placed on his head and he was captured.

Taken to Edinburgh, Montrose was charged by Campbell of Loudoun with 'atrocities most inhuman' and he was condemned to death. The night before his execution he wrote a poem mocking his own plight:

> Let them bestow on every airth a limb
> Then open all my veins that I may swim
> To Thee my maker in that crimson lake
> Then place my parboiled head upon a stake.

He met his death clad in scarlet and gold, an exhibitionist to the last, on the scaffold in Edinburgh aged only thirty-eight. Also executed was the serial turncoat Sir John Hurry; young John Spotiswood, grandson of the former archbishop; plus Montrose's long-term lieutenant, Sir Francis Hay of Delgattie. A fourth condemned prisoner, James Crichton, Lord Frendraucht, one of Montrose's old friends from the Gordon connection, had begged him not to waste his life dying at Carbisdale, but then Frendraucht either committed suicide to avoid the humiliation of public execution, died of his wounds after the battle or escaped, depending upon which version you believe. Their master the would-be-king Charles II had promised to disown them if they failed and unusually for him he carried out his promise.

Chapter 24

THE ROAD TO DUNBAR AND THE THIRD CIVIL WAR

God's gracious goodness in changing the king's heart and turning him from the evil of his former ways.

Part of a proclamation by the Scots pouring scorn on Cromwell's assertion that Charles II was insincere.

By May 1650 the would-be Charles II was running out of options and credibility. The fanatical lawyer Warriston and Sir John Chiesley of Carswell were both advising that there was no point any longer in trying to negotiate with him, but it was Argyll who surprisingly made a strong stand for proceeding with an agreement, even pointing out to Charles that his secret letters to Montrose had now been discovered, so he and his colleagues were on the lookout for any further deception. Charles would now promise anything, presuming that if by some unlucky chance he had to fulfil his oath, at least he would have the crown. He spent two months resisting the demands, particularly the imposition of Presbyterianism in England and also the exclusion from office of all those who had worked or fought for his father during the Preston campaign. The negotiators were adamant, though perhaps a little naïve, about the reliability of oaths and signatures. After all, Charles was undoubtedly charming and a fair actor, for even the learned and worldly-wise Robert Baillie described him at this time as a 'gentle, innocent, well inclined prince'.

Thus Charles had signed the First Treaty of Breda on 1 May and soon afterwards set sail for Scotland. He landed at Garmouth (now further away from the sea than it was then and once famous for its slave market), at the mouth of the Spey, on 23 June. He was met by the commissioners who would not let him land until he had confirmed acceptance of the Covenant. His new oath, promising adherence to the Covenant, was administered by John Livingston, a minister who had been one of the church commissioners at Breda and who had a long record of staunch support of the Covenant having been one of the rebels against the bishops in 1638 and having served in one of the Ulster parishes with Robert Blair. So Charles II, formally, at last, signed the Covenant.

Livingston was clearly convinced that Charles was genuine at this point. Ten years later Livingston was to be deeply disappointed that he had been wrong. Ironically he was dismissed from his parish in 1654 and exiled to Holland, where he died a disillusioned man.

The Scottish Parliament, determined not to let Charles off the leash, ordered him to dismiss all his so-called malignant adherents who had shared the crossing with him, including Lauderdale and the new Duke of Hamilton together with several English Royalists who had also been exiled in Breda. Charles was ordered to make his surviving English courtiers sign the Covenant or leave his service and some of them made a joke of obeying.

With the prospect of yet another invasion of England by the Scots, Cromwell was recalled from Ireland where his work of suppression was virtually complete. The need for him to command the New Model Army was now all the greater because Tom Fairfax, up to this point the front runner, had refused to fight the Scots, influenced perhaps by his strongly Presbyterian wife. Cromwell was therefore now the undisputed leader of the new republican state.

Thus on 22 July 1650, Cromwell crossed the border with 16,000 veteran troops to deal with the new threat posed by the arrival of Charles II on Scottish soil. This was the Third English Civil War, and the Scots and their religious demands were the main cause of it, for without them, Charles had no army.

The English army headed towards Edinburgh from Mordington but there was an acute food shortage in the eastern counties due to accidental and deliberate destruction of crops, so Cromwell had to have his supplies delivered by sea to Dunbar. Aiming to avoid a battle if possible, he issued propaganda sheets accusing the Scots of giving up all their earlier ideals by pandering to the 'untrustworthy wastrel' Charles II. He put out conciliatory proclamations, offering peace and reconciliation, but there was no response from those in power.

Thus Cromwell reached Haddington to find that David Leslie had made considerable efforts to fortify Edinburgh ready for his attack.

There were new batteries on Calton Hill, Salisbury Crags and at Leith. In bad weather Cromwell stormed the fortifications on Arthur's Seat, only to lose them again. He set up a battery by St Anthony's Chapel to discomfort Leslie's left wing, but fire was returned from the quarry on Calton Hill.

Finding no easy route to victory Cromwell retreated to Musselburgh, pursued by David Leslie and the Scots army. He nearly lost his second-in-command John Lambert in the process, for he was captured and only escaped with difficulty. The Scots also tried a bold night attack with 800 men under generals Strachan and Montgomery at Stoneyhill, Musselburgh, but after initial success against the cavalry, they met strong resistance from the infantry with the result that they retreated with heavy losses. Cromwell, as ever when trying to win over his enemies, did the decent thing and provided wagons for the wounded and some prisoners to be taken back to Edinburgh.

The allegedly reformed Charles II had meanwhile appeared at the army's camp, bringing with him a jolly crowd of Malignants who arrogantly strutted around to the horror of the Covenanters. Eighty more Malignant officers were dismissed from the army, Charles was sent back to Dunfermline and forced to apologise again for his former misconduct, for his mother's idolatry, and for the bloodshed caused by his father. If many of the Scots were worried about the man on whose behalf they were fighting, he must also have quietly cursed the men on whose gullibility he had to rely. He was out hunting near Dunfermline when he was sent another copy of the Covenant for him to sign, but he conveniently forgot.

The new committee's banner read

IN THE DEFENCE OF GOD AND THE KINGDOM

in that order. In due course Charles reluctantly signed the Dunfermline Declaration endorsing the Covenant.

Meanwhile there was a military stalemate, with Leslie well protected in Edinburgh and refusing to fight, while Cromwell and his men were struggling to get supplies and frustrated by the lack of action. Cromwell did try to cut off Edinburgh's supply routes, but Leslie kept them open. There was a small skirmish at Colinton but it did not develop. As August wore on, the English lack of decent food and their overcrowded camps led to a decline in health and morale so Cromwell retreated again towards Dunbar, waiting for his ships.

The Scots, elated by these apparent signs of weakness, decided to cut him off. This they nearly managed at Haddington but the plan failed because the moon was obscured at the crucial moment.

The English retreat continued with Cromwell occasionally offering battle but with Leslie refusing and keeping to the high ground while Cromwell stayed near the coast as both armies made their way to Dunbar. Leslie reached Cockburnspath and dug his army into a good position on Doon Hill that would prevent Cromwell from heading south to safety. With at least 14,000 men, perhaps as some sources claimed as many as 27,000, Leslie outnumbered Cromwell's allegedly sick 11,000 drawn up in the fields near Dunbar. Cromwell was himself still suffering from 'some weakness in the flesh'.

It was at this point, according to some accounts, that the members of the Committee of Estates, who as usual accompanied the army to supervise affairs and who included a number of ministers, decided to argue with the opinions of their professional and experienced general, David Leslie. With their conviction of the superiority of their cause and the support of God, and their belief that Cromwell's men were still weak from illness, it was they who probably made the decision that snatched defeat from the jaws of victory.

Against his better judgment, it is suggested that Leslie was ordered to descend from his good defensive position. Thus his troops had to make the awkward descent after dark to the narrow coastal plain so that they would block Cromwell's route to the south. However, the weather was very poor and the newly recruited Scottish officers were inexperienced, as were many of their troops, due to the culling of Malignants, so the manoeuvre was badly executed. Leslie was perhaps overconfident because of the rumours that Cromwell was too weak to attack, so his scouting was poor.

Meanwhile Cromwell and his second-in-command John Lambert were in a house at Broxmouth, from which they could see the movement quite clearly. Backed by General Monck, they agreed that the best time to attack the Scots would be at dawn just as they were arriving at their new position. As the morning mist cleared on 3 September, an anniversary date that was remembered again in 1651 and 1658, the New Model Army infantry attacked with pikes and the butt end of muskets, while Cromwell's cavalry dealt with their Scottish opposite numbers. Leslie's army lost any advantage due its superiority in numbers because it was hemmed into such a narrow pass between the hills and the sea. His army had been deprived of some 300 of its most experienced officers, and many more rank and file, who had been at Preston and therefore came under the heading of Malignants. Of those who fought, Campbell of Lawers and his men were amongst the few on the Scottish side who distinguished themselves.

It was a humiliating rout with more than 3,000 Scots killed and approximately 10,000 taken prisoner, who were then marched southwards, exhausted and half-starved, so that many of them died en route. It was said that they were so close to starving that by the time they reached Newcastle, they ate raw cabbage from the fields. A mass grave with a large number of victims' bodies was unearthed near Durham Cathedral in 2015. One of those killed in the battle was the negotiator George Winram, from Inch House, Edinburgh, who had helped forge the treaty at Breda.

Of the prisoners of war who survived the terrible march to Durham, 500 were indentured into the French army and most of the rest sent to Virginia or the West Indies as indentured slave labourers, so the vast majority of them never returned. For entrepreneurs such as John Becx who bought and sold them, it was a profitable business. A total of 150 were taken to Boston on the ship *Unity* and those who were fit enough, were sold off as indentured labourers, mostly as forge hands or charcoal burners at the New England Iron Works of Linn, Saugus and Braintree. Others went to the Reader Saw Mill at Berwick on the River Pascataqua in Maine and some to a linen works. For most of them the conditions were extremely arduous with 12-hour shifts and indenture for at least seven years. However, some survived to start new families so that names such as MacShane, Mackall and Tower appeared in the registers. Some also seem to have gone to Barbados, which had been bought in 1626 by James Hay, Earl of Carlisle, and where sugar cane was being planted.

The Battle of Dunbar was one of the rare occasions when church ministers serving with the army were given little sympathy; the English blamed them for the war, whilst the Scots perhaps knew enough to blame them for losing the battle. A number of surviving ministers hid in Edinburgh Castle. One of those captured was John Carstares, the Covenanting minister from Cathcart, whose son William was to play a prominent role in the fall James II.

Remarkably ten years after the Fife militants had first led Scotland into war, at least seven of them were serving in senior positions at Dunbar: David Leslie as commander-in-chief, plus generals Arnot, Browne, Holbourne, James Lumsden, Pitscottie and Balfour.

For Charles II, who was kept away from the battlefield, it appeared to be the end of his hopes for a military invasion of England. But for the time being it gave him some respite from the bullying of the Covenanters, for it appeared God had not been on their side after all. So he was far from depressed by Dunbar but rather regarded it as freeing his hand to recruit a new Royalist army in the north, a project which his adviser General Middleton was keen to pursue.

> The Philistines will come down against me to Gigal
> > 1 Samuel 13, cited by the church ministers before the Battle of Dunbar as divine justification for General Leslie to abandon his excellent position above the town.

The three Leslies

Above left: Field Marshal Alexander Leslie of the Swedish army, later Earl of Leven.

Above right: John Leslie Earl of Rothes, chief co-ordinator of the Fife Conspiracy.

Below: General David Leslie, later Earl of Newark.

The three Leslie castles.

The burned-out shell of Leslie House or Palace, which incorporated parts of Leslie Castle, home of the Earl of Rothes.

Left: Balgonie castle, 3 miles from Leslie, was bought by Field Marshal Leslie in 1635.

Below: Newark Castle on a cliff near St Monans was bought by General David Leslie in the 1640s.

Three ministers

Alexander Henderson of Leuchars
Church, Fife, chief instigator of the
Covenant.

George Gillespie of East Wemyss
Church, Fife, key propagandist
and negotiator for the Covenant
campaigns.

Zachary Boyd of the Barony Church,
Glasgow, trained at a Huguenot
college in France and was a major
west coast supporter of the Covenant.

Three churches

Leuchars Church, East Fife, where Alexander Henderson was based after a spell teaching at St Andrews.

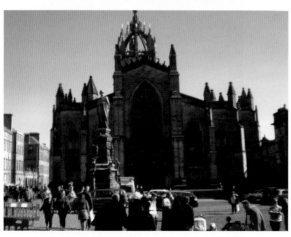

St Giles, Edinburgh, scene of the Jenny Geddes stool-throwing episode.

Greyfriars Churchyard where the Covenant was signed in February 1638.

Two Campbells

Above left: Archibald Campbell, Earl then Marquis of Argyll, ex-student of Henderson's, potential King of Scotland.

Above right: John Campbell, Earl of Loudoun, probably the ablest politician and negotiator in Scotland; led his own regiment at Marston Moor.

Montrose and Warriston

Above left: James Graham, Marquis of Montrose, chief enemy of the Campbells and first Covenanter to change sides to the Royalists.

Above right: Archibald Johnston, Lord Warriston, Edinburgh lawyer and co-author of the Covenant.

Left: The Tailors Hall, Edinburgh, now a hotel, site of the main Fife Conspiracy meeting on 27 February,1638.

Below: Burleigh Castle, on the Fife border, home of General Robert Balfour.

Above: The entrance to Dunfermline Palace in Fife where ironically Charles I was born within a few miles of the men who were to initiate his downfall.

Below: Carrickfergus Castle was held by the Scots till captured by General Monck in 1648. (Courtesy of Donna Marijne under Creative Commons 2.0)

Three Stuart Kings

Above left: Charles I.

Above right: Charles II.

Left: James II.

Two generals

Tam Dalzell of the Binns.

John Graham, later
Viscount Dundee.

One archbishop and three rebel ministers

Above left: James Sharp, Archbishop of St Andrews.

Above right: Alexander 'Prophet' Peden.

Below left: Donald Cargill.

Below right: Richard Cameron.

The Whiteadder Conventicle.

The Battle of Bothwell Bridge.

Two monuments at Magus Muir near St Andrews

Above: The pyramid marking the spot where Archbishop Sharp was murdered.

Left: The tombstone nearby of four innocent men hanged in retaliation for the murder and for refusing to give evidence.

Three prisons

Greyfriars churchyard, used as an open-air prison in 1680, with its monument to those who died, particularly those drowned when the convict ship carrying 200 prisoners sank off the Orkneys.

The interior of St Giles. Haddo's Hole was a very cramped prison, built under a corner of the cathedral. (Courtesy of Graeme Anderson under Creative Commons 2.0)

The Bass Rock prison.

Above: The thumb screw, allegedly brought to Scotland from Russia, was used to gain information from suspected Covenanters. (Courtesy of David Monniaux under Creative Commons 2.0)

Left: Physician wearing plague preventative costume. (Courtesy Wellcome Library, London)

Above: St William's College, York, which housed the Royal printing presses during the Civil War. (Courtesy of Chapter of York)

Right: Oliver Cromwell, Lord Protector, unkown artist. *c.* 1650. (Courtesy of Rijksmuseum, Amsterdam)

Left: *James, Duke of Monmouth*, by Jan van der Vaart, after Edward Cooper. (Courtesy of Rijksmuseum, Amsterdam)

Below: *The Man of War Brielle on the River Maas off Rotterdam*, by Ludolf Bakhuyse, 1689. This ship carried William of Orange to England. The Latin inscription on the red flag translates as 'for faith and freedom'. (Courtesy of Rijksmuseum, Amsterdam)

Chapter 25

MORE OF THE MALIGNANTS

If this be refused by you ... God who hath once borne his testimony
will do it again on the behalf of us his poor servants.
>   Oliver Cromwell's offer of peace, warning that
>   God will give him another victory.

As usual the Committee of the Estates still had their complement
of church ministers and therefore blamed the defeat at Dunbar on
godlessness, so they proceeded to a further purge of 'all profane,
scandalous, malignant and disaffected persons'. All this they had
to do from Stirling and Perth since Cromwell was on his way to
Edinburgh, which, apart from the Castle, the Scots could no longer
hope to defend. Even Perth looked vulnerable and Leslie concentrated
on extending the fortifications at Stirling.

Cromwell occupied Edinburgh within a week of Dunbar, though the
castle under its commander Walter Dundas held out until December
1650. In Edinburgh itself there was now no longer any fellow feeling as
there had been a few years earlier between the Presbyterian Covenanters
and Parliamentarian soldiers occupying the city, for these men were
almost all now Independents who despised the rigid structure of the Scots
kirk. Independent ministers from the New Model Army even started
preaching on street corners, to the annoyance of the locals. Cromwell
himself, however, wanted reconciliation between the Presbyterians and
the Independents and a united front against the Royalists. Though he was
at times bedridden with fevers, he made diplomatic efforts to win back
the moderates by hosting a banquet in the Great Hall of Edinburgh
Castle and holding meetings at Moray House and in Glasgow.

Meanwhile with affairs in chaos there was a new rebellion in the Highlands, encouraged by Charles and his advisers. It was initially led by Lords Ogilvy in Atholl and Dudhope (John Scrimgeour whose father had been killed fighting for the Royalists at Marston Moor) in Angus, with Huntly also joining in from the north east. With around a thousand men, it was sufficient to inspire the frustrated Charles II to make a move. He pretended to go out hawking on the South Inch at Perth but his plan was really to rendezvous with the Earl of Buchan. This incident known as The Start was botched and he ended up in a small cottage in Glen Clova where he was soon afterwards arrested by Colonel Montgomery and dragged back for a sermon in Perth, after which, as usual, he blamed the entire escapade on 'wicked advisers'. Doubtless he used the same excuse when he was caught playing cards, another example of sinful behaviour.

Naturally The Start further eroded the king's fragile credibility and the division between the Resolutioners and the Remonstrants increased. The believers accepted his usual reassurances that he had learned his lesson, whilst the doubters professed astonishment. Now instead of purging Malignants, the Committee offered indemnities to former rebels in the north east and Highlands, for there was now a serious manpower shortage in the army.

Leslie, meanwhile, made such a good job of the defences at Stirling that Cromwell gave up the idea of storming them and retired to Linlithgow Palace from which he issued offers of armistice except for the 'blood-guilty Stuarts' and warned of the dangers of war, hunger and disease. His offer was rejected.

Now to make matters worse for the struggling Committee there was a rebellion in the south west, the Covenanting heartland, led by two colonels, Strachan and Kerr. Both had refused to serve under Leslie and joined the Western Association. Cromwell marched against them and they withdrew to Dumfries without a battle, but sent a remonstrance to the Committee denouncing Charles for having used the 'apostate rebel James Graham (Montrose)' and for being totally untrustworthy. Argyll led the opposition to this diatribe, surprisingly defending the man who was a decade later to order his execution.

When the Scottish Parliament met, with Campbell of Loudoun as president and Charles on a makeshift throne, the would-be king pronounced with studied sincerity that 'He (God) hath moved me to enter in covenant with His people.' The parliament happily passed a decree for two days of fasting for the sins of the king and his family and nobility.

Meanwhile Lambert had headed west to Clydesdale to deal with the rebel Covenanter force under Kerr – his colleague Strachan had been dismissed for suggesting an alliance with Cromwell – and easily defeated it by the Cadzow Burn near Hamilton in December 1650.

There was now a deep rift between the two branches of the Scottish Covenanter movement and a potential split within the Church of Scotland. On the one hand the hard line Remonstrants, mainly in the west, rejected any deal with Charles unless there was an absolute guarantee of his fulfilling the Covenant and they also refused to allow any so-called Malignants back into the army. They had Warriston as their chief spokesman along with two ministers, James Guthrie and Patrick Gillespie.

Against them, still with a slight majority, were the Resolutioners led by Campbell of Argyll, with the two earls, Alexander Lindsay of Balcarres, and William Kerr of Lothian. Balcarres, who had fought at Marston Moor against the Royalists, had become a Covenanter-Royalist like others who accepted the terms of the Engagement in 1648, but was now a strong Royalist and later suffered for it as he died in exile in Holland in 1654. Lothian had been a semi-professional soldier, serving with Monro in Ireland as a Covenanter. He had been governor of Newcastle after its capture by Leven, joined Argyll to fight against Montrose but then had been one of the negotiators with Charles I at Holdenby House and ended up a Covenanter-Royalist aiding Leslie at Dunbar. This group regarded Charles II's oaths as trustworthy and favoured relaxing the rules to allow the so-called Malignants, most of whom were good soldiers, to come back into the army even if they had fought under Hamilton or Montrose. Their arguments were that the army had lost so many men that they needed every one they could get and even with his frailties, there was more chance of fulfilling the Covenant by supporting Charles II than by submitting to Cromwell.

The two groups were now so bitter in their recriminations that they began to hold separate church services. The new Duke of Hamilton was organising recruitment for the army against the 'unjust invasion', freely letting in English Royalist courtiers and ex-Montrose supporters. In contrast the General Assembly was unrealistically strict and wanted to vet all applicants for signs of malignancy. For example, Dundas the governor of Edinburgh Castle, which had surrendered just before Christmas, was branded as a traitor.

On New Year's Day 1651 Charles II was crowned at Scone with a gaggle of earls doing the honours; Loudoun announcing the Covenant oath, Argyll carrying the crown, Crawford-Lindsay the sceptre, while the moderator Robert Douglas gave a sermon based on Kings II. 'And Jehovah made a covenant before the Lord and the King that they should be the Lord's people.' He urged Charles not to repeat the sins of his grandfather. Then the Solemn League and Covenant was read aloud. So the next war, like the others, was to be a holy war, and for the second time it would be Presbyterians against Independents.

Chapter 26

THE SCOTS INVADE ENGLAND
FOR THE FOURTH TIME

The Lord will purge the crown of the sins and transgressions of
them that did reign before him.

Prayer spoken at the coronation of Charles II

The Scottish Parliament met in March 1651 and the king was already
throwing his weight about, removing Loudoun as president and
packing the Committee of Estates with Royalists, English nobles and
rehabilitated Malignants. They sponsored a vote of censure against
the minister James Guthrie for daring to oppose the admission of the
Malignants back into the army, while the king had himself declared
commander-in-chief, with Leslie and Middleton as his major generals.
Argyll accused Charles of violating his oath so he too was removed;
thus both the two main Campbells were out of power and the new
Covenanter/Royalists were preparing for war. They even devalued the
Scottish currency as a means of covering their deficit.

However, the Scots only controlled half of their own country, for
Edinburgh and almost everywhere else south of Stirling was in the
hands of Cromwell. The defences of Stirling were improved with a
new rampart to Torwood and the River Carron. Cromwell had now
recovered from his 'ague', perhaps malaria, and was preparing for an
invasion of Fife, but Burntisland proved too well fortified for him to
land there and he retired to Linlithgow.

Subsequently a force of 1,400 under Colonel Overton mounted a
surprise attack on North Queensferry. Cromwell then sent for General
Lambert to join him and they were faced at Inverkeithing by about
3,500 Scottish Covenanter-Royalist troops sent from Stirling under

Sir John Browne of Fordel. The result was a decisive Parliamentary victory with 2,000 Scots killed and 1,200 prisoners, including Major General Browne whose castle nearby was demolished by the victorious Roundheads. Of the 2,000 deaths, it is estimated that some 700 came from a single clan, the Macleans, brought there by Sir 'Red' Hector Maclean of Duart. This delivered a crippling blow to the populations of Mull and Tiree, from which they arguably never recovered.

After this victory Cromwell was able to subdue Fife and most of Perthshire so that Stirling was becoming an isolated outpost of the Scots and the king. Charles's solution to the problem was to ignore the advice of the Committee of Estates, except for its ultra-Royalist members, and to head for London with his army, fondly expecting the English to join him in large numbers as he marched south, a mistake to be copied by his nephew in 1715 and his grand-nephew in 1745. Argyll was one of those who protested and he was called a coward so he left the court. Thus on 1 August 1651 a predominantly Scottish army of 18,000 men set off for the border to the delight of Cromwell, who thought that the move made it far easier for him finally to defeat the Royalists than it would have been had he needed to chase them through the wilder parts of Scotland. Charles left garrisons in Perth and Stirling to defend his few remaining bases in Scotland. Cromwell left Monck with 5,000 men to besiege Stirling, whilst he with the rest of his army followed Charles back to England.

As Charles crossed the border he still had to keep on the right side of the accompanying Covenanters, who made up a significant portion of his army and for whom this was still a holy war. So to please them, he gave orders that all English Royalists who joined him should sign the Solemn League and Covenant, but apparently then told his officers privately to ignore the orders, a secret which soon became known and thus seriously disturbed the Covenanters in the army.

When he reached Carlisle, Charles had himself proclaimed King of Great Britain. He was still several days ahead of Cromwell's main force, but the advance guard of the New Model Army was harassing the Covenanter/Royalists' rear. For a while Charles acquired a false sense of security when his men beat off an attack by Lambert at Warrington Bridge, but the experienced David Leslie was not deceived and already foresaw disaster. This feeling began to spread amongst the Scots as there was by this time an obvious absence of English Royalists coming to join the Covenanter/Royalist army as they moved further south. On the contrary many local militias were coming out to attack the king's army, still angry at the depredations inflicted by the Scots three years earlier during the Preston campaign.

With his army badly tiring after its long marches and shrinking in size due to desertions, Charles now gave up the idea of a quick attack on London, just as his father had done soon after Edgehill. Instead he made for Worcester still hoping for English or Welsh supporters to join him, but very few did. A force of 1,500 men raised by the Earl of Derby was routed before it could reach him. Charles himself was by this time close to panic and contemplated a quick retreat back to Scotland, at least for those who had horses. However the infantry threatened mutiny if they were left behind and dug strong entrenchments to defend themselves in Worcester where Cromwell's army caught up with them on 28 August.

Initially the Scots performed well in preventing the Parliamentarians from crossing Powick Bridge, but were eventually forced back into the city. Then they did a sortie on the opposite side of Worcester, hoping to destroy one of Cromwell's divisions before it could join up with the rest of the army. This battle lasted for three hours and almost succeeded, until the Parliamentarians sent reinforcements. Again the Scots were forced back and this time it was even further, for their entrenchments had been stormed by the New Model Army.

Charles, who according to one legend was resting in a house, woke up to find disaster and began to prepare his escape in disguise, a quick haircut, less conspicuous clothing and dismissing all his attendants except two. He left by St Martin's Gate and later hid in what became his emblematic oak tree.

Estimated Scottish casualties were 3,000 killed, including the Duke of Hamilton who died of his wounds, and at least 6,000 prisoners were taken, most of whom were condemned to transportation as indentured labourers to Virginia and the West Indies. Lauderdale was one of about 150 Scottish noblemen, including eleven earls, who surrendered and got rather better treatment, usually a spell in the Tower of London. Even the Earl of Leven, who had taken no part in this conflict, was arrested and condemned to death and only reprieved after a special plea from the Queen of Sweden.

Amongst those who got away were a party of Glencoe Macdonalds, including certainly the clan bard Ranald who had written a poem to honour Charles I, and almost certainly his massive young chief Alastair who was to die forty-one years later in the Massacre. Of the other Highland clans that had been at Worcester, the worst sufferers were the Macleods who had sent a thousand men and lost so many of them that, like the Macleans after Inverkeithing, their home territory suffered a crippling loss of manpower from which they took many years to recover.

The previous three Scottish invasions of England had been almost exclusively by lowland troops plus a few southern clans, but the Worcester campaign had attracted the support of quite a few Highland clans in a pattern that was to be repeated in 1715 and 1745. Ironically the main Battle of Worcester had taken place on 3 September, the same date as the Battle of Dunbar only one year earlier, and it was to be on this same date seven years later that the victor died.

Back in Scotland the Remonstrants were happy to be proved right, while the ministers declared a day of national humiliation and confession of sins. It now looked very unlikely that the English would be forced to accept Presbyterianism or that Charles II would regain the throne in the foreseeable future. A succession of seven holy wars that had begun with the Fife Conspiracy of 1637 had caused massive loss of life throughout the British Isles and after thirteen years of campaigning the future of Presbyterianism was still in doubt.

Chapter 27

SCOTLAND BECOMES PART OF A REPUBLIC

Cemented with the blood of their dear sovereign
who loved Presbyterianism and hated toleration
From a proclamation put out by the Earl of Glencairn

Back in Scotland the country was suffering from malnutrition and disease due to the devastation and loss of so much manpower. General Monck had steadily been overcoming the remaining Scottish Royalist garrisons and Stirling had been surrendered by the Highlanders on 14 August. Dundee, despite its fine fortifications, was taken by storm on 1 September when its garrison were the worse for drink at lunchtime, and there followed three days of looting and killing. Monck picked up substantial deposits of gold held for many of the local lairds in the city's vaults. The garrison commander Sir Robert Lumsden was either killed or put to death as a traitor.

The Royalist earls of Huntly and Balcarres held out for a while in the north east before they too surrendered. Argyll offered to surrender to Monck on terms, but these were refused, so General Dean was sent to capture him, but the surrounding land had been so badly wasted that there was no food for his troops. He gave up and eventually tracked down Argyll to a bedroom in Inverness where he was recovering from an illness.

Meanwhile the two Covenanter parties, the Remonstrants and Resolutioners, were still rowing with each other, the former willing to accede to union with England and a republic, whilst the latter disliked the Cromwell regime both for its religious 'oddities' and its rejection of the monarchy. Cromwell offered to preserve the Church of Scotland but not the Scottish Parliament, so it was dissolved, and an Act of Union passed in 1653. All tariffs between the two countries were removed for the benefit of Scottish commerce; the powers of hereditary chiefs, many of whom had been Royalists, were also abolished, with the concept of vassalage. Though it survived briefly the General Assembly of the Church of Scotland in July 1653 was so acrimonious that it too was abolished by Cromwell. A year later the monarchy was formally abolished and Scotland became part of the Protectorate with an allocation of 30 MPs to be sent to Westminster.

Despite all this, the Royalists were not yet dead. In August 1653 those old stalwarts, the Earls of Balcarres and Glencairn, were encouraged by the exiled king to stage a new rising. Alexander Lindsay, Earl of Balcarres (1618–59), one of the original Fife conspirators, had initially been strong for the Covenant and fought against the Royalists at Marston Moor, but then became one of the group that half changed sides to support Charles I so long as he accepted the Covenant; so he had supported the Covenanting Engagers at Preston in 1648. On the other hand, William Cunningham, Earl of Glencairn, was different, for he came from Kilmaurs in the Covenanting heartland of Ayrshire, yet from the start had been a Royalist and well regarded by Charles I. Thus he had opposed the Solemn League and Covenant and the invasion of England to help the parliament in 1644 and had been removed from office. He had then been implicated in the plot to rescue the king in 1648. Glencairn's proclamation for a rebellion in 1653 did, however, reflect the Solemn League for it was in favour of the Stuart monarchy and Presbyterianism. Meanwhile he was joined by the usual suspects, the Glengarry Macdonalds, the Camerons of Lochiel, and Argyll's heir Lord Lorn with some Campbell adherents. There were a couple of skirmishes in the Trossachs, which suggested more might follow. They raided Atholl and Kenmore and ranted in their publicity about 'the monstrous republic'.

Just as they were making some progress the two main leaders fell out, Balcarres refusing to take orders from the hot-headed Glencairn who did not like Balcarres's idea of bringing in a committee or compelling his men to swear the Covenant oath. So Balcarres went off to exile in Breda in disgust and Lorn tried to withdraw his Campbell contingent but was prevented from doing so.

Glencairn was undaunted and received a new batch of English ultra-Royalists brought by a mercenary colonel called Wogan, who unfortunately died after their first skirmish at Drummond in Atholl. Glencairn made for Elgin to wait for a promised delivery of supplies. He then headed to Sutherland to join up with General Middleton who was also again raising a rebellion and welcomed him to a bibulous feast at his base near Dornoch. Probably after too much drinking had taken place, Sir George Munro, a professional and veteran of the Antrim and Preston campaigns, referred to Glencairn's forces as 'a band of robbers', and things got out of hand. A duel between the two ensued, in which Glencairn had the best of it, followed by another duel between two of their supporters, which resulted in the death of one and the execution for murder of the other. Glencairn headed south in disgrace.

Meanwhile Cromwell had sent General Monck back to Scotland, a man well capable of dealing with this dysfunctional rebellion. His assistant Morgan heavily defeated the Royalist force at Lochgarry, Middleton fled to France and Glencairn surrendered soon afterwards on terms, but he was to stage a comeback in 1660 when his loyalty to the Stuart dynasty was rewarded. Balcarres on the other hand never returned from exile and died in Breda. For the time being it was the end of armed opposition to the Protectorate in Scotland and Cromwell, with Monck's aid, had achieved a more comprehensive subjugation of the Scots than any previous English leader.

The next six years were almost uneventful. Scotland was run by a council of nine men, only two of whom were Scots, the Quaker judge Swinton and the former mercenary Sir William Lockhart of Lee (1621–75). Lockhart from The Lee near Lanark was almost unique in having been a Scottish Royalist for the Civil War period but then in 1652 switched to the republican side, the opposite direction to most of his fellow lairds. Having served in the French army he had risen to be a cavalry general for the Preston campaign where he fought doggedly during the retreat to Wigan, but he then remarkably switched over to the English Parliamentarians. Perhaps having fought for Charles I he had less liking for Charles II who rejected his services for the Worcester campaign. Soon afterwards he met Oliver Cromwell in London and was made a commissioner for Scotland working with Monck. He then became Cromwell's ambassador to France and later governor of Dunkirk. So he was lucky to escape execution after the Restoration.

Under Monck's regime the Church in Scotland functioned with presbyteries but no assembly, so there were no major confrontations.

The Scottish economy improved partly due to the increased cross-border trade and partly due to the cessation of warfare. The first Edinburgh-London stagecoach service, taking 14 days, was established. Cromwell had his worries in England but in Scotland, Monck kept a tight grip and all went smoothly. The moral influence of the Church also continued, as it did in England. In 1656 an Act was passed making it a crime to do any of the following on a Sunday: visit taverns, dance, play profane music, wash, carry water, sweep houses, make bread or beer or travel anywhere. Discipline was enforced by kirk sessions that paid watchdogs to report breaches of the rules, particularly in Glasgow and Aberdeen. Sessions also ensured children were punished for playing games on the Sabbath.

On 3 September 1658, the anniversary of Scotland's two disastrous battles, Dunbar and Worcester, Oliver Cromwell died, probably of malaria caught either in his East Anglian marshes or in the bogs of Ireland; apparently he had rejected quinine as a drug because it was a Jesuit priest who had discovered its properties. His son Richard or 'Tumbledown Dick' took over as Lord Protector but failed to inspire confidence and as England plunged into chaos it was Monck, based in Scotland, who coolly assessed the situation and, helped by William Lockhart, started negotiations again with the king. This time it was a mainly English army under Monck that marched to Coldstream, occupied Berwick, and headed south over the border to London where he sensed that the country was ready to take back its king. And this time Charles II would not be required to sign the Solemn League and Covenant, nor to make a promise he would have no intention of keeping.

> While Darwen streams with blood of Scots imbrued,
> And Dunbar field resounds thy praises loud,
> And Worcester's laureate wreath ...
> From John Milton's poem in praise of Oliver Cromwell

PART TWO

SCOTLAND'S OTHER CIVIL WARS AND THE SECOND FIFE CONSPIRACY: 1660–1689

He (Charles II) was now in such a situation that he could renew the attempt that had been so destructive to his father without any danger of his father's fate.

> Thomas Macaulay: *History of England*

The number of desperate rebels increases.

> From Covenanter report 1666

The Scots having fought and won two wars to get rid of bishops in Scotland and having helped to win a third to get rid of bishops in the whole of the British Isles, had then been deprived of the promised rewards. Then they had fought and lost two more wars with the same objective and ended up losing what they had won in the first two. They had lost 60,000 men for nothing. But many of them were still determined to stop the reintroduction of bishops. Yet for quite a few, including according to legend Jenny Geddes herself, the Restoration meant some welcome relief from the funless asceticism of the extreme Calvinists with their Sunday curfews and general disapproval of earthly pleasures.

The English Parliamentarians, mostly Puritans and Presbyterians, had also started and won a civil war against the high Anglicans, but in the process had their army so heavily infiltrated by members of independent sects that they mislaid their own victory. In turn the New Model Army, having finished winning the war that would create freedom of worship for the varied sects of which its men were members, also in the end failed; due to the unpopularity of the republican regime and its self-destruction after 1658, they lost all the religious freedoms for which they had fought. So the Puritans, Presbyterians, Quakers, Congregationalists, Fifth Monarchists, Shakers and others who had been the backbone of Cromwell's success, all lost in the end. The only religious sectarians who won were the high Anglicans and perhaps also the Catholics, for they were to enjoy a period of reduced persecution. Yet 28 years later, everything was to change again.

Meanwhile in Scotland the hard-core Covenanters were to endure more than two decades of relentless persecution, but showed no signs of giving in. This time Fife was initially less prominent in planning the opposition, for Ayrshire and Lanarkshire had become equally dedicated to the Covenant. However it was to be a second Fife conspiracy that resulted in one of the most dramatic events of the next period, the murder of Archbishop Sharp. And it was a Fife minister, Richard Cameron from Falkland, who both gave his name to a new sect but also to a military regiment that was to win the last battle of the nine wars. What is more, his parents came from Leuchars, the parish of Alexander Henderson, the man who co-wrote the Covenant.

The last two wars like the first seven were both closely linked to the Covenant, separate yet closely intertwined. The Covenanter rebellion of 1666–1683 was essentially to become a civil war between the oppressed surviving Covenanters and the repressive Edinburgh Royalist regime. The last of the nine wars from 1685–9 was a more widespread reaction to the even less popular regime of James II, whose threat to bring back Roman Catholicism was far more alarming than anything his father had ever even considered.

Chapter 1

THE PEOPLE AND
THE REGIMENTS

> It is odd to think how cruel men fall upon such methods to torment
> their fellow creatures.
>
> Robert Wodrow: *A History of the Sufferings of*
> *the Church of Scotland*

Of the many people involved on both sides in the seven wars of
religion begun in 1639 many were now dead, retired or on the run, so
it is worth reviewing the new breed of decision-makers whose careers
influenced the next two decades after the Restoration in 1660.

Of the ten bishops whose unpopularity had caused the long series
of wars, only one was still alive after two decades had passed. He
was one of the least popular, Thomas Sydserf of Galloway, and was
reinstated but sent to a more remote see, the Orkneys, to keep him
out of trouble; he died there a couple of years later.

Amongst the new bishops created in 1660, James Sharp was
the most important for, as the new Archbishop of St Andrews, his
aim was the elimination of Presbyterianism in Scotland. Both as
a clergyman and politician he was obsessively authoritarian in a
way that was largely responsible for the next bout of holy wars in
Scotland. Having been a reluctant Covenanter (he had managed
to avoid actually signing it when he was made minister of Crail
by his patron the Earl of Crawford) he had served as a negotiator
for the Kirk Party and spent a year in the Tower of London after
Worcester, thus giving him time to think of the future. Now in
1660, he readily negotiated the return of episcopacy with himself
in the leading role.

Of the other new bishops Robert Leighton (1611–84) at Dunblane was the most respectable, pious and learned. His father had been persecuted as a Presbyterian and he himself had served as a Covenant-signing minister at Newbattle before resigning in 1652, perhaps unsympathetic towards his more fanatical colleagues. He became Principal of Edinburgh University and after Dunblane, was Archbishop of Glasgow.

Andrew Fairfoul (1606–63), born in Anstruther so one of the Fife group, was his predecessor as the new Archbishop of Glasgow in 1661. He had been chaplain for the influential new Earl of Rothes and had served as a Covenant-signing minister first in Leith, then Duns, but found it convenient to change sides. He was inducted by the resurgent Royalist Earl of Glencairn but died two years later on the way to Edinburgh.

Alexander Burnet (1615–84) could at least boast of having refused to sign the Covenant and then suffered dismissal from his charge in 1639 and exile to England. He had the advantage, however, of being chaplain to the Earl of Traquair. So having become Bishop of Aberdeen in 1661, he was promoted to Archbishop of Glasgow in 1664.

Montrose's former chaplain, the anti-Covenant George Wishart, was restored after three spells in prison and became bishop of Edinburgh in 1662.

Of the main Covenanter ministers, Alexander Henderson had died whilst vainly trying to get Charles I to accept the Covenant in 1647. Henderson's tomb was vandalised by the Royalists out of spite, as was that of George Gillespie who had been in London negotiating the Solemn League. James Guthrie the minister of Lauder, who like Sharp had once been episcopalian, was the only minister executed after the Restoration, mainly because he had made an enemy of General Middleton by excommunicating him. Two others escaped execution, Samuel Rutherford because he died in prison and Patrick Gillespie because he managed to escape.

David Dickson and Andrew Cant died shortly after the Restoration in their seventies, whilst Cant's nephew, the bloodthirsty John Nevoy, was one of those ministers dismissed for refusing to accept bishops in 1661 and died in exile in Holland. Zachary Boyd who had famously preached to Cromwell in Glasgow and wrote a poem extolling the victory at Newburn, had died in 1653 aged seventy. Robert Baillie who had become Principal of Glasgow University and been one of the main negotiators of the Solemn League died in 1662.

Two of the survivors were the evangelical Robert Blair who had become a popular preacher in both Ireland and London; he lasted till 1674, as did Robert Douglas, five times moderator of the General Assembly who had crowned Charles II at Scone and at eighty preached the sermon at the first Scottish parliament after the Restoration.

Of the other parish ministers in post in 1660 approximately 300 were dismissed for refusing to accept the return of bishops. Many became mendicant preachers, addressing huge conventicles (preaching in a field) on remote hillsides and constantly on the run. A number also were later executed for such non-cooperation, including James Renwick from Moniave when only 26 years old in 1688, and Donald Cargill, from Blairgowrie, the ex-minister at the Barony in Glasgow in 1681 after being wounded in the Battle of Bothwell Bridge. Numerous other ministers were dismissed after the Restoration for refusing to accept bishops: Matthew Ramsay of (Old) Kilpatrick; Robert Law of New Kilpatrick, though he later got his post back as one of the 'indulged'; John Dickson of Rutherglen, another conventicler who was imprisoned on the Bass Rock; Henry Forsyth of Kirkintilloch; James Blair of Cathcart, who was shot; Thomas Melville of Cadder, who held conventicles at Bearsden; John Low of Campsie, who was also imprisoned on the Bass Rock; Patrick Simpson of Renfrew, the father of 17 sons but no daughters; and James Walkinshaw at Baldernock, accused of holding conventicles. Many such men suffered eviction from their homes and loss of stipend, many were imprisoned and some killed. Some who succumbed to the temptation of being 'indulged' later recanted and were punished accordingly. Those who accepted episcopacy without complaint were looked down on as 'curates' and dismissed when the regime changed again in 1688. The charismatic Fife preacher Richard Cameron (1648–60) from Falkland was killed fighting at the Battle of Airds Moss.

Of the other influential new ministers Alexander Robertson in Edinburgh, and John Guthrie of Tarbolton, both were ejected from their parishes but continued to preach in the open and were present at the Covenant oath renewal at Lanark. Inspired by Guthrie was Alexander Peden (1636–1686) known as Prophet Peden, son of a local laird who became a schoolteacher at Tarbolton and then minister at New Luce in Wigtonshire. William Guthrie of Fenwick (the third of the three Guthrie brothers) and Hugh Crawford of New Cumnock were also prominent opponents of the Sharp regime. Another popular preacher who lost his living, William Carstairs (1649–1715), returned to Scotland after he had been tortured in 1682 for alleged connections with the Rye House Plot and became an agent for William of Orange.

By far the most influential of the lay supporters of the clergy had been Archibald Johnston, Lord Warriston, joint author with Henderson of the Covenant and legal brain behind the Solemn League and Covenant. He had been an opponent of the Preston campaign and remained cynical about the oaths of Charles II during the Dunbar and Worcester campaigns. He had preferred serving Cromwell rather than the king, so he fled to Germany at the Restoration. Unfortunately he paid a visit to Normandy and was arrested in Rouen, then extradited home to be tried and executed. Though appearing almost senile at his trial, he suffered his fate with dignity leaving his wife and many children in penury.

Of the noblemen who had mainly been Covenanters in 1639 but mostly drifted back to half-Royalism by 1648, Montrose, the first to change sides had been executed in 1651 but was exhumed and given a State funeral on the orders of the king in 1660. His was an extreme case but clearly the first flush of aristocratic support for the Covenant had begun to wear off when the nobles found themselves being ordered about by middle-class clerics with vaguely egalitarian views and a deep distrust of human pleasures.

One of the others to change sides early was John Lindsay (1598–1678), Earl of Lindsay from 1633, then Earl of Crawford from 1642, who had been the patron of James Sharp at Crail Church back in 1648. A namesake and neighbour of Alexander Lindsay of Balcarres who had died an exile in Breda just before the Restoration, he now came into his own.

The two Hamilton brothers, James as the 1st Duke, and William as the 2nd, were both dead, James executed after Preston and William killed at Worcester. Both had been staunch but conciliatory Royalists using allegiance to the Covenant as camouflage for their campaigns and in death had been deprived of all their estates. Since neither of them had produced sons the 3rd Duke was William Douglas (1634–94), who had married James's daughter Anne. He himself was a supporter of Lauderdale and pro-Covenant, but he played no major role till 25 years later he was significantly one of the first to switch allegiance from James II to William of Orange. Of the other Douglases, his father William the Marquis (1589–1660), had signed the Covenant, but changed sides to join Montrose in 1645, had escaped after Philiphaugh but been captured a year later until released from Edinburgh Castle in 1647. He refused to join the Worcester campaign, and was past seventy when he died. Archibald Douglas, Earl of Angus (1609–85), had signed the Covenant but went into exile in 1641, returning only to be a commissioner sent to London in 1643 to further the cause of Presbyterianism. His teenage son was to be founder of the Cameronian Regiment and to die with them at Steinkirk. One new branch of the Douglas clan came to the fore, the Drumlanrig Douglases who became Earls then Dukes of Queensberry. Queensberry Hill near Drumlanrig was ironically a favourite site for illegal Presbyterian services.

Of the two Campbells who had played a major part in encouraging the wars first against and then for the Stuarts, Archibald of Argyll, to his huge surprise, was arrested in London in 1660 and later executed. Despite having played a significant part in the king's restoration, he had perhaps made himself too powerful with too many enemies and had not stood up to Cromwell. His heir, another Archibald (1629–1685), became the 9th Earl of Argyll and was also destined to have an ambivalent and ultimately fatal relationship with the Royal Stuarts, executed by the Maiden, just like his father. As a youngster he had taken a part in the Glencairn rebellion of 1653 as a Royalist for Charles II, but was to lose his life trying to prevent the accession of Charles's brother, James II. As his second wife, Archibald married the remarkable Anna Mackenzie, widow of his fellow rebel in 1653, the Earl of Balcarres who had died in Holland. His elder son refused to fight on his side in 1685 and was later to be rewarded with a dukedom.

John Campbell of Loudoun who had been sacked as Chancellor at the Restoration died soon afterwards in his mid-sixties. The next two Earls of Loudoun, James Campbell (d. 1684), and Hugh Campbell (d. 1731), played no major part in affairs. Their Ayrshire neighbours the Campbells of Cessnock, however, fell foul of the authorities and as a result were to pioneer settlements in America, as did Neil Campbell (1630–1692), the Earl of Argyll's brother who went into exile after the 1685 rebellion and sailed for East New Jersey where he briefly became its governor and expanded the Scots colony at Perth Amboy. Other Campbells active in the period included the new Duncan of Auchinbreck, son of the instigator of the Rathlin massacre, 'Slippery John' of Glenorchy, Earl of Braedalbane and Campbell of Ardkinglas. One of the Campbells who suffered most from the Macdonald depredations encouraged by the Stuart regime was the later infamous

Robert Campbell of Glenlyon (1632–1696), who had lost so much money that he had to enlist in the new Argyll regiment and in 1692 won notoriety as the man who started the shooting in Glencoe.

Another founding member of the Fife Conspiracy had been the avuncular John Leslie, Earl of Rothes, but he had died on a mission to London in 1641 aged only forty. His son, also John Leslie (1630–81), the replacement earl had diametrically opposing views partly perhaps because he was orphaned at the age of ten and brought up by the now strongly Royalist Lord Crawford (John Lindsay) whose daughter he married and whose post as Lord Treasurer he took over in 1663. Rothes had been one of the first to greet Charles II at Breda in 1660 and was made a duke shortly before he died. He had been imprisoned briefly in 1651 after being captured at Worcester and again for philandering. The old castle was too cramped for him so he built the magnificent Leslie Palace, which burned down a century later. As Justice he was involved in numerous incidents of torture.

Lord Balmerino, another prominent early Covenanter who played a major role in the resistance to Charles I and sent his son to fight at Marston Moor, was later the civilian commissioner advising General Baillie during the Montrose campaign, died of a stroke in 1649. His son, another John Elphinstone, kept a lower profile, making only a brief protest against the revival of bishops.

Of all the Covenanter lords who changed sides after the capture of Charles I the one who came off best was undoubtedly John Maitland, Earl and later Duke of Lauderdale, who had been a vital negotiator with both Charles I and II, had been imprisoned after Worcester and exiled but came back in 1660 to huge wealth and the position of Secretary of State. He held out for the continued abolition of bishops in 1660 and had a major fallout with the king's other main leader in Scotland, General Middleton. He quickly saw that this would not aid his career so he assented, becoming not only a duke but also the L in the CABAL that ran Britain in the 1670s. A huge, ill-co-ordinated man with an over-large tongue and shaggy red hair, he needed the funds to keep his new wife, the extravagant Lady Dysart, in the style she wanted.

Cunningham of Glencairn, builder of Kilmaurs Place, had an erratic career as a diehard loyalist, hot-tempered, unpredictable and easily offended, but he too survived to get his reward at the Restoration. He had been an isolated Episcopalian Royalist in an area full of Covenanters, close to his long-term rivals the Kennedys of Cassilis and the Montgomerys of Eglinton.

Overall in this period we see a relative increase in prominence of Border lairds, as opposed to those further north. Families like the Maitlands of Lauderdale, the Johnstones of Annandale, the Hays of Tweeddale, and the Douglases of Drumlanrig, all came to the fore. These families were on the rise, had no special loyalties to any dynasty or religion and found it fairly easy to change sides to which ever one was winning. They were also richer than the old families further north who had suffered so badly from the depredations of the past few decades.

Of the professional soldiers, one of the main survivors from the years of war was John Middleton who, after serving in the Covenanter army till 1646, then spent many years of battling vainly in the Covenanter/Royalist cause. He at last got his reward when he was made the king's commissioner in Scotland in 1660 and as Earl of Middleton opened the Parliament on behalf of Charles II. Noted for heavy drinking, a riotous lifestyle and bearing grudges (one that led to the execution of a Covenanter minister) he rowed with his civilian rival Lauderdale and was recalled to London in 1666, then sent as governor to Tangier, which had come to Charles as part of his wife's dowry. While there, Middleton fell down the stairs after a drinking bout and died of his injuries.

So far as the two great Leslie generals were concerned, Alexander, Earl of Leven, had been captured in 1651 despite taking no part in the Worcester campaign, was condemned to death but then had been released from the Tower in 1654 after an appeal from Kristina, the Queen of Sweden. Now in his early seventies, he retired to his castle at Balgonie and died seven years later just short of eighty. His heir, Lord Balgonie, who had served as a colonel both in Germany and the Marston Moor campaign, and was a son-in-law of Rothes, seems sadly to have had some form of nervous breakdown and died before his father in 1645, leaving three young children. Leven's son-in-law, the brilliant dragoon commander Hugh Fraser, seems also to have died quite young. David Leslie, Earl of Newark, spent nine years in the Tower before he too was allowed to retire to his Newark Castle on the Fife coast with his young Yorkshire wife; he died in his eighties.

The mysterious Sir Robert Moray, former commander of the Garde Ecossaise in Paris, agent for Cardinal Richelieu, and important early supporter of the Fife Conspiracy, returned to London at the Restoration and, as a highly gifted amateur scientist, aided Prince Rupert in founding the Royal Society.

James Livingston, Earl of Callendar, who had been an erratic Royalist ever since The Incident, fled to Holland after the defeat at Preston but was allowed to return home in 1650 and like other wealthy ex-mercenaries could buy himself a castle, near Falkirk. But four years later, he was back in prison and deprived of his properties until the Restoration. He lived until he too was in his eighties. In the next generation his cousin Sir Thomas Livingston (d. 1711) was to serve in the Dutch army and be a prominent supporter of William of Orange.

William Baillie from Lamington had suffered the disadvantage of bastardy but made good in Swedish service and with the Covenanters, though he lost twice to Montrose. He married a Janet Bruce of Glen House, settled down in an estate at Letham in Fife and, with his profits as a mercenary general, bought Castle Cary near Cumbernauld – which is allegedly still haunted by his granddaughter's ghost.

Sir James Lumsden (1598–1660) was one of three brothers who fought in the Swedish army and returned to Scotland, settling in Fife. Sir James, founder of Lumsden's Musketeers, was a veteran from Marston Moor and Dunbar who retired soon afterwards, having bought two castles with his earnings, Innergellie and Mountquhanie. His brother Robert was governor of Dundee when it was stormed by Monck in 1650 and he was killed or executed there. His third brother, William, also fought at Marston Moor and was captured at Worcester.

The old campaigner Sir Robert Monro fell into disfavour after his defeat at Benburb in Ireland as he had sent half his troops back to Scotland for the Preston campaign, but after a spell in the Tower he was allowed to retire in Antrim, where he had married a well-endowed widow during his long service there.

The least fortunate of the professionals was Sir John Hurry, who paid the price of changing sides too often and had been executed. His brother, Colonel William Hurry, was less controversial and survived.

Amongst the new breed of professionals emerging in 1660 was Tam Dalzell (1615–85) of the Binns in Linlithgow. He had started soldiering at the age of thirteen at La Rochelle then served in the Covenanter army in Antrim under Robert Monro, becoming a prisoner of war there on the capture of Carrickfergus Castle in 1650. Apparently he refused to shave his beard after Charles I's execution and fought for the Covenanter/Royalists at Worcester where he was once again taken prisoner. He escaped from the Tower in 1654 to join Glencairn's rebellion in the north, and then went to Russia where he fought for the Romanov Tsar Alexei till the Restoration. Known as Bluidy Tam and the Muscovite Devil, he became a ruthless opponent of the Covenanters.

His cousin Robert Dalzell (1611–54), Earl of Carnwath, was accused of Royalist leanings in 1643 and went to England to fight for the king at Naseby, where he encouraged Charles to escape and was blamed for thus causing a general retreat. He also was taken prisoner at Worcester and sent to the Tower, dying soon afterwards. His son Gavin (1627–74) was also a prisoner after Worcester but survived and the next generation were to be fervently Jacobite.

Equally ruthless was Sir James Turner (1615–86), the son of a minister in Dalkeith, who had been a junior officer in the Swedish army, returned to fight for the Covenanters in 1640, spending several years under Monro in Ulster where ill-treatment of the populace was standard practice. He spent some of this time with Lord Sinclair's Foot, notorious for their outrageous billeting habits, referred to as 'a noxious weed in the gardens of godliness'. He fought for the Covenanter/Royalists at both Preston and Worcester and on both occasions was captured. Described as dissolute in his private habits and vindictive as a soldier, he was employed after the Restoration to terrorise the south west counties until he was captured by the Covenanters in a surprise attack.

James Graham of Claverhouse (1648–89), later known as Bonnie Dundee from Claypotts Castle by Dundee, had served with the Scots Regiment in France under the Duke of Monmouth and in Holland for the Prince of Orange. In 1678 he was to be appointed captain of the force intended to wipe out the Presbyterian rebellion in south west Scotland, suffered a humiliating defeat at Drumclog, and ten years later was to become the first great Jacobite martyr at Killiecrankie. A number of witnesses recorded him shooting Covenanter prisoners out of hand.

William Drummond (1617–88) of Cromlix, later Viscount Strathallan, was the son of the Drummond who supported Montrose, and had, like Dalzell, served with Monro in Antrim but turned Royalist for the Preston and Worcester campaigns. Taken prisoner in the latter he escaped, joined with Glencairn in the 1653 rebellion then rose to the rank of general in Russia. Described as 'loose and profane' and an enemy of Lauderdale's, he nevertheless married the daughter of the strong Covenanter Lord Warriston and was slightly milder in his treatment of the rebels than Dalzell or Turner, though he was rumoured to have introduced the thumbscrew because of his experience in Russia. He modernised Strathallan Castle and his descendant, the 4th Viscount, was killed at Culloden.

His two cousins, James Drummond (1648–1716), Earl of Perth, and John (1649–1714), Earl of Melfort, also became prominent Jacobites. Both of them converted to Catholicism, presumably to please James II for whom the elder became Chancellor of Scotland and the younger Secretary of State, between them effectively running Scotland for the three years during which King James tried to establish absolute rule. James Drummond, like his cousin, is remembered for introducing torture by the thumbscrew in Scotland, and for organising a settlement in New Jersey. He spent four years in prison from 1689, whilst his brother John managed to escape to France. Both of them died in exile in Paris within a year of each other.

Sir Mungo Murray of Garth, brother of the Earl of Atholl and from a long-term Royalist family, was another officer noted for intimidation and torture of suspect Covenanters.

A feature of life in this period for the professional soldiers was the formation of a number of new regular regiments replacing the casual militias of the previous generation. Amongst these, as we have seen, were the Scots Guards who derived from the 1642 Marquis of Argyll's Regiment, which fought for the Covenanters in Ireland, then emerged under Argyll's son Lord Lorn as the Scottish Troop of Life Guards, which fought in 1651 at Worcester, then revived ten years later as the Horse Guards under the Earl of Newburgh.

As officially the senior regiment in Britain, the Royal Scots evolved from a number of Scottish mercenary units that had fought in Germany and France: Lumsden's Musketeers, the Hepburn Regiment and Mackay's Highlanders, known at this period as the Garde Ecossaise, legitimised by Charles I in 1633. They transformed into the Douglas Regiment of 1678, then the Earl of Dumbarton's, hence their regimental march Dumbarton's Drums. They fought for James II against his nephew Monmouth at Sedgemoor in 1685 and at many other battles till emerging as the Royal Scots, nicknamed Pontius Pilate's Bodyguards, then finally, in 2006, as part of the Royal Regiment of Scotland. George Douglas, unusual for a Douglas in being a Catholic, was made Earl of Dumbarton (1635–92) by Charles II but made a poor job of defending the Thames against the Dutch. He helped suppress the rebellions against James II in 1685, but followed his master into exile in 1689 and died soon afterwards at St Germain.

Similarly the Earl of Mar's Regiment of Foot, founded in 1678 to fight Covenanters, was amongst the first to have the new French muskets or fusils and provided the foundations for the Royal Highland Fusiliers. The first grenados or grenades appeared round about this time and provided the concept of Grenadiers. Monck's regiment became the Coldstream Guards.

The Royal Scots Greys had begun life in 1678 as the Royal Scots Dragoons to chase the Covenanters, but acquired their name from the grey cloth ordered for his troops by the eccentric General Tam Dalzell when he took over in 1681, making them pioneers as cavalry with bayonets to fit to their muskets.

Most remarkable were the Cameronians, raised at Douglas in 1689 in the name of the teenage James Douglas (1671–92), Earl of Angus, and named after the Covenanting preacher Richard Cameron since their objectives were definitely to support Presbyterianism, as R. Money Aimes put it 'unique in being the only regiment named after a religious reformer.' Under Colonel William Clelland they were to hold back the Jacobites at Dunkeld, despite being hugely outnumbered. Colonel Clelland, a diehard Covenanter and ex-gamekeeper, was killed there at the age of 28. The unfortunate young Earl of Angus was killed three years later, fighting for William of Orange at Steinkirk in the Netherlands.

Of the two restored royals King Charles was now thirty and unmarried but with a string of mistresses and some bastard sons and daughters. He had endured periods of considerable hardship and uncertainty over his career, but had inherited his father's near obsession with absolute authority and a religion based on tight discipline imposed by bishops. He also had plenty of time at St Germain to witness the apparently efficient practice of absolutism by his cousin Louis XIV of France and he determined to copy him. He was to be married two years after the Restoration to the relatively unattractive Catherine of Braganza, but she did bring the useful dowry of two major ports, Tangier and Bombay. Charles was realist enough to appreciate that he could not convert Britain back to Catholicism, but clearly he was determined on what was for him the next best thing, a high Anglican church controlled from the top by himself with bishops as his instruments of power. So like his father he was sure to make himself unpopular in most of Scotland.

The king's younger brother James, Duke of York, was only twenty-seven at the Restoration but already had behind him an impressive career as an army officer, fighting with distinction in both the French and Spanish armies and the Spanish navy. If anything he was even more influenced than his brother by the autocratic atmosphere of the French court and the Catholic Church so that unlike Charles, he was to be less realistic about the idea of converting Britain back to the old faith, a delusion that in the end was to cost him his crown. Meanwhile, whereas Charles seemed personally careless about the duty to provide legitimate heirs, he ordered his reluctant brother to marry his pregnant Protestant mistress Anne Hyde, who in 1662 produced the first of two queens, Mary and Anne, who were to be the last reigning members of the Stuart dynasty, and both of them were brought up in England as Protestants. Meanwhile James was destined to adopt even more extreme measures than his elder brother and became intent on self-destruction for the sake of his religion.

Especially worrying was James's second wife, Mary of Modena (1658–1718), mainly because she was a Catholic and still young enough to produce a male heir. They had married in 1673 and she had seven pregnancies all resulting in infant deaths until, in 1688, she finally gave birth to James (the Old Pretender) whose fairly robust health caused severe alarm for the Protestants both north and south of the border.

There were two other significant fringe members of the royal dynasty, both of them bastards. James, Duke of Monmouth (1649–85), otherwise known as Mr James Crofts, was perhaps Charles II's favourite child, an easy-going if somewhat lightweight Protestant who was a useful figurehead for the opposition to Charles and James. He was popular in Scotland for his relative leniency towards the Covenanters and became closely associated with the Argyll plot of 1685, which led to both their deaths.

The other bastard was James Fitzjames (1670–1734), Duke of Berwick, James's son with Arabella Churchill, brought up a Catholic and a successful career soldier, eventually a marshal of France, though his efforts at the Battle of the Boyne were to be in vain.

Overall the change in personnel reflected the changed mood across Scotland. The Covenant was no longer so popular with the upper classes or the establishment generally, partly because it had been socially too subversive and partly because it had led to military disaster. It had also caused a short-term crackdown on earthly frivolities and self-indulgence, which had perhaps overreached itself. Similarly the Covenant no longer attracted many professional soldiers, doubtless partly because the Covenanters had no money to pay them, and also because the Thirty Years war was long since over, so holy wars were less fashionable. Nevertheless, there was still a hard core of dedicated ministers who would sleep rough and preach for nothing rather than accept a return of bishops. In turn they attracted a hard core of mainly middle-class supporters willing to give their lives for their faith and this was to cause two new holy wars, which finally resulted in the expulsion of the Stuart kings and of the last bishops in the Church of Scotland. But before that happened there were to be many deaths in battle and by murder or execution.

Chapter 2

THE BISHOPS' REVENGE

Do not ascribe the faults of Presbyterians to Presbyterianism.
Attributed to the Earl of Crawford

On his restoration Charles II began to reward the hard-line Royalists who had shared some of his exile and fought on his behalf. The hard-drinking and strongly episcopalian General Middleton was appointed the king's commissioner in Scotland, whilst his great rival, the Presbyterian John Maitland of Lauderdale, became Secretary of State based in London. Then came the three favourite earls; Rothes was to be President of the Council in Scotland, the hot-tempered Glencairn was made Chancellor and Crawford the Treasurer. The old Committee of Estates was revised to manage affairs but all friends of Montrose were excluded. The Campbells too were out of favour, Loudoun dismissed as Chancellor and Argyll suddenly arrested in London and sent to the Tower.

So far as religion was concerned, Charles moved cautiously and his first letter suggested that he would allow the Church of Scotland to stay Presbyterian and function without bishops. Lauderdale favoured that solution but Middleton and Glencairn did not. The main royal adviser at this point on Scottish ecclesiastical affairs was James Sharp, the ambitious minister of Crail who had been a reluctant Covenanter since 1648, spent a year in the Tower after Worcester and was strongly attracted by the idea of becoming a bishop himself. It is suggested that he first offered the post of Archbishop of St Andrews to Robert Douglas who preached at the first Scottish Parliament of 1660, but doubtless he expected a refusal so he lost nothing by his offer and took the job himself. This made things easy for Charles who followed both his father and grandfather in believing that bishops were a useful prop for the monarchy. At the same time the progress that the Scottish Parliament had made since 1638 in asserting its authority was reversed, for Charles was voted a massive annuity of £480,000 Scots, meaning the parliament need hardly ever be called as there was no longer any need to ask its permission to raise taxes.

Some hefty bribery also smoothed the way. Three large parcels of land earmarked for government forts in Leith, Inverness and Ayr were given to the three earls, Murray, Lauderdale, and Eglinton. Only two members of the Parliament refused to take the oath endorsing Charles as supreme head of the Church, Cassilis and the Laird of Kilbirnie, but Lords Balmerino, Crawford and Cowper were also unhappy, as was the new Duke of Hamilton, William Douglas. Most of the lairds, however, particularly the Chancellor Glencairn and the President, the allegedly dissolute Rothes, were happy to see the discomfiture of the more fanatical and dictatorial church ministers who had wielded such power over the previous two decades.

As the new parliament led by an often-tipsy Royal Commissioner General Middleton steadily eradicated all the policies of its predecessor, Presbyterianism and the Solemn League and Covenant, the majority was for the time being happy to see the return of stability, which meant a hierarchy of king and nobles coupled with a parallel hierarchy of king, bishops and subservient clergy. The new council consisted of eight bishops, eight nobles chosen by the bishops and eight burghers chosen to make up the two dozen.

Montrose was accorded a much-delayed State funeral by the king who perhaps had a twinge of guilt for disowning him ten years earlier. Meanwhile Montrose's arch enemy Argyll was confined to a commoner's cell in Edinburgh whilst his mock trial could find no crime except for his co-operation with Monck, though the real reason was probably his bullying of the king to sign the Covenant. His fellow Campbell, the Earl of Loudoun, was one of the few who stood up for him, but his execution was inevitable and he died with unexpected courage under the sharp blade of the Maiden. 'I could die like a Roman but I choose to die rather like a Christian.' His headless body was taken down the Clyde from Old Kilpatrick to the Holy Loch for burial at Kilmun. His son and heir Lord Lorn was also arrested and threatened with losing all his estates, but he had wisely married Lauderdale's niece, so he survived with all his titles except marquis.

Of the other political trials designed to intimidate the population, the ex-judge Swinton escaped death by becoming a Quaker and of the three church ministers selected as scapegoats for the aggressions of the Covenant only James Guthrie, who had turned down a bishopric, was executed on the gallows, mainly because he had made an enemy of Middleton by excommunicating him; Patrick Gillespie escaped, and Samuel Rutherford died in his cell. Hanged at the Mercat Cross on the same day as Guthrie was one strongly Presbyterian army officer Major William Govan, an opponent of the Preston and Worcester campaigns accused of various unlikely acts of treason, but a useful warning to other soldiers to toe the new party line.

Meanwhile the new Archbishop of St Andrews, James Sharp, arrived in Edinburgh with uniformed footmen and a smart carriage. Not only was he wielding supreme power over the Church of Scotland but also significant political power. All church ministers were given a month either to swear the oath to accept bishops and royal supervision or face eviction from their parishes. Some 300 out of a total of 900 ministers refused and were dismissed, which in most cases meant that they and their families were evicted from their homes. The renegade Covenanter, Archbishop Fairfoul of Glasgow, complained of the reluctance of his charges to accept his orders and recommended the use of force, which soon became the standard practice.

The result was a chronic shortage of reasonably qualified clergymen, so that fairly mediocre candidates were brought in to fill the vacancies and were mockingly referred to by their parishioners as 'curates', a disparaging nickname that rapidly acquired popularity. The parishioners in large numbers, particularly in the south west, began to avoid their churches and instead attended unofficial, often outdoor, services held by their former and now unsalaried ministers. As laws were enforced making attendance at the official church compulsory, the unofficial conventicles or field preachings were made illegal and the services had to be moved to remote localities where they were less likely to be discovered. Heavy fines and whipping were introduced as penalties for non-attendance at the official churches, and masters were punished if their servants did not attend, and lairds if their tenant farmers failed to conform.

This system of fines soon became corrupted by the fact that they were imposed by the soldiers of the new Scottish army who could double them or pocket them with the connivance of unscrupulous officers. Notorious in this role was General Sir James Turner who was directed to harsher extremes by Archbishop Burnet of Glasgow, Fairfoul's replacement. Turner in particular used the device of obtaining free billeting for his troops from likely conventiclers, using up all their food and animal fodder and destroying what they could not carry, thus reducing many areas to starvation and destitution. Even the Chancellor, the old Royalist Glencairn, was shocked by the level of persecution and was criticised by Archbishop Sharp for his lack of zeal. The Courts of High Commission were brought back to enforce penalties, which now included whipping, branding and forced emigration to Ireland or the colonies.

In 1666 Glencairn died and the ruthless Rothes increased his power by taking over the dead man's post as Chancellor, while Crawford, the other mild opponent of persecution, was removed as Treasurer. So Sharp's position grew even stronger as he was now allowed to maintain a standing army to enforce his policies and pay for it by using the vast number of fines that it collected. General James Turner was sent on three devastating missions to the western counties, with heavy billeting that acted like a scorched earth policy. Male householders who had for many years been allowed to keep arms in case they were required to act as militia were now forcibly disarmed. The 'curates' were allowed to fine whom they pleased for making their churches look empty and the soldiers collected the money with whatever violence it required. As Wodrow put it, 'the widow, the fatherless, the old and infirm are not spared, the poor must beg to pay the church fines.' In tiny Lochrutton near Dumfries sixteen families were 'utterly broken' and there were numerous examples of families driven from their homes by the soldiers, ruined by the destruction of crops.

Chapter 3

THE ROAD TO RULLION GREEN AND THE EIGHTH HOLY WAR

... having forfeited to save their lives and fortunes by their former rebellious practices under the cloak of religion.

Government proclamation November 1666

The new standing army of 3,000 men was now given a replacement commanding officer, Tam Dalzell of the Binns, a veteran Royalist who after the Glencairn rebellion had gained more military experience in Russia as had his new second-in-command William Drummond of Cromlix. They were given orders to clean up the south west along with local militias under the Duke of Hamilton, Lords Annandale, Airlie and Kincardine.

However all did not go according to plan for on 15 November 1666, an extraordinary incident occurred. Sir James Turner was in Dumfries, one of the hotbeds of Conventiclers or Wanderers as they were often called and was persecuting the locals with his customary vigour. Four of his badly disciplined soldiers had allegedly put an old man on a red-hot gridiron in Dalry, 17 miles away, but the man was freed by four Covenanters who were passing by and witnessed the cruelty. In this process they injured one of the soldiers and killed one of another platoon nearby, thus disarming and capturing seven. At this point some local lairds including Maclellan of Barscobe from New Galloway joined the four rebels as they foresaw heavy reprisals. Gathering around fifty recruits, they surprised and captured General Turner in Dumfries, apparently a travelling Edinburgh merchant Andrew Gray being the man who actually grabbed the general when he was least expecting an attack.

For professional soldiers, including one of high rank, to be ambushed and kidnapped by total amateurs was both a shock and severe humiliation for the government. The Earl of Rothes, at this stage still based in London, was informed and Archbishop Sharp called up reinforcements. Five earls, Cassilis, Glencairn, Lothian, Fife and Newark, as well as Lord Drumlanrig, were told to muster their militias, the Edinburgh guard was doubled under Colonel Hurry and Major Thompson, while General Dalzell with his troops was sent to Glasgow to prevent the rebellion from spreading. Some officers offered the Covenanter rebels 24 hours to submit, but Sharp refused any quarter.

Barscobe's band of rebels now had nothing to lose and began to look for public support. Recruitment, however, proved difficult; the populace had been so intimidated, so reduced to utter poverty and with their weapons confiscated that only the hardiest joined in, about 300 from Galloway. There were some additional troops from further north including some professional soldiers, Colonel James Wallace of Auchens, Captain Robert Lockhart and Captain Arnot of Lochridge. They were aided by a rebel clergyman Alexander Robertson from Edinburgh plus Alexander Nisbet of Tarbolton and Gabriel Semple of Towhead. Major General Montgomery and the Laird of Gadgirth were also regarded as promising recruits but they were dissuaded by Tam Dalzell in a meeting at Eglinton Castle.

The Covenanters held a council of war at Ochiltree and decided to head for Edinburgh, adding recruits on the way, but failed to gather many more. In fact they actually lost one troop under John Ross who was ambushed by the Duke of Hamilton's militia. The remainder floundered on in foul November weather bringing with them as their prisoner James Turner who had only avoided a lynching by producing letters from the bishops which ordered him to be even harsher than he had been. They arrived at Lanark for a sermon by John Guthrie and a renewal of the Covenant oath; then they were joined by a Major Kilgour and a clergyman J. Scott from Hawick, followed by an embassy from the Duke of Hamilton, begging them to stop the rebellion.

The government was seriously alarmed by these events because at this time Britain was at war with the Dutch. Tam Dalzell nearly caught up with the rebels near Bathgate, where there was no food or accommodation. Then the citizens of Edinburgh came out under young James Graham, 2nd Marquis of Montrose (1631–69), second son of his famous father and his heir since the eldest son had died at Bog of Gight in 1645. James had joined the Glencairn rebellion of 1653 but fallen out badly with his hereditary enemy Archibald Campbell, Lord Lorn.

There was now a further offer of quarter in return for surrender, but not from Dalzell. So when Colonel Wallace replied there was no answer and he retreated into the Pentland Hills with his remaining force of about 900 men to Rullion Green. On 26 November 1666, he formed his troops in three divisions, his own plus those of Major Learmont and Captain Arnott and a small cavalry detachment under Maclellan of Barscobe. Dalzell cut through from Calder but his advance troops were put to flight by the Covenanters, though two Irish ministers were killed in the action, Andrew MacCormack and John Crookshanks, who had apparently had considerable influence in promoting the rebellion. Wallace's infantry fought remarkably well against the professionals but by nightfall fifty had been killed and fifty taken prisoner. As Wodrow put it 'thus was the body of the good people broken and dissipated.'

In the aftermath of the battle Colonel Wallace escaped to Holland and never returned. John Welsh also escaped. The various lords such as Annandale, Drumlanrig, Murray of Teviotdale and Nithsdale were briefed to round up the stragglers – most of whom died of exhaustion, cold or were robbed and murdered by villagers on their path. Fifty, however, were captured alive and crammed into the tiny dungeon beneath St Giles known as Haddo's Hole The unfortunate Royalist Sir John Gordon of Haddo (1610–44) who had fought both against and for Montrose had been held here in 1644 until, despite being promised his life by Argyll, he was beheaded by the ruling Covenanters. It was so narrow that prisoners had to stand upright all the time. Despite orders from Charles II to be lenient, Sharp wanted them executed.

Meanwhile in other respects there were some improvements in daily life for many people. Edinburgh was provided with its first proper supply of fresh water from Comiston in 1675 and the beginnings of some more hygienic drainage, the city had its first coffee houses and a new physic garden, even its first newspaper, the *Mercurius Caledonius*, founded by Thomas Sydserf, son of the notorious former bishop of Galloway who had played his part in the provocations of 1637. Overall the atmosphere for most people was more relaxed, pleasures were less frowned upon and the intolerant curfews of the ministry less obvious. There was, however, no relaxation for the surviving Covenanters who still took huge risks to gather for worship on remote hillsides and were still relentlessly pursued by the authorities.

Chapter 4

MARTYRS AND MURDERERS – THE OTHER FIFE CONSPIRACY

The peculiar character and prejudices of the Covenanters are easily accounted for.

Sir Walter Scott: *Tales of a Grandfather*

There now followed an even more paranoid persecution of the Rullion Green prisoners and other Covenanter rebels, in which Archbishop Sharp was the obsessive leader. He was at odds with the army as General Dalzell had promised quarter to those Covenanters who surrendered. Sharp, however, had the full support of the ruthless Justice Clerk John Hume and his colleague William Murray. The prisoners were executed, their right hands cut off to signify the fact that they had broken the coronation oath and their heads were displayed on poles in Edinburgh, Kilmarnock, Kirkcudbright and Hawick.

Not satisfied with merely punishing the rank-and-file Covenanters the paranoid archbishop was desperate to unearth some secret conspiracy amongst those in command and to do so he resorted to torturing even the most unlikely suspects. The chosen instrument of torture was the boot, a wooden contraption into which a leg was inserted and then wedges were gradually hammered in to crack the bones and induce excruciating pain. Two of the victims were a brilliant young preacher, Hugh Mackail, and Robert Neilson of Corsock, both of whom had been harshly persecuted and forced to leave their homes.

General Turner to his credit tried to intervene to have Corsock reprieved as he had been one of those who dissuaded his colleagues from lynching him earlier in the year. Turner was overruled as the curate of Corsock's local church in Parton (near Castle Douglas), Mr Dalgleish, accused him of being a ringleader of the rebellion. The torture of Mackail was supervised by the Earl of Rothes who was suspiciously enthusiastic about this practice, and when his leg was broken in eleven places Mackail allegedly commented that he was more worried about his neck than his leg. Those worries were justified as despite pleas from the Duchess of Hamilton and the Marchioness of Douglas, he was executed.

Rothes set out on a tour of Ayrshire and Dumfries to organise further executions and torture, though he was held back somewhat by the disappearance of the Ayr hangman and the refusal of his Irvine colleague to act as substitute. It is understandable that Covenanter eulogies perhaps exaggerate some of the stories of cruelty and debauchery amongst the dragoons, the 'booted apostles', but were probably fairly close to the truth. Stories such as James Graham of Claverhouse being bulletproof and in league with the devil were popular items of folklore as were notions of angelic forms appearing at conventicles. One of the quainter but probably genuine tales was that of the green plover, or peesweep, which was regarded as a treacherous bird because it liked to hover near people and therefore sometimes enabled the dragoons to find otherwise totally hidden conventicles.

Meanwhile Generals Dalzell and Ballantyne, using Kilmarnock as their headquarters, were destroying wide swathes of farmland and using paid informers to bring in new suspects who were often tortured and left in the prison known as the Thieves' Hole. David Finlay of Newmilns was tortured to find evidence of so-called 'rich Whigs' who supported the Covenanters, but gave nothing away and was executed. Women were reportedly kept in cells full of toads. Sir Mungo Murray, an officer in the army and brother of the Earl of Atholl supposedly had two prisoners strung up by their thumbs. In Balmaghie near Castle Douglas Sir William Ballantyne, one of the most ruthless and greedy of the senior officers, is said to have molested a woman in a local inn, shot her husband, then tied up and heavily fined a bystander who came to her defence, drank all day on Sunday and stripped the inn of all its contents before leaving. The wife of David Macgill in Earlston near Dalry was tortured by Ballantyne's men with lit matches between her fingers for supposedly helping her husband to evade capture by wearing his clothes; she died a few days later.

Clearly things had got out of hand and the more moderate Lauderdale stepped in to put an end to the excesses of Sharp, Rothes and their henchmen, particularly Dalzell, Turner, Drummond and Ballantyne. The bishops and generals who between them dominated the Council wanted to topple Lauderdale, so they sent the Archbishop of Glasgow and General Drummond to London to get the king's approval for a new proposal to sequester the estates of exiled Covenanters. As it happened Lauderdale was forewarned; there was a government purge. Sharp's main ally in London was sacked for his failure to win the war against the Dutch and his main ally in Scotland, the Earl of Rothes, was demoted for similar reasons, letting the Dutch navy shell the port of Leith. Sharp could then be removed from the Privy Council and confined to his ecclesiastical duties. The Scottish army in the west was to be disbanded, Turner was dismissed and Ballantyne both dismissed and sent into an exile, from which he never returned.

With the slight reshuffle of the government there was greater relaxation in the treatment of Covenanters, though conventicles were still nominally illegal. However, Sharp was determined to maintain the pressure backed by Honeyman, the aggressive Bishop of Orkney. In July 1668 the pair of them were returning from dinner on their way to the archbishop's Edinburgh house in Blackfriars Wynd when an unemployed church minister and veteran of Rullion Green, James Mitchell, jumped into their coach and fired his pistol at them. He missed Sharp but hit the bishop, who died soon afterwards. Mitchell changed his clothes in his lodgings at Stevenslaw Close then reappeared on the scene, without anyone attempting to stop his escape. As a result, a number of innocent Presbyterian families in Edinburgh were persecuted. Mitchell was apparently promised his life by Lauderdale if he surrendered but he refused and was only caught five years later. He was then left for four years on the Bass Rock until 1678 when his execution was demanded by Sharp.

There was now a renewed attempt to calm down the atmosphere by the Chancellor John Hay, the Earl of Tweeddale (1625–97), a strong Presbyterian who had himself had a varied career. He had fought for Charles I in 1642 but against him at Marston Moor in 1644, then for him again at Preston. He had served in the London Parliament in the 1650s and at the Restoration been sent to prison for defending the Covenanter minister James Guthrie. Despite all this he rose to be Chancellor and stuck his neck out both at this time and later in

1692 when he demanded an inquiry into the massacre of Glencoe. By that time he had changed allegiance in 1688 from the Stuarts to the House of Orange and been made a marquis. Meanwhile his new reforms allowed the reappointment of previously sacked Presbyterian ministers so long as they signed up to accept bishops, and even those who did not were to be allowed a reasonable stipend for preaching. It was a compromise that failed to satisfy the extremists.

Rothes, Sharp and his bishops naturally opposed this move and did their best to thwart it, but forty-three previously sacked minsters were allowed back to parishes. The only problem was that the extreme Covenanters regarded this as a betrayal of the cause because it implied that these ministers and their followers accepted the heretical idea of the king having control over the Church. It was a repeat of the Engagers versus Resolutioners crisis that had split the Presbyterians fifteen years earlier and was similarly to induce considerable bitterness.

Meanwhile pressure was still coming from London to create an Act of Union, to make Charles II more of an absolute monarch and to keep bishops as a means of enforcing conformity. The Act of 1669 was seen by some as a prelude to the re-establishment of Roman Catholicism by the king's heir James, Duke of York, for Charles still had no legitimate children and James was a Catholic.

Not surprisingly the Archbishop of Glasgow strongly opposed the new toleration of Presbyterian ministers, but more surprisingly opposed the king for decreeing it, so he was forced to resign and was arrested. Sharp voiced the same opinion, but got away with it, since sacking one archbishop seemed good enough for the time being.

In tandem with the king at every stage, re-emphasising his total power over Church and State, the Earl of Lauderdale, as both his Commissioner and Secretary of State, was building up his own absolute control of Scotland, bullying the Scottish Parliament to a humiliating extent, using what was referred to as 'licentious language' that shocked the members. He was also feathering his own and related family's nests by granting valuable new monopolies on key products such as brandy, salt and tobacco. He needed the money himself even more when his wife died and he was able to marry his long-term mistress, the extravagant Elizabeth Murray, Countess of Dysart (1626–98, born in Dysart) whose home was now in London.

This remarkable lady was countess in her own right and had, unusually for a woman in this era, received a formal education. She had become a dedicated Royalist, noted for her political manipulations, which were sometimes even attributed to witchcraft. Her father had been a childhood friend of Charles I and his 'whipping boy', later carrying out missions to Montrose and the French. She had married an English Royalist and with him had eleven children, yet at the same time dabbled in politics to the extent of joining the Sealed Knot Society and communicating with Charles II in his exile. Her main residence was Ham House near Richmond and she had spent considerable sums doing it up. When widowed in her early forties in 1669, she became Lauderdale's mistress and in due course his duchess. It was at this time that Lauderdale also commissioned the architect William Bruce to remodel Thirlestane Castle near Lauder as a huge baroque mansion.

Alongside this extravagance, the diehard Presbyterians were still organising field preaching in ever more obscure locations to avoid the law. In mid-June 1670 a conventicle was held on Beak Hill by Dunfermline with the main preacher John Blackadder, who left a graphic account of people coming in all directions, many sleeping in the open the night before, some from as far away as Galloway brought by the irrepressible Maclellan of Barscobe, armed in case of attack. Some kind of large tent was erected on the hillside and the first preacher John Dickson spent most of the morning on the appropriate text from Corinthians: 'He must reign till he hath put all his enemies to flight.' A new Act produced by Parliament under Sharp's direction described such people as 'maliciously wicked and disloyal' suggesting punishment by death, confiscation of all property or transportation to 'His majesty's plantations in the Indies'. In Parliament the only man who dared vote against this was the Earl of Cassilis.

The Beak or Beath Hill conventicle was seen as the start of a new trend in conventicles where the participants would come armed, as James Mackenzie described it 'the first armed conventicle on the smooth green hill of Beath', and Fife began to take over from Galloway and Lanarkshire as the most active area. It was perhaps partly because this was the archbishop's home county and he had displayed his power there ostentatiously: 'he loved to ride in his archiepiscopal carriage, to be attended by liveried attendants and accosted as "My Lord".' This added to the irritation felt by his opponents, and their resultant increased defiance by attending conventicles on his doorstep led him to intensify his persecution of them. This in turn led to them justifying retaliatory violence. Such in fact was the strength of the Fife's population's antipathy that when the archbishop ordered the baillies to collect fines, they disobeyed and refused to take the money from offending conventiclers, thus adding still more to his annoyance. So large conventicles were held at Kinkel Ness, near St Andrews itself, in the Lomond Hills, on Balcarres Crag and in Dora Glen. In response a hundred outside militiamen were ordered into Fife, according to William Crookshank 'because Fife was where the (armed) conventicles had started'.

In contrast the new Archbishop of Glasgow Robert Leighton was pursuing a more enlightened policy, trying to promote peace between the ministers who had accepted the compromise known as The Indulged, and those who had refused, the Unindulged, but in vain. At a meeting in Paisley in December 1670 he was met with rejection and exclaimed ominously: 'Is there no hope of peace? Are you for war?'

In 1673 there was an attempted political coup against Lauderdale, led by the two men with the same name, William Douglas – the Duke of Hamilton (1635–94), and the Earl of Queensberry (1634–95), later to be made a duke and a pillar of the Royalist community. It was Hamilton who posed the question: 'Is this a true parliament or not?' Lauderdale was, above all, a planner and a survivor, so he made a few concessions but kept the confidence of Charles II for the time being. He implied a reduction in persecution of conventicles but in effect encouraged it and let Sharp intensify his efforts.

There was a huge meeting, again organised by John Blackadder, this time by the River Whiteadder where, despite the local laird the Earl of Home threatening that his horses would drink the communion wine, some 3,200 people attended an all-day service on the hillside and took communion. There were now also groups of women banding together to protest about the persecution. Even the Duchess of Rothes defied her husband and gave shelter to Covenanters. The Covenanters bore arms more often and sometimes assaulted the soldiers sent against them. The officious Sir Mungo Murray was involved in another scandal when he led a party to take over Cardross Castle near the Lake of Menteith from its owner, a suspected Presbyterian, when he was away from home and his wife was there and expecting a baby. Three bishops even protested against their superior, but Sharp retaliated, and two of them withdrew their complaints, leaving only one, the Bishop of Dunblane, to take the blame; he was demoted. As Wright quaintly puts it, 'it was actually made criminal to be suspected of being suspected.'

Sharp and his allies now aimed to make use of what was in effect a self-liquidating army, by inviting down what came to be known as the Highland Host, northern militias recruited by men such as the new Campbell Earl of Caithness. The Highlanders could patrol central Scotland extracting their wages from the local populace, treating suspects with intimidating brutality and living off the land.

Archbishop Sharp had recruited two unsavoury new assistants for his mission. One was Captain Carstairs, who specialised in entrapment and extortion by pretending to be a fellow-Presbyterian in order to get evidence. The other was a bankrupt Edinburgh merchant called William Carmichael, 'a man of very dissolute life and abandoned manners' (according to James Cleland), who was appointed a sheriff depute in Fife to hunt down suspects using paid informers. It was Carmichael who would cause the archbishop's downfall by provoking the Second Fife Conspiracy.

The Conspiracy was a group made up of a number of minor lairds with farms close to each other in central Fife. It included and was perhaps led by John Balfour of Kinloch, whose home in Fife had been invaded by Carstairs. Balfour hatched a plot to ambush and kill Carmichael on 3 May 1679 whilst he was out hunting at Blebo Hole near Magus, though the group seems to have also had Archbishop Sharp as a future target. According to Hewison, they consulted the Bible for words justifying their acts and 'confessed to having got encouragement therein for their homicidal mania.'

This reflected the new militancy of the Covenanting clergy including Richard Cameron and John Blackadder, both of whom had been born in Fife, Cameron in Falkland and Blackadder at Blairhall near Dunfermline. Also born in Fife, at Elie, was the powerful preacher Robert Traill, who fought at Rullion Green, was a prisoner on the Bass Rock and did most of his preaching in London. Blackadder in particular had recently addressed a large conventicle in Fife and other preachers including Donald Cargill had begun to hint at biblically justifiable violence against the persecutors.

Other plotters included James Russell of Kettle near Ladybank, George Fleming of Balboothie in the Lindsay territory west of Elie, George Balfour of Gilston which is a few miles south at Largo, Andrew Gillan a weaver from Balmerino, two Henderson brothers from Kilbrachmont near St Monans, Robert Black of Baldinnie near Cupar and the fiery David Hackston of Rathillet near Balmerino. The latter had refused the leadership of the group in case his motives should be misconstrued because he owed money to the archbishop.

This mixture of local lairds, tenant farmers and a weaver was from lower social strata than the conspirators of 1637, they were more extreme in their views and more personally violent – but they did all come from exactly the same small area of Fife. The covenanting ministers similarly came from a lower stratum than their 1637 forbears, both socially and academically, for most of them had not come from church families nor had they studied theology in Scotland as the universities were at this point controlled by episcopalians. Thus in many cases they had done their training in Holland and acquired a more apocalyptic vision, having no hope of a proper parish appointment and under constant threat of arrest as they moved from one illegal conventicle site to another.

In this context it is worth recalling that the previous attempt to murder Archbishop Sharp, the shooting in Blackfriars Wynd, had been by James Mitchell who had read theology at Edinburgh but never managed to get his own parish, though he had been helped by the strange Major Weir. Mitchell was from Midlothian rather than Fife but one of his alleged accomplices was from Strathmiglo. Mitchell himself was executed after a spell on the Bass Rock and became a martyr; there was no hint from the struggling Covenanters that it was wrong for a man of the cloth to attempt murder against an enemy of Presbyterianism. The new atmosphere endorsed by the preachers was sympathetic to violence, thus in the meeting before the new attack on Archbishop Sharp, the wife of one of the plotters, Robert Black, allegedly gave his colleagues encouragement with 'a holy kiss' and a suggestion that they kill the local 'curate' at Cupar while they were at it.

Sheriff Carmichael, however, the intended first victim of the conspiracy, never appeared as his hunting trip had been cancelled. Instead the plotters heard that Archbishop Sharp had been spotted smoking his pipe with the curate of Cupar and was about to pass nearby on the so-called Waterless Road from Kennoway to St Andrews. One of the group, James Russell, who wrote an account of the incident, recorded that they had responded, 'God hath delivered him into our hands.' So they changed targets, overtook the archbishop's coach, pulled him out and killed him despite the presence of his daughter Isabella and despite his own pleas for mercy. It was, in its way, a crime of passion, and the Covenanters in general did not repudiate the criminals; in fact five Covenanters in December 1651 chose to be executed rather than provide evidence: Thomas Brown of Edinburgh, James Wood from Newmilns, Andrew Sword from Galloway, John Weddell from Monklands and John Clyde from Kilbride.

Thus the Second Fife Conspiracy, which led to the death of James Sharp, was a pivotal moment of 'heroic' violence, which committed the Covenanters to all-out war. It was a much less gentlemanly affair than the conspiracy of 1637/8 and the participants were both more desperate and less scrupulous but, just like the first conspiracy, it eventually helped to cause the deposition of a king. The key differences were the fact that the supporters of the Covenant were now little more than an outlawed minority, they had no access to serious money and there was no longer an available pool of good ex-mercenary officers to give them leadership. Their defiance was little short of suicidal. The moderate Presbyterians were shocked by the murder, regarding it as rash and not in the spirit of Presbyterianism, but the majority seems to have regarded the Fife plotters as heroes while they lived, and martyrs when they died.

Chapter 5

BLUIDY CLAVERS –
THE KILLING TIMES

Some perished at the hands of the common executioner and of those who were sent to the plantations only a few ever reached their destination in consequence of the way they were treated.

Thomas Wright: *History of Scotland*

The downfall of Archbishop Sharp coincided with the rise of Colonel James Graham of Claverhouse, later Viscount Dundee, otherwise known as Bonnie Dundee or Bloody Clavers. A professional soldier of thirty, he had served in both the French and Dutch armies and his temperament was ideally suited to strict discipline and ruthless retaliation against miscreants. His orders were to pursue all Covenanters, break up their conventicles, and treat them as traitors for whom summary execution was perfectly legitimate. Instead of softening the approach to the dissenters after the archbishop's murder, the government treated it as a reason for intensified persecution.

The result of this was that the hard-line Covenanters were treated as outlaws and behaved as such, responding to violence with violence. A prime mover in this was Sir Robert Hamilton (1650–1701), a member of the Hamilton family that had settled at Preston Tower, Prestonpans. His father had fought as a colonel for Charles II at both Dunbar and Worcester. Robert Hamilton was shortly joined by the group that had murdered the archbishop: John Balfour of Kinloch and Balfour of Gilston, James Russell of Kettle, Andrew Gibson, the two Hendersons, William Dalzell and David Hackston of Rathillet (d. 1680) in Fife who had withdrawn from the murder plot at the last minute. The teenager William Clelland (1661–89), a gamekeeper and poet from Douglas just out of Glasgow University, appeared as did John Nisbet of Hardhill.

Hamilton's first exploit was in Rutherglen on 29 May 1679 where his men ostentatiously doused all the bonfires lit to celebrate the anniversary of the Restoration and instead staged a ceremonial burning of all the government proclamations in favour of bishops, followed by a posting of the Solemn League and Covenant. They then made off towards Loudoun Hill where a minister called Douglas was due to preach on the nearby moor.

Claverhouse, who was stationed in Glasgow, headed south with three troops of dragoons to Hamilton where he caught fourteen Covenanters who were on their way to the Loudoun conventicle. Having learned of their destination he bound them and drove them in front of his troops towards the hill. To his surprise as he neared the site of the conventicle some 240 armed Covenanters came out to meet him and there was an exchange of fire. Some 30 or 40 government soldiers were killed and the dragoons took flight, Claverhouse himself escaping with difficulty as his horse had been shot from under him. At this skirmish, given the name The Battle of Drumclog Moor or Loudoun Hill, apparently not even half a dozen Covenanters were killed and young William Clelland was given credit for the success, perhaps his training as a ghillie gave him a good idea of ground cover – he eventually rose to be a colonel and was killed at Dunkeld fighting for William of Orange. The other able soldier was Hackston who seems to have been effective on the day.

This unexpected reverse sent shock waves through the establishment, just as had occurred with the capture of General Turner thirteen years earlier. Claverhouse retreated to Glasgow where he had to put up barricades to prevent the Covenanters invading the city. In frustration they challenged him to come out and fight but he refused. Soon afterwards he was deprived of his command and George Livingston (1616–90), the Earl of Linlithgow, put in over his head.

Unfortunately for the Covenanters they failed to exploit this early success and instead of training and equipping their makeshift army ready for the next onslaught they began to bicker amongst themselves. It was the Engagers and the Remonstrants all over again, the Indulged versus the Unindulged, those who were willing to compromise with the bishops and those who would accept nothing but total abolition. Robert Hamilton and the squad which had murdered Sharp were so adamant that many of the moderates began to drift away.

Meanwhile Charles II, in alarm, sent up his favourite bastard son, the Duke of Monmouth, to take charge of the Scottish army of 10,000 men, which he did on 22 June. Only four days later he was at Bothwell where some 6,000 Covenanters were camped on the south side of the River Clyde with a troop of men guarding the then narrow bridge over the river. Lack of artillery amongst the rebels put them at a serious disadvantage and the troops holding the bridge were eventually driven back by cannon fire despite a gallant one-hour stand led by David Hackston.

Then George Livingston's 300 dragoons crossed over and began the slaughter. Some 400 Covenanters were killed on the spot and 1,200 captured and frogmarched to Edinburgh where many of them were crammed into the Greyfriars Kirkyard for five months with only minimal food and without any form of shelter, despite the onset of winter. Monmouth, to his credit, had ignored his father's orders and halted the slaughter. He organised doctors for the wounded and only a token 300 prisoners were transported to Barbados and elsewhere. However one ship carrying prisoners, the *Crown of London*, was sunk off the Orkneys and as the prisoners had been locked in the hold, some 200 of them drowned.

Sir Robert Hamilton, who at Bothwell Bridge seems to have spent more time erecting a symbolic gibbet rather than preparing for battle, had quickly given up the fight and made his escape. Panic or cowardice were suggested and he headed into exile in Holland where he stayed until able to return in safety with William of Orange. Perhaps more of an eccentric than a serious rebel he was to die in his bed soon afterwards. Hackston escaped but was later executed after Airds Moss. Clelland escaped, to be killed fighting gallantly against the Jacobites at Dunkeld in 1689.

Meanwhile Monmouth was recalled to London and the policy of vindictive pursuit of even the mildest connection to the rebels was intensified. The king's brother, James, Duke of York, who made little attempt to hide his Catholic allegiances, had just returned from exile and was posted to Scotland to keep him out of trouble, so he used the opportunity to cultivate a relationship with the highland clan chiefs, most of whom were episcopalians if not actually still Catholics. This was the first stage of his plan to develop an undercover powerbase for his future ambitious plans to re-catholicise Britain, the preliminaries of Jacobitism. He also made clear his extreme contempt for the rebellious Covenanters, and the need to be rid of them.

Claverhouse was sent to Galloway to root out Covenanters using whatever force was required. By this time there were only two unindulged ministers left, Richard Cameron and Donald Cargill who, with their small band of followers, were known as the Cameronians. One of them, Hall of Haughhead (Campsie Glen), was captured with incriminating letters complaining about the tyranny of Charles II and these were used as government propaganda to justify the efforts to exterminate the group. The same theme was proclaimed at Sanquhar and General Dalzell sent a troop of 120 dragoons to face a Cameronian force of sixty under Hackston at Airds Moss on the River Ayr near Muirkirk. Two of them were killed. Hackston was himself wounded, then tortured on Dalzell's orders and condemned to the death as a traitor, hung, drawn and quartered. Cargill survived and while preaching at Torwood near Stirling, he publicly excommunicated the king along with his brother Duke James, his son Monmouth, Lauderdale, Rothes, General Dalzell and Sir George Mackenzie. Cargill said 'deliver up to Satan Charles Stuart king for his high mocking of God ... and his great perjury in breaking and burning the Covenant.' He was to be executed for his impertinence.

In November 1680 James, Duke of York, was back in Edinburgh and when the castle garrison attempted to fire a salute from Mons Meg, the old cannon exploded, an ill omen according to some. Lauderdale was now showing signs of old age, so he was replaced by the Earl of Moray who shared the Duke's views. With paranoid thoroughness, the government unveiled what was probably an imaginary plot to murder the duke by Archibald Stuart of Bo'ness and a Glasgow pharmacist called Spreul. The students of Edinburgh and Glasgow Universities tried to make fun of the neurotic regime by wearing the banned blue ribbons and burning an effigy of the Pope at Christmastime. Everywhere juries were bullied to condemn people on the flimsiest evidence of connection to Covenanters. Two almost certainly innocent young women, Isobel Allison from Perth, and Marion Harvey from Bo'ness, sang the 23rd Psalm before they were hanged. Donald Cargill, one of the last survivors of the rebel ministers, was at last captured and also hanged, but the Cameronians carried on without ministers.

There were a number of violent attacks in retaliation. An anti-Covenant church minister or 'curate', Peter Pierson of Carsphairn, was murdered in his home by a gang of five men, including James Macmichael. Several government soldiers were killed in an ambush by armed Covenanters at Enterkin. Two guards were murdered at Swineabbey near West Calder in 1684.

A new extreme group known as the Gibbites or Sweet Singers and consisting mainly of women had been started by a sailor from Bo'ness called James Gibb. They headed for the top of the Pentland Hills expecting 'the fate of Sodom and Gomorrah to fall on the wicked city of Edinburgh'. They were rounded up by the dragoons at Woodhill Craigs and given a good scourging in the Tolbooth but regarded as too eccentric to be worth prosecuting.

Under this tyrannous and violent regime the Scottish lairds who had so far mostly supported the government began to become restive. The king's brother was not only a Catholic but pompous and arrogant, so many began to dread what things would be like when Charles II died and James succeeded to the throne. To make matters worse, he bullied the Scottish Parliament to bring in a new test oath, which not only demanded acceptance of bishops but also Catholics by all officials. Fletcher of Saltoun opposed it and shortly afterwards went into exile in Holland whilst another opponent, Lord Belhaven, was put in prison.

The Earl of Argyll tried to alter his own version of the oath, but was trapped by Montrose, son of his father's great enemy, so he too was imprisoned in 1682. Thanks to the ingenuity of his step-daughter Sophia Lindsay of Balcarres, he escaped dressed as her ladies' maid and after a dangerous trip through England he too made it to Holland, where he was later joined by his fellow Campbell, the Earl of Loudoun, and several other prominent figures. The news that Argyll was being stripped of all his estates sent shockwaves not just through the Scottish landowners but also their English counterparts, so the unease about the heir to the throne was spreading; property, after all, was sacrosanct.

There was also a new breed of Covenanter ministers coming forward, young men like James Renwick (1662–1688) and Alexander Shields (1660–1700). Renwick was the son of a Moniaive weaver and referred to as 'praying even at the age of two.' While at Edinburgh University, he witnessed the execution of Donald Cargill and was so moved that he joined the United Societies, a group of Covenanting congregations who no longer had ministers. They funded his training as a minister in Holland where he mixed with other radical Protestant groups, returning to become a wandering open-air preacher in Scotland who could attract large crowds. He reacted to constant pursuit by the dragoons with his

Apologetical Declaration announcing that Covenanters had the moral right to punish their persecutors, following this up with his even more revolutionary Sanquhar Declaration, which pronounced that James, the king's brother, was unfit to be the next king. This was what Mark Jardine describes as a call for an 'apocalyptic war' and caused the government to intensify efforts to capture him. This they eventually achieved and he became the last Covenanter martyr in 1688. His colleague Alexander Shields from Earlstoun in Berwickshire also became a highly popular preacher at conventicles and like Renwick became in 1682 involved in the fringes of the Rye House Plot against Charles II. Other Scots associated with this plot to murder both the king and his brother were George Campbell of Cessnock, John Cochrane and William Carstairs, an ex-minister working as an agent for Argyll. Whilst preaching in London, Shields was arrested in the Embroiderers Hall, Cheapside and shipped back to Edinburgh, after which he was imprisoned on the Bass Rock but apparently managed to escape dressed as a woman. After the fall of James II in 1688, he became chaplain to the Cameronian regiment and was later one of four ministers ordered by the General Assembly to accompany the Scots fleet sent to capture Darién in Panama from the Spaniards. Like many others on that expedition, he died of fever.

For the period 1661–80, the first two decades of Charles II's reign, a figure of 18,000 deaths was estimated by Daniel Defoe, apparently based on some official sources, so it was probably reasonably accurate but would exclude all the collateral casualties due to starvation, hypothermia and disease attributable to compulsory billeting of soldiers and their destruction of crops. To this should be added the significant numbers who died in prisons, such as Dunnottar Castle or the open yard at Greyfriars Church in Edinburgh, and also the numbers condemned to transportation to the plantations, who probably died early deaths as a result.

Chapter 6

THE ATTEMPTED CATHOLIC TAKEOVER AND THE NINTH WAR

... the royal power which we do now resolve to maintain in its greatest lustre ... against fanatical contrivances, murderers and assassins.

James II Proclamation, 1685

I die not only a Protestant but with a heart-hatred of popery, prelacy and all superstitions whatsomever.

Earl of Argyll's last words, 1685

As Charles II's health deteriorated and his brother prepared to take over the crown, the scene began to change. Decrepit old Lauderdale died in 1682, James had gone back to London, and in Scotland there was a new strongly Royalist regime under the Marquis of Queensberry, the Earl of Perth and Gordon of Haddo, who was made Earl of Aberdeen. The hunting down of suspected Presbyterians continued and Dalzell, with Claverhouse and Meldrum, was sent down to the hotbed of the south west. People were arrested on the slightest of pretexts. Lady Douglas of Cavers in the Borders was in a cell for two years for refusing to swear the test oath. Hume of Hume was executed for no good reason. A pedlar called James Robertson was tortured and hanged. One of the ruthless new enforcers, Irvine of Bonshaw, a descendant of Robert the Bruce's armourer, arrested thirty people in Hamilton for non-attendance at church, pushed them into a deep rubbish pit in November, then tied them to horses, with their feet bound underneath, and made them gallop to Edinburgh. Forty Cameronians who met at Lesmahagow and burned copies of the test oath were arrested and the town of Lanark received a massive fine as punishment. The dragoons collecting cash fines still went hand-in-hand with persecution, which was hugely profitable both for the Crown and the collectors.

One possible escape from this torment was devised by the Campbells of Cessnock in Ayrshire who began negotiations to buy a large tract of land in Carolina to provide freedom of religion. They do not seem to have been conventiclers themselves but had been prosecuted for not keeping a tight enough rein on their tenant farmers. Other supporters of this scheme included Lords Haddington and Callendar, who whilst negotiating in London for the purchase became mixed up with English opponents of the Stuart regime. Somehow they were involved in the so-called Rye House Plot, a scheme allegedly to murder the king on his way home from the races at Newmarket. Other Scots supposedly involved were John Cochrane of Ochiltree, Baillie of Jerviswood, Crawford of Crawfordland, Alexander Gordon of Earlston, and Stuart of Cultness. Through an exiled minister from Cathcart called William Carstairs (1656–1715), previously employed as a secretary by Argyll, they were in turn put in touch with the Earl of Argyll in Holland and Walter Scott, the Earl of Tarras, who was linked by marriage to the Duke of Monmouth. Thus the North Carolina project, which after initial difficulties did eventually take off, meanwhile provided a diversion for the Argyll and Monmouth party in Holland, which was planning a far more serious attack on the Stuarts. Amongst the early plotters caught was Hugh Campbell of Cessnock who was acquitted of being at Bothwell Bridge, but nevertheless sent to the Bass Rock. Carstairs was tortured, Baillie was executed and Cochrane managed to escape. Another Argyll aide William Spence was given both the boot torture and the newly introduced thumbscrew.

In January 1685 Charles II died and his brother at last took over, having already made sure that his close adherents dominated the Scottish executive. James had already alienated not just the extremists but many of the moderates too. In April 1685 he called a Scottish Parliament and urged them to eliminate 'the wild inhuman traitors' and he also enforced a new test oath asserting his absolute supremacy over the Church and since he was a Catholic, this had to be controversial. His Scottish Chancellor John Drummond, Earl of Perth (1648–1716), who like his soldier namesake was rumoured to have pioneered the use of the thumbscrew, actually converted to Catholicism, as did his brother Lord Melfort, who was rewarded with some of the huge Argyll estates. Perth was later involved, with fellow dissenter William Penn, in the founding of Pennsylvania as a bigotry-free state.

But the more the persecution intensified under the aggressive Earl of Perth, the more the surviving Covenanters thrived. The rebel minister Alexander Peden returned from Ireland, as did his colleague James Renwick from Holland. Peden was famous for wearing a mask and allowing a second identical mask to be worn by an accomplice so that the authorities would be confused about his movements. Renwick did without a mask but relied on having a fast horse near his outdoor pulpits so that he could always make a quick escape. More conventicles were organised despite the large numbers of dragoons being deployed to hunt them down. On one occasion dragoons taking a captured minister to his trial were themselves ambushed at Enterkin in Dumfries and the minister released. General Drummond was given additional troops and Hamilton of Orbiston had permission to bring down more of the dreaded Highland Host to spread fear, devastation and what were sportingly called 'field murders'. Claverhouse and Queensberry's brother Colonel Douglas shot six men out of hand at Minigaff while Captain Bruce of Earlshall shot four and hanged two at Lochenkit. A widow and two young girls were tied to stakes on the beach near Wigton and left to drown. Yet the Cameronians and the Wanderers still kept going despite numerous executions without proper trial, transportations to the colonies, and confiscations of property, which went to the king or his henchmen.

That same month there was a meeting in Rotterdam of the main Scottish opposition figures in exile, led by Archibald Campbell, Earl of Argyll, Patrick Murray and John Cochrane. Even at this stage they had differences with each other about tactics. They had in common a desire to support the Presbyterian Church, but they of course also had political and personal motivations, so the invasion they proposed can only be partly classified as a war of religion.

In early May the advance force sailed in three ships for the Orkneys, with a promise that Monmouth would be sailing to England with the English rebels a week later. One experienced English officer, Richard Rumbold, was sent with Argyll to demonstrate Monmouth's support. As news spread of the impending invasions the Edinburgh regime called up the militias and had 240 suspects arrested and herded into the foul dungeons of Dunnottar Castle, after which many of the men had their ears cropped and the women had their cheeks branded.

After leaving the Orkneys, Argyll's three ships sailed on to Islay before assembling with 300 men at Campbeltown, then Tarbert, where Argyll's younger son Charles brought in 1,200 extra men. But in general recruits were very hard to find as the government had such an effective system of intimidation. Amongst those refusing to support Argyll was his own eldest son and heir, another Archibald Campbell, Lord Lorn (d. 1703), an ambitious young man who had done the Grand Tour and enjoyed what was referred to as 'a profligate life'. Disapproving totally of his father's idealistic stance he grovelled to the new king, even implying that he would become a Catholic, until having won no new honours he changed sides three years later to support William of Orange, for whom he administered the coronation oath. It is remarkable that of the four Earls of Argyll in this period all of them quarrelled with their fathers and three of them were condemned as traitors. This last one was certainly a traitor but instead of being condemned he was made a duke, and raised the first official Highland regiment with Duncan Campbell of Auchinbreck, son of the villain of the Rathlin Island massacre, as its commanding officer. He was to die in his forties in a brothel brawl in Northumberland.

Hesitantly meanwhile the Argyll force of 1,500 men came to Inveraray where they had a skirmish with Atholl men, followed by another at Ardkinglass, whilst some of their force under Duncan Campbell of Auchinbreck fortified Ellengreg Castle on the tiny island Eilean Dearg in the Kyles of Bute. They stored their ammunition there with orders to blow it up if English navy frigates threatened its capture. Then they headed over Loch Long to the Gareloch, then Dumbarton, but crossed the River Leven 3 miles up from the town, losing time and men in a muddled diversion past Gartocharn. The able Rombold was captured at this point and later executed. Argyll himself crossed the Clyde to Renfrew, hoping for help, but was recognised and captured by the River Cart at Inchinnan, so he too faced inevitable execution like his father.

Sir John Cochrane of Ochiltree (actually from Johnstone) led the surviving troops over the Clyde at Erskine and headed south, hoping for reinforcements from the Wanderers. With him was Patrick Hume of Polwarth, a moderate Covenanter who left an account of the events and, after escaping to Holland, became a key negotiator for the replacement of James II by William of Orange. Cochrane, like Hume, had been in exile in Holland till 1685 for his connections with the Rye House Plot. On 18 June they fought and lost a small battle at Muirdykes above the village of Howwood. Ironically the Royalist force was led by Lord Ross who was Cochrane's uncle and had offered a truce. Captain Clelland was killed and Cochrane, having marched his men in a circle during the night, hid in a convenient barn. He was captured but his father saved his life by paying a massive fine. Naturally Ellengreg Castle was blown up, as was Carnasserie, the other arms depot of the rebellion and current home of Auchinbreck since his father's other castle on Loch Sween had been ruined by the Macdonnells in 1646. Meanwhile, according to a dubious source, John Cochrane's daughter, the feisty Grizel, took to the road and twice held up the Edinburgh-London mail-coach dressed as a highwayman.

The unfortunate minister with the troops, Thomas Archer, had been wounded in the skirmish and was taken to Edinburgh to be hanged. The only winners from the Argyll rebellion, and they did not keep their rewards for long, were the two men who pocketed the entire Argyll estates, Argyll's fellow clansman Slippery John Campbell of Braedalbane and the half-Jacobite John Murray, Marquis of Atholl, after Atholl's men had plundered the whole area. Others, however, did win promotion as the new king favoured ministers who were either Catholics or pretty close to it.

The three Drummonds, the Earls of Perth and Melfort plus General William Drummond fitted well into the new regime, as did the obligingly Catholic George Gordon, the new Duke of Gordon, who was given custody of Edinburgh Castle and several other posts including membership of the newly founded Order of the Thistle (1687). This was one of King James II's methods of winning loyalty without much cost. Referred to as a foppish libertine and a veteran of two years' service in the French army, Gordon did not hold out in the castle for long and was soon to flee the country. Eventually allowed to return, he was arrested as a suspected Jacobite in 1717. His son Alexander, the 2nd Duke, was also a Catholic and a Jacobite who brought 2,300 of his men to fight at Sheriffmuir in 1715 – such was the ability of the Gordons, like the Campbells, to raise men.

Of the two main Douglases, Queensberry's face no longer fitted, so he retired to spend time supervising the building of his massive new chateau at Drumlanrig, but the Duke of Hamilton was made king's commissioner. It was the opening stage of a new royal coup d'état, designed not only to give James II absolute control over Scotland but also to turn it back to Catholicism. The two Drummonds and Gordon were now openly Catholic, as was the Marquis of Traquair. It was becoming fashionable again in order to show loyalty to the king. It would later prove to be a step too far.

The execution of Argyll had triggered another great invasion of Campbell estates by their traditional enemies. Three Campbell castles, Dunstaffnage, Dunoon and Carrick, were trashed, and huge numbers of cattle were carried away by the Macdonalds of Islay, Glencoe and Keppoch. Numbers of Campbells were killed off in retaliation for the atrocities of 1647, including several hung from their own gallows tree at Inveraray. Others had their ears cropped or were sent off to the plantations. The executed earl's younger brother, Lord Neil Campbell, led a group of survivors across the Atlantic to found a new settlement in East New Jersey – he had previously tried and failed with a similar venture in South Carolina. A second ship, the *Henry and Francis* followed in 1686 with a group of Covenanters, but many of them died during the voyage.

Chapter 7

THE DUTCH SOLUTION

The throne is become vacant.
                    Scottish Parliament Proclamation 1689

We never could be of that mind that violence was suited to the
advance of true religion.
          Moderator Hugh Kennedy at the 1690 General Assembly

If the reign of Charles II had meant severe persecution of Presbyterians,
the reign of his brother was to be even worse for the diehard Covenanters
who had survived. Even the church ministers who had accepted bishops,
the so-so called 'curates' or the Indulged, were alarmed to see the first
stages of decriminalising Catholicism, followed by the open royal
encouragement of the old religion, and the sudden conversions amongst
those who wanted positions of power.

There was soon evidence of public dissatisfaction. The baker
apprentices of Edinburgh began a riot in late January 1686 and
were condemned to be publicly whipped along the Canongate.
They were rescued by another mob, but the militia then fired into
the crowd and killed three bystanders. A fencing master called
Keith was hanged on a false charge of drinking a toast against
papists. Three bishops were demoted for disapproving of the
new royal policy, as was the old Royalist Sir George Mackenzie,
a staunch prosecutor of the Covenanters but quite unwilling
to condone a drift towards Catholicism. He was replaced by
Sir John Dalrymple, from a family to be known for its role in the
Massacre of Glencoe six years later. Two other earls, Penmure and

Dundonald, were sacked from the Privy Council and the Duke of Hamilton was given a severe reprimand.

As all restrictions on Catholics were removed by 1687, many of the Presbyterian ministers who had compromised with the bishops gave up their charges and fled to Holland. The king's illegitimate son James Fitzjames, the Duke of Berwick, was briefed to bring troops from the Border to hunt down Covenanters and many who were caught were sentenced to transportation. The latest charismatic Covenanting preacher, James Renwick from Moniaive, was in 1688 the last of his kind to be condemned and hanged in the Grassmarket; his head and hands were removed and put on spikes at the city gates. He had studied at Edinburgh and in Holland before returning to preach in the open air for five years. When captured he said of James II, 'I cannot own this usurper as a rightful king.' He was only 26 when he was executed.

Despite the number of Scots asylum-seekers in Holland it was a group of English Parliamentarians, the so-called Immortal Seven, who in June 1688 wrote inviting William of Orange to become King of Great Britain and Ireland. This of course was far more interesting to William than a rebellion in Scotland. However the new Earl of Argyll was near The Hague, as was Lord Cardross back from America, as well as Lords Drumlanrig, Annandale, Glencairn, Dundonald, Tarras and Crawford.

In September 1688 there were rumours of a possible invasion of Scotland from Holland so the government troops, including the dreaded Highland Host, were put on alert. Two agents liaising with Holland were captured, Captain Mackay, a relation of the general, and Dr Blackadder. There were also rumours of a Jacobite invasion from Ireland and various defensive measures were taken by opponents of the regime.

The Presbyterian ministers organised a meeting at Wanlockhead for men to take up arms. King James ordered two regiments from Scotland to head for England, leaving only the militia under the none-too-reliable George Monro to hold Scotland. Lord William Ross with the anti-Jacobite volunteers manned the border and blocked communication between the Scottish Royalists and King James. William Ross (1656–1738) was a friend of Claverhouse and had served under him as a major. He had resigned and been wounded during the 1685 Argyll rebellion but was to find an excuse not to fight against his old friend at Killiecrankie. Having been briefly an anti-Jacobite, he was later to join Montgomery's Plot and spent some time in the Tower before returning to respectability.

Meanwhile King James II's chief men in Edinburgh, the earls of Perth (Drummond), Atholl, Tarbat (George Mackenzie), Balcarres (Colin Lindsay, 1652–1722, second son of the great Covenanter and Engager who had died in 1659), the Archbishop of Glasgow (John Paterson 1632–1708 a staunch supporter of James II) and George Lockhart, sent a letter to the king that instead went to William of Orange. Perth quit the scene and hid in Drummond Castle while there were anti-Jacobite riots in Edinburgh, chapels were vandalised, religious images trashed, and the pope burned in effigy. Perth set sail for Europe but was arrested when his ship was becalmed near the Bass Rock. There were more rumours of an Irish Jacobite invasion and 6,000 Covenanter troops gathered on Douglas Moor.

In the meantime William of Orange had landed in Torbay and as he headed for London was meeting very little opposition from James II and his army. At the end of January 1689, William had his first formal meeting with the Scottish peers when the Duke of Hamilton acted as their spokesman. As insurance, Hamilton was making sure that as far as his family was concerned it did not matter which side won, so he sent his son to console the panicky James II. Despite his record as a robust commander on both land and sea, James, now in late middle age, seemed to have lost confidence, was being deserted by his own senior officers and was suffering from embarrassing nosebleeds. Soon he had abandoned all efforts to retain the crown and was being dispatched from Rochester harbour. The London meeting resulted in a vague promise from William but no indication that he would restore full Presbyterianism. His own preference was for modified Presbyterianism firmly under State control, a prospect that would horrify the Covenanting ministers. The Scots generally were again deeply divided between the diehard Covenanters at one extreme, the moderates in the centre and at the other extreme the strong Episcopalians such as John Paterson with their allies including Viscount Dundee (Black Jack, alias Ian Dhu Graham, alias Claverhouse) and Thomas Livingston.

Obviously by this time the vast majority of the clergy, the so-called curates, had been appointed by bishops and could not easily revert to Presbyterianism even if they wanted to and were anyway still utterly despised by the Covenanters. At the end of April 1689, Lawrie of Blackwood, with the help of the young Douglas heir, Lord Angus, formed the new regiment of Cameronians, some 1,200 men whose officers all had to take the Covenant oath and whose stated objective was the 'defence of religion'. Patrick Hume of Polwarth (1641-1724), a die-hard Covenanter who had joined the ill-fated Argyll campaign of 1685 and spent some time in prison, later Earl of Marchmont, became chief spokesman for the Covenanting party, demanding impeachment of their former persecutors and a purge of episcopal church ministers. Laws were demanded against any soldiers guilty of 'debauchery, drunkenness, swearing or other vices'.

At this point the Earl of Atholl (John Murray) changed sides from the Jacobites to the Whigs, as did the ambitious Annandale, so the balance was clearly swinging. A Presbyterian army was put together with 800 Cameronians, 400 of Argyll's (Archibald the new Earl) and the Scottish regiment of General Hugh Mackay (1640–1692) who had crossed over from Holland and landed at Torbay ahead of William of Orange. An experienced officer credited with inventing the socket bayonet, Mackay had fought with the French, Venetian and Dutch armies as well as alongside Marlborough in King James's army but as a strong Protestant had gone over to William in 1688.

Dundee and Livingston were ordered to surrender but escaped. There was now a new council in charge with the usual suspects taking the main roles: Atholl, Argyll, Crawford, Sutherland, Patrick Hume, William Scott and the unpredictably ambitious Montgomery of Skelmorlie. In April 1689 they proclaimed the Scottish throne vacant as they waited to see what kind of settlement William would offer. That same month the new king was crowned in England and the oath included the words 'gainstand all false religion' with still no mention of bishops.

Argyll was one of those on hand and pronounced 'our religion exposed and laid open to be ruined by the treachery of our clergy.' But there was still no resolution of the Scottish problem as William had more urgent problems to deal with and whatever he said would not satisfy all of the Scots.

Thus Scotland again drifted towards civil war. A garrison was sent to Arran to watch out for the Irish invasion and supplies were shipped to Londonderry to help with the defence of the city against the Jacobites. All shipping on the west coast was deployed to block any Irish armada. Dunnottar Castle was refurbished to help dominate the north east and General Mackay was appointed commander of the army. Melfort, acting for James II, sent a letter to Balcarres suggesting he keep his powder dry and wait for a reinforcement of 5,000 men James was intending to supply, but the letter was intercepted and decoded. Balcarres was arrested and Dundee headed for Inverness to raise the Highland Host.

Recruitment was difficult, however, as the Keppoch Macdonalds turned up but were unreliable, as were the Camerons who were already laden with booty and soon most disappeared back home. The devious young Simon Fraser of Lovat (1667–1747, executed after Culloden) was allegedly helping to recruit men, though his elder brother Alexander was killed fighting for the other side – hence Simon got the inheritance. Even the promised contingent from Ireland was smaller than expected and led by the uninspiring Irish commander Alexander Cannon. There was also some unrest in Dundee's camp when the Jacobite Earl of Dunfermline James Seton (d. 1694) had some of his cavalry transferred to the command of Sir William Wallace. However, the Murrays who under Mackay's command were defending the Pass of Killiecrankie deserted him and went over to Dundee, thus providing a potential ambush point for the Jacobites.

The scene was now set for the asymmetric clash between Dundee's relatively small force of 4,000 Highlanders and the new Scottish army under Mackay. Dundee won a spectacular victory due to the overconfidence of Mackay who unwisely sent his army through the narrow pass at Killiecrankie where his superior numbers were of no advantage. Dundee used the MacColla technique of one last-minute close-up firing of the muskets followed by a fast gunless charge against the enemy pinned together in the narrow gorge. It was successful but very expensive, since although Mackay suffered about 4,000 casualties not only was Dundee himself killed but also a large number of his Highlanders. Dundee, who had been understandably vilified as a violent persecutor of lowland Scots, was now the first great Jacobite martyr, Bonnie instead of Black Jack. Amongst the victors who survived were the ill-fated chieftain of the Glencoe Macdonalds and the teenage Rob Roy Macgregor, yet to make his name as a heroic outlaw.

After Dundee's death Mackay retreated to regroup whilst the cautious Cannon took over the victorious Jacobites and kept to the hills as he led his men south in mid-August 1689 to capture the arms depot at Dunkeld. Despite hugely outnumbering the defenders of Dunkeld, and despite the absence there of Mackay's main force, Cannon with more than 4,000 men proved quite unable to dislodge a small but determined troop of 800 Cameronians led by Colonel William Clelland, the young hero of Drumclog. They were joined by 100 fusiliers under John Campbell and some dragoons under the remarkable Henry Erskine, Lord Cardross (1650–93). He had been imprisoned as a Covenanter by Lauderdale and then emigrated to start a settlement at Charlestown Neck, Carolina, but been driven out by Spaniards, then joined William of Orange in Holland. He had been with Mackay at Killiecrankie but now came to the aid of the beleaguered Cameronians at Dunkeld. His half-brother John Erskine (1662–1743 known as 'The Black Colonel') had landed with William at Torbay.

The situation of the Cameronians was still desperate (members of the Clan Cameron were of course on the Jacobite side). At one point they were cutting lead from the town roofs to make bullets. They set parts of the town on fire to trap groups of Jacobites who had taken cover. It was ironic that this regiment of extreme psalm-singing Covenanters was unpopular not just among the Highlanders but also the vast majority of Lowlanders, but Clelland and his men stopped the Highlanders in their tracks. Dundee had won a glamorous battle but Clelland and Cardross won the war: 300 Jacobites were killed compared with two dozen Covenanters. It was reported the Highlanders 'could fight against men but not against devils.' Like Dundee, Clelland was killed in the moment of victory and he was only twenty-eight.

Amongst the survivors of both the Battles of Killiecrankie and Dunkeld was Alastair MacIain Macdonald, chief of the Glencoe Macdonalds, who had lost several of his small clan in the fighting. Nevertheless he joined with a number of other clansmen in swearing to continue the fight against William of Orange, the king who three years later was to sign his death warrant, perhaps having hardly read it. MacIain meanwhile used the interlude as an opportunity to renew his profitable raids on the Campbell heartland. For him this was hardly religious warfare but for some of the others, religion did play a part, as with the Camerons' attack on the Grants who favoured the Protestant, perhaps even the Presbyterian side.

Ironically, one of the main victims of MacIain's raiding was Robert Campbell of Glenlyon (1630–96), who was already in deep financial trouble due to the extravagant improvements he had made to his little castle at Meggernie, his drinking and his gambling. When the Glencoe Macdonalds headed off with his cattle, his wine and his furniture, it was the final blow and despite being over fifty he was allowed to enrol in the Argyll Regiment of Foot so that he could earn a modest salary. It was in this capacity three years later that he was, by accident or design, in charge of the soldiers sent on royal orders to wipe out the little clan that had destroyed his home.

Another survivor from the Highland army at Killiecrankie and Dunkeld was a much younger man, the still teenaged Rob Roy Macgregor (1671–1734) who was to have an even more remarkable career than Alastair MacIain as a cattle raider and professional drover but, unlike him, had a Campbell wife so received some Campbell protection. Despite this, however, he remained an active Jacobite.

At the end of June 1689 there was another significant success for the pro-William establishment when at last Edinburgh Castle was surrendered by its Jacobite governor, the newly promoted Duke of Gordon. In Edinburgh, however, there was growing impatience about the absence of a firm settlement with William of Orange, who was still expected to want royal control of the Church. In fact his influential chaplain, William Carstairs (1649–1715), was nicknamed Cardinal Carstairs. The son of a Glasgow minister who had been captured by Cromwell at the Battle of Dunbar, Carstairs had acted as a spy for William for some years, travelling to England under a false name as William Williams. He was later to be an influential chancellor of Edinburgh University and be moderator of the General Assembly four times. So bishops were abolished by the parliament but not for true Presbyterianism in the eyes of the Cameronians. They regarded any form of State control of the church as 'to be detested' and ostentatiously renewed the Covenant oath at Borland Hill near Lesmahagow.

Also upset were all those Presbyterian lairds who had been deprived of their estates by James II and were fretting about their return. On top of this, several ambitious lairds who were banking on earldoms and high positions in the new regime were frustrated by the slow response. The most neurotic of these were Sir James Montgomery of Skelmorlie; William Johnston, Lord Annandale; and Lord Ross, who were all fondly expecting promotion from William of Orange and in their disappointment founded what became known as The Club with a rather vague plan for a reverse coup d'état.

Employing two agents called Fergusson and Payne, they bribed Atholl to raise an army for them – but he simply pocketed the cash. Their big idea was to strike while the king was busy in Ireland, raise the Highland Host, and get French naval help. Most naively of all they extracted a promise from James II that he would allow the Presbyterian Church in Scotland – the third time a struggling royal Stuart had made such a promise with no intention of keeping it. However, for the time, being the plot was plausible enough to gather a few more recruits: Queensberry, Atholl, Tarbat and even Arran, who was still imprisoned in the Tower. (Arran was James Douglas, later Duke of Hamilton, prominent in the Darién Scheme and in the passing of the Act of Union in 1707). Two others also in prison were Balcarres and Dunmore.

The Club's plan was to push through the Scottish Parliament an Act endorsing the abolition of bishops and royal control over the Church in the full expectation that William would veto it and thus provoke an anti-Orange riot. In the aftermath Montgomery expected an earldom and to be Secretary of State. To make this more likely when the king summoned the Scottish Parliament for April 1690 Lord Tarbert/Tarbat plotted to create a Jacobite majority, so many of those attending had to perjure themselves in swearing the oath of allegiance to William or they would have been excluded from the proceedings. Montgomery's complicated plot began to unravel for two reasons: firstly because William was far more relaxed than expected about abolishing bishops and thus there was little risk of a split between king and Parliament. Secondly, the deviousness of their tactics discouraged new participants.

At this point a Jacobite spy called Strachan was arrested in Greenock and a letter from James II revealing the plot was found in the sole of his shoe. The only real sticking point for William was that he still wanted some form of royal supremacy over the Presbyterian Church, the situation which he was used to in Holland but was branded as Erastian by the more extreme Covenanters who could not tolerate the idea of lay patrons. So a delegation of Crawford, Stair, Cardross, Hume and Irvine of Drum was appointed to sort out the detail.

Meanwhile the members of The Club, having lost the opportunity of a popular row against William, were also feeling let down by James. Of the ambitious plotters Montgomery still had not received his promised earldom from James II, while Annandale, Ross and Arran had not received the promotions, albeit somewhat theoretical promotions, that they thought they deserved. James had, however, sent a contingent of 1,500 troops from Ireland with Generals Cannon and Thomas Buchan (1641–1724) in command. They added 400 local Jacobites to their force but in late April 1690 were both caught literally napping at Cromdale in Speyside by an official pro-Orange force under Sir Thomas Livingston. As a result, 400 Jacobites were killed and after brief efforts to revive the campaign in Aberdeenshire, Buchan gave up and took shelter in Lochaber. His position was further undermined by the surrender of Seaforth.

At about the same time The Club was further unravelling as one after another the main members claimed immunity by betraying their fellows. Ross confessed to Queen Mary, followed by Montgomery, whilst the unprincipled Annandale moved to Bath and handed over the agent Payne to be tortured for additional information by the authorities.

With the plotting and fighting more or less over, Melville proposed a new church settlement in which Presbyterianism would be restored with the numbers of lairds acting as patrons greatly reduced and royal supremacy kept fairly discreet. Former patrons were to be compensated and 400 formerly attainted Covenanter lairds were to get their estates back. Apart from dedicated Episcopalians and extreme Covenanters, the vast majority of Scots were satisfied. The Cameronians were naturally not amongst this number but were tolerated as long as they did not resort to violence. Then in July news arrived of William's final victory over James Stuart on the River Boyne.

Thus in October 1690, the General Assembly of the Church of Scotland met again for the first time in thirty years, celebrating the occasion with a one-day fast and a sermon by the diehard Covenanter Gabriel Semple, who had presided over the Rullion Green campaign. The huge losses incurred by the Scots in pursuing the goal of UK-wide Presbyterianism were brushed under the carpet, along with the Solemn League and Covenant. There had been an estimated 60,000 deaths in the Civil War period with another 20,000 after the Restoration, a high price to pay for Scotland to be free of bishops. To this should perhaps be added the death toll attributable to the Jacobite risings, which were so overtly based on, or akin to, the model of the four invasions of England by the Scots in 1640, 1643, 1648 and 1651. Thus in just over a century after Jenny Geddes, there were 100,000 unnecessary deaths, huge hardship and long-term economic damage.

Chapter 8

THE JACOBITE POSTLUDE – TWO MORE SCOTTISH INVASIONS OF ENGLAND

(Prince) Charles proceeded to give a practical dose of divine right in expecting obedience to and acquiescence to his decisions.
    Allan Macinnes: *Clanship, Commerce and the House of Stuart*

After nearly fifty years of altercations and wars related to the Presbyterian Church it is not surprising that in 1690 there remained significant fault lines in Scotland. The traditional one between the Highlands and Lowlands had also become a religious and cultural divide with the Highland clans being almost entirely Episcopalian with a tiny Catholic minority, whilst the Lowland families were almost entirely Presbyterian.

The divide was also economic for the central belt, including Perthshire and Argyll, had suffered far more from war degradation, plunder and depopulation, especially of able-bodied males, whereas the border country, which had formerly been vulnerable to warfare and Border Reivers, had seen a significant decrease in violence except amongst pockets of extreme Covenanters.

This divide had now also acquired a fourth dimension, political. From 1640–60 the Presbyterian Lowlanders dominated the Edinburgh establishment, but lost out to those north and south of the Central Belt after the Restoration, then recovered to support first William III, and later George I. Thus the Episcopalian Highlanders then became the frustrated opposition who found a focus for their yearnings in the exiled Stuarts, first in ex-king James II, then his son the Old Pretender and finally his grandson Bonnie Prince Charlie. However, there were always exceptions due to local feuds, as in Ayrshire between Episcopalian Cunninghams and Presbyterian Kennedys.

So while it would be absurd to call the civil wars of 1715 and 1745 religious wars, the Jacobites were fighting consciously for the restoration of a Catholic royal dynasty and the downfall of a Protestant one, so they did have at least some element of religious motivation. There was therefore a strong preponderance of men with episcopalian or Catholic sympathies in all the Jacobite risings and the vast majority of Scottish Presbyterians, in fact the majority of all Scots, were against them, as were the vast majority of English Anglicans.

It is clear that the two main Jacobite campaigns followed closely the example of the four earlier Scottish invasions of England. The first two, in 1640 and 1643, had been via the east coast route and had been successful, while the other two, in 1648 and 1651, had followed the west coast route and been disastrous. In fact the 1715 invasion ended up in almost exactly the same place as that of 1648, except that it was in the streets of central Preston rather than spread through the outskirts. The sixth of this series of invasions was in 1745 and also followed the western route and like the previous three, the expected help from English sympathisers failed to materialise.

The self-destructiveness of the Scots' renewed support for the Stuart dynasty after 1648 soon became apparent when they switched from the winning Parliamentarian side to the losing Royalists after gullibly accepting the barely credible promises first of Charles I and then of Charles II that they would hand over England, Wales and Ireland to Presbyterianism. Invading England from the north perhaps became habit-forming, especially for the Highlanders who had never before showed any liking for the Stuarts until they became a lost cause and when based in London were much less likely to interfere with their way of life than when based in Edinburgh. Perhaps also there were fond memories of looting, and amnesia when it came to recalling the deaths and destruction of previous campaigns.

A fourth aspect of the unfortunate Jacobite learning curve was that they aped the battle tactics of the so-called Highland Charge developed by Alastair MacColla and Montrose in 1644. Even then it had been an anachronism, relying on shock, brute strength and sword power in an era dominated by disciplined musket fire. However, it had, on many occasions, been successful, especially against inexperienced musketeers, as it was at Tippermuir, Inverlochy, Kilsyth, Killiecrankie and Prestonpans. Such successes gave the Highlanders an undue confidence in what was essentially an archaic form of warfare that proved to be far from perfect at Sheriffmuir and disastrous at Culloden.

PART THREE

GAZETTEER: THE BUILDINGS, RUINS, MONUMENTS AND BATTLEFIELDS OF SCOTTISH WARS 1639–1689

One of the features of this period is the huge destruction of castles and towns by the opposing Scottish factions during the civil wars and also by the English invaders both in the Cromwell and Hanoverian periods. It also shows how many land- and castle-owning lairds faced bankruptcy due to their expenditure on the war effort or the attrition of their territory, so that they often had to sell or abandon their traditional homes. In many cases it also demonstrated that old family tower houses were no longer much protection against artillery, so the new rich, those who made money by being on the winning side in the wars, chose not to rebuild medieval castles but instead spent their money on lavish new mansions like Drumlanrig, Floors, Hopetoun House and Thirlestane, using the new breed of architects such as William Bruce (1630–1710) and later William Adam. Bruce from Kinross was a Royalist merchant, based in Rotterdam, who assisted in the Restoration of Charles II, became Royal Surveyor in Scotland and was referred to as the 'Kit Wren' of Scotland. In 1689 he was imprisoned briefly as a Jacobite sympathiser. William Adam, father of Robert and James, was one of his assistants.

Another use found at this time for medieval castles was as prisons. Dunnottar Castle was one of the largest and least pleasant. Edinburgh, Blackness, Strathaven, the Bass Rock and Newmilns Tower all featured alongside the Tolbooths at Glasgow and Kirkcudbright. Even St Giles Cathedral had its basement converted to a prison, Haddo's Hole.

It is also evident that many of the expensive fortifications built in places like Leith, Inverness and Ayr in the 1650s were largely pulled down again in the 1660s when the regime changed.

Another feature of the landscape particular to this period is the large number of little memorials to the Covenanter martyrs that are scattered across Southern Scotland.

Scotland

Cathedrals and Bishops Palaces
St Andrew's Cathedral. This building is now roofless, as is St Andrew's Castle, which was for many years the residence of the archbishops. The See also had Inchmurtach Castle, of which little is now left, and Archbishop Spotiswood's home at Dairsie, which has survived. There are also limited remains of Stow Castle near Lauder, a 15th century palace of the St Andrew's See.

Aberdeen: St Machar's Cathedral. It was founded around 950 but mainly rebuilt after 1350, it still survives but nothing remains of the Bishop's Palace that stood to its west as it was demolished to make space for Cromwell's Citadel. Aberdeen also had Fetternear Castle near Kemnay but it was burned down in 1919. Another vanished palace was at Loch Goul or the Bishop's Loch near Dyce.

Argyll: Lismore Cathedral. This still stands as a tiny parish church and there are ruins of the old bishops' castle at Achadun from before 1512 when they moved to Saddell Castle, now restored, in Kintyre south of Carradale.

Brechin Cathedral. The mainly 13th century cathedral still survives as a parish church, as does a 10th century Irish-style round tower, but only one gateway survives of the Bishop's palace.

Caithness: Dornoch Cathedral. It replaced the earlier one at Halkirk, still stands and nearby Dornoch Palace, the bishop's residence, has been converted into a hotel. Similarly the bishop's country residence at Skibo, where Montrose was once imprisoned, was demolished to make way for Andrew Carnegie's more modern Skibo Castle, now also a hotel. The site survives of another Bishop's Palace at Scrabster.

Dunblane Cathedral. It survives as a parish church with an 11th century bell tower and 13th century nave. Only a few vaulted arches remain of the Bishop's Palace here but the Library of Bishop Leighton has been preserved.

Dunkeld Cathedral. Part of the cathedral survives as a parish church but only the site survives of the Bishop's Palace

Edinburgh's St Giles Cathedral. This was the scene of the epic stool throwing by Jenny Geddes, or someone dressed in that fashion. In the late 1630s it was subdivided into four parts beneath one of which was the dungeon known as Haddo's Hole. There are monuments to Montrose, Argyll and Jenny's stool. Archbishop Sharp's city dwelling was destroyed. Cramond Tower was the Edinburgh home of the Bishops of Dunkeld.

Galloway: Whithorn Priory. The scene of much remedial archaeology, the Priory was turned into a small cathedral by Bishop Sydserf.

Glasgow Cathedral. This is the oldest medieval cathedral left with its roof on in mainland Scotland and was the scene of the famous 1638 Assembly. The Bishop's Castle on the High Street, where many of the bishops hid for safety during the 1638 meeting, has long vanished but the contemporary house Provand's Lordship, built in 1471 as part of a hospital, survives and foundations have recently been unearthed of the Archbishop's country residence at Partick Castle. They also had a hunting lodge at Lochwood near Bishop's Loch, where three lakes were apparently once linked by canal to allow the episcopal barge easy access. Nearby is Provan Hall a well-preserved building of this period associated with Francis Livingston. The cathedral has a monument for nine martyred Covenanters.

Moray: Elgin Cathedral. It was ruined long before this period but the Bishops of Moray were well supplied with magnificent Spynie Palace nearby, which was besieged by Robert Monro in 1640, as well as the Bishop's House, a 15th century tower-house on North College Street.

Orkney: St Magnus Cathedral. This large medieval building dates from 1167 when the Orkneys still belonged to Denmark and were ruled by Norse earls. There is also the three-storey hall block of the bishop's palace.

Ross: Fortrose Cathedral. This ruined cathedral on the Black Isle dates from the 13th century when it replaced Rosemarkie, but was seriously dilapidated by the Reformation. The bishops' castle may have been Craig.

Other Churches and Conventicle Locations
The spread of rebel parishes, Covenanter tombs, battle sites, remote conventicle venues, pulpit stones and caves used as hiding places helps us understand the geographic hotspots of the Covenanters. Significantly whilst the main lairds of Fife and Ayrshire dominated the drive for rebellion in the 1640s, their sons two decades later had mostly reverted to the establishment side and became oppressors of the Covenanters.

Fife and nearby Counties

The close-knit community of anti-episcopal ministers and lairds in Fife played a key role in the start of the two Bishops' Wars, which in turn led to the English Civil Wars. The number of Fife ministers who accompanied the Scottish Army to Marston Moor is a clear indication of their commitment.

Abdie. The church near Lindores was patronised by the Balfour family.

Aberdour Kirk. This is the burial place of prominent Covenanter minister Robert Blair, d. 1666. He was exiled to a parish in Ulster where he tried to organise a colony in America, but later a key Presbyterian preacher in London.

Anstruther West. David Murray the minister was arrested and deposed for praying for King Charles II in 1653. Alexander Leslie was his predecessor and had been chaplain to General David Leslie but was later friendly with the future Archbishop Sharp at Crail.

Auchtermuchty. The minister here was suspended in 1641 for failing to hold a communion service for two years. The birthplace of David Leslie was nearby.

Balcarres Crag. The site of a major conventicle close to Balcarres Castle.

Balmerino. This was the base of Covenanting minister Walter Grieg (d. 1672), chaplain to the Earl of Balcarres and present with the army at Marston Moor. The anti-episcopal Earl of Balmerino owned the former monastery.

Burntisland. The minister John Michaelson was deposed in 1639 for refusing to sign the Covenant.

Carnock. The now-ruined church was the base of the strongly pro-Covenant John Row.

Ceres. There are monuments and tombs of Lindsay Earls of Crawford. William Row was appointed minister here by Ludovic, Earl of Crawford, in 1634, and became a strong Covenanter, deposed as such in 1668. The church was rebuilt by the Leslies in 1806.

Crail. In east Fife was the first charge of future Archbishop Sharp, which was given him by his patron, the Earl of Crawford, in 1648.

Culross. The minister John Duncan was prominent in the 1638 rebellion and was chaplain to General Leslie during the siege of Newcastle in 1647. The church is part of the original abbey. Many of the local indentured coal miners were conscripted for the Covenanter army.

Cupar. David Dalgleish, the minister here was vocal in the 1638 Assembly. The tower of the old church survives; two women were hanged at Newburgh for burning the manse here in 1661. Buried here were the hands and feet of three of the murderers of Archbishop Sharp. Nearby Kembach has its ruined 16th century church plus a Covenanters cave. The Dura Den gorge was scene of a huge conventicle of 8,000 people in 1674. Nearby lived the Lindsays of Pitscottie.

Dalgetty. The minister Andrew Donaldson was chaplain to the Dunfermline Regiment at Marston Moor and again with the Scottish troops in 1649. After the Battle of Kilsyth 'it pleased the Lord to visit a pestilence on Dalgetty.' Fine ruins survive.

Dron Church, south of Perth. It has a monument to the Covenanter John Elway.

Dunfermline Abbey. John Row, minister here and later at Carnock, a 13th century church, was a strong supporter of the Covenant in 1638. His brother William at Ceres held similar views. Nearby on Hill of Beath or Beak was the major conventicle, noted as the first where the participants came armed.

Dysart. The minister James Wilson was tutor for the Rothes family, supported the Engagers and was deposed in 1661. The impressively strong tower and other parts of the old church survive.

Fossoway, in Glendevon. William Spens, the minster here till 1679, was deposed for supporting the Argyll rebellion of 1685, was tortured with the boot and suffered sleep deprivation but was then restored to his parish.

Inverkeithing. Only the tower now survives of the medieval church, notable for its role in the Great Scottish Witch Hunt. The town suffered severe devastation during the Battle of Inverkeithing between Cromwell's troops and the Scottish Royalists.

Kilconquhar. Three arches survive of the old church patronised by the pro-Covenant Balcarres family.

Kilrenny Church. It has a medieval tower and a monument to the Lumsden family of mercenary soldiers who fought for the Covenant.

Kinghorn. John Moncrieff was minister here till 1656 and was a Scottish army chaplain at Marston Moor.

Kingsbarns Church. It was a base of strong covenanting minister Bruce and rebuilt in 1630.

Kinkell Ness, near St Andrews. This was the site of a major conventicle on ground owned by Hamiltons of Kinkell

Leuchars. St Acheads, the church built in 1187, was the base of Alexander Henderson, main author of the Covenant of 1638. He accompanied Leven's army to England in 1642 and after the king's capture in 1647 was given the task of trying to convert him to Presbyterianism.

Lomond Hills. The site of major conventicle.

Markinch church. It is ruined except for a medieval tower but the graveyard was used for Lindsays and had the tomb of Field Marshal Leslie.

Moonzie. This is a 17th-century church building in a strong area for Covenanters.

Muckhart. The minister John Govan served as chaplain with the Kirkcudbright regiment of the Covenanter army at Marston Moor. His parish stretched to Castle Campbell in Dollar, lowland base of the Earls of Argyll, key leaders of the Covenanters.

(East) Wemyss. The leading Covenanter George Gillespie was minister here till 1642, when he moved to Greyfriars in Edinburgh. Ruinous church now converted to house.

Central Belt and Ayrshire
Airdrie. It had a now-vanished Covenanter's cave on the North Calder.

Ayr. It has a monument to seven Covenanters who were hanged here, the local hangman refused orders to execute them so another prisoner took over the job. There is a Peden's cave at Craigie.

Barr. There is a Peden's Stone on a conventicle site here.

Bathgate. The Old Church, now roofless, has the Covenanter Stone of James Davie, shot by dragoons during a conventicle at Blackdub, Armadale.

Biggar. Two hundred people signed the Covenant and the local laird, Lord Fleming, raised troops here. His home at Boghall Castle was occupied by Cromwell in 1650. Biggar has a revevant Museum.

Cadder. Thomas Melville the minister was dismissed in 1674 for holding conventicles in Bearsden.

Campsie. John Law the minister was gaoled on the Bass Rock for holding conventicles near Kippen.

Carmunnock. The minister of the church was Andrew Morton who was dismissed as a Covenanter rebel in 1662, then gaoled in Stirling Castle for holding conventicles. He is buried here.

Cathcart. The churchyard has a memorial to three murdered Covenanters. The original church had John Carstairs as its minister who was one of the committee men wounded and left naked at the Battle of Dunbar and was imprisoned afterwards. His son William

Carstairs became friendly with William of Orange whilst a student at Utrecht, acted as his spy in England where he suffered imprisonment and torture, eventually becoming Moderator of the General Assembly four times. Another minister here, James Blair, was sacked in 1662, accused of holding conventicles and shot at Dalry.

Cleland near Bothwell on the South Calder Water. This is the site of a large Covenanters Cave also credited to William Wallace.

Colmonell in Ayrshire. – It has a gravestone with a rhyming inscription beginning

> I Matthew McIlwraith in the parish of Colmonell
> By Bloody Claverhouse I fell

Dalry. In nearby Lynn's Glen is Peden's Pulpit, site of a major conventicle.

Dolphinton. Black Law near Biggar has the tomb of the prominent Covenanting officer Major Joseph Learmonth, who was taken prisoner at Bothwell Bridge and then imprisoned on the Bass Rock.

Eaglesham. A favourite haunt of Covenanters on moors nearby, it has a monument to Gabriel Thomson and Richard Lockhart, both shot by dragoons led by Maclay of Ardincaple after a conventicle. On nearby Whitelee Windfarm are a Preacher's Stone and a Covenanters' cave plus a monument to dead Covenanters near Glengoin Farm, which they used as a safe house. Robert Train the minister here was dismissed for supporting Montrose in 1645.

East Kilbride. This was a strong Covenanter area and Conventicles were held in Muirhouse Glen. A monument near Priestknowe Roundabout commemorates ten local martyrs including five who were drowned in the convict ship *Crown of London* on its way to the Americas.

Edinburgh, Greyfriars Kirk. Founded in 1602, it was the scene of an unofficial Assembly meeting to sign Covenant in February 1638. A monument records when the churchyard was used as an open air prison for 1,200 Covenanter prisoners taken at Bothwell Bridge and kept without proper food or shelter for several months in winter weather.

Edinburgh, Magdalen Chapel. Built as a chapel for the local blacksmiths or hammermen in 1541, it was used for conventicles in the 1670s and also for taking care of the bodies of executed Presbyterian martyrs such as the Marquis of Argyll.

Edinburgh, Braids Crag. It was the site of illegal outdoor preaching.

Fenwick Church. The village in Ayrshire was home to weavers and Covenanters. The church built in 1643 had the minister William Guthrie (1620-65) who was tutor to the Loudoun Campbells and had two brothers also prominent Covenanter ministers, John at Tarbolton Church and James who was executed in 1661. The executed Covenanter James White is buried here.

Glasgow Barony. Donald Cargill succeeded the great Covenanting preacher Zachary Boyd here but was later dismissed, was wounded at the Battle of Bothwell Bridge and hanged in Edinburgh as a rebel. Cargill's Stone near Maybole marks the site of some of his conventicles.

Glasgow Tron. Robert Baillie was minister here for some time with David Dickson, both of them major Covenant supporters. Baillie was chaplain to Lord Eglinton's regiment as well as negotiating in London in 1640. The surviving Tron Steeple was completed in 1636.

Gourock. It has a Covenanters or Whites Well with a Pulpit Rock nearby.

Kilmaurs Church. It houses the monument to the Earls of Glencairn.

Kippen in Stirlingshire. This was the parish of rebel Covenanter James Muir who held conventicles on Kippen Muir and led 400 volunteers at Bothwell Bridge, which he survived. His mother was arrested and held in Glasgow Tolbooth. He died in 1746 and was buried here. Conventicles were held below nearby Dunmore Hillfort which has a Covenanters' Hole.

Lanark St Kentigern's. An obelisk marks the site of the signing of the Lanark Declaration in 1682, also the tomb of William Herig who was executed at Bothwell Bridge in 1680.

Hamilton Old Parish Church. It has the graves of fallen Covenanters from Bothwell Bridge.

Lesmahagow. It was the home of the Steel family including John, captain of the Lesmahagow Covenanters; Thomas, shot by dragoons at Yonderton; his brother David, murdered; and his wife Isobel, who was first imprisoned and then transported to Barbados but remarkably survived to return home. Nearby is the remote conventicle site of Auchengilloch.

Loudoun. This was the ruined home church of the Campbell Earls of Loudoun and former parish of infamous minister John Nevoy, instigator of the Dunaverty massacre. In his time it was replaced by a newer church at Newmilns.

Maybole. It has a Covenanters memorial. A large conventicle was held at Cargill's Stone in 1681. The Carrick Covenanters mustered at Muster Lea in 1681 and were amongst 1,000 Ayrshire men fighting at Bothwell Bridge, of whom 400 were killed or imprisoned.

Neilston. Nearby is the Covenanting Stone Circle of Moyne Moor.

Old Dailly in the Girvan valley. It has a ruined 14th-century church with several Covenanter gravestones.

Shotts/Kirk o' Shotts. It has a stone for William Smith, killed at Rullion Green. There was a contingent of 150 Shotts men at the Battle of Bothwell Bridge. Nearby is the Fortissat Stone with Covenanter associations.

Sorn. It has a 17th-century church and was the birthplace of the prophet Alexander Peden. Nearby is Peden's Cave in Cleugh Glen and there is a Covenanter Stone in Old Auchinleck kirkyard.

Stirling. The Church of the Holy Rude has a monument to the Wigton martyrs.

Stonehouse Church. It has the grave of James Thomson of Tan Hill killed at the Battle of Drumclog. His wife and son were both imprisoned.

South West Scotland and Borders

Anwoth. The minister here, the anti-episcopal Samuel Rutherford, was dismissed by Bishop Sydserf for alleged immoral conduct with his future wife; he later delivered a sermon in Latin to an unwilling Charles II.

Barscobe. Site of Conventicles at Holy Linn, Holy Croft and Mulloch Hill.

Carsphairn. The anti-Covenant curate of this church near Dalmellington was murdered in 1684 by James Macmichael, who was later captured at Auchencloy Hill. He also shot a supposed Royalist informer at Stroanpatrick. His brother Daniel was shot in the Dalveen Pass.

Crossmichael, on Loch Ken. It has an 18th century church including a tower from 1611 and has the tomb of William Graham, allegedly shot by Claverhouse in 1682 but otherwise perhaps executed in 1684.

Dumfries. St Michaels's numerous Covenanter gravestones. Robbers Cave is also known as Covenanters Cave.

Durisdeer. Burial place of Daniel Macmichael, brother of the murderer of the Carsphairn curate and himself shot in the Dalveen Pass by Sir John Dalzell. Also here is the Queensberry Aisle of the Drumlanrig Douglases, one of whom was an active persecutor of Covenanters.

Earlston. This was the home of the Covenanter Alexander Shields, who preached at Conventicles nearby, as did James Renwick.

Ewes Valley. Langholm was reported to be used for secret conventicles by the Eskdale Covenanters.

Gameshope. It has Peden's Pulpit, site of Alexander Peden's preaching.

Glencairn. There are a number of Covenanter graves here and nearby is the Preaching Stone of Breconside.

Glen Trool. This was the site of a conventicle held by Alexander Peden on Craig Minn, and nearby six of the United Societies men were killed at Caldons.

Irongray. It was the parish of the fiery preacher John Welsh, great-grandson of John Knox and two Covenanters were hanged on the oak tree here in 1685. Four martyrs' tombs and communion stones are on Skeoch Hill.

Jedburgh. Rubers Law has Peden's Pulpit at about 1,300 feet above sea level.

Kirkcudbright Old Church. It has tombs of four Covenanters allegedly shot by Claverhouse.

Lilliesleaf Moor, near Hawick. This was the site of a major conventicle held by John Wellwood of Tindergarth.

Moniaive. It has the monument to James Renwick the last Covenanter minister hanged in Edinburgh. The Caitloch Cave with Covenanter connections is nearby.

Sanquhar. A monument has now replaced the old town cross where the Sanquhar Declaration was proclaimed. There is a Covenanters' Well nearby on the Southern Upland Way.

St John's Town of Dalry. There are martyrs' graves here.

Troqueer Church. It has a monument to the prominent Covenanter minister John Blackadder who was minister here from 1653 till dismissed for refusal to accept bishops in 1663. He became a popular open-air preacher addressing huge crowds at the three major Fife conventicles: Hill of Beath, Balcarres Crag and Kinkell. When Archbishop Sharp called in the militia to arrest him he was told that the militia were all attending the service. Blackadder escaped to Holland but returned and was imprisoned on the Bass Rock and died whilst still a prisoner in 1685. He was buried in North Berwick. The Covenanter James Kirko was shot near Troqueer.

Tweedsmuir. Graves here include John Hunter, shot near the Devil's Beef Tub at Corehead by James Douglas of Drumlanrig.

Tala Linn. This was the scene of meeting place of 'Hillmen', followers of Richard Cameron. They nearly captured Claverhouse in 1682.

Tynron. It has the grave of William Smith, Covenanter shot at Moniaive. Nearby at Craigellar was a skirmish in 1685, noted for the use by Covenanters of the so-called Galloway Flail, a weapon designed by a local blacksmith.

Wanlockhead. Nearby is Glendyne where Peden hid from his pursuers. Martyrs' Knowe at Cogshead commemorates three Covenanters who avoided capture by Drumlanrig. Allan's Cairn near the Whig Hole recalls another well-hidden site for conventicles.

Wigton. The Old Kirk has martyrs' monument commemorating amongst others the two Covenanter women who were tied to stakes so that they would be drowned by the incoming Solway tide, also three men hanged on the orders of Major Winram. On the hill above is the Covenanter Windy Hill Monument.

Castles and Houses

Central Lowlands
Airdrie House. A ruin west of Airdrie was the home of Covenanting Hamiltons, one of whom fought at Drumclog.

Almond Castle, west of Linlithgow. Now ruined, the keep was taken over by Livingstons of Callendar, including Lord Almond, Callendar, ally of Montrose and general under Leslie at siege of Newcastle and later Earls of Linlithgow – forfeited 1715.

Argyll's Lodging, in the Castle Wynd at Stirling. This is a fine Renaissance palace bought by the Earl of Argyll in 1666 and refurbished when he married Balcarres' feisty widow.

Barnton Tower/House. Now demolished, it was the Edinburgh base of Earl of Balmerino, key member of the Fife Conspiracy.

Bass Rock. Only ruins remain of the artillery station used to fight off Cromwell's ships in 1650 and the prison where several Covenanters, such as John Blackadder and Alexander Shields, were kept in solitary confinement. Shields remarkably managed to escape.

The Binns. This was the West Lothian home of the Dalzell family from 1612 including the ex-Russian army General Tam Dalzell, severe persecutor of Covenanters. It is now a National Trust property.

Blackness Castle. The late medieval rock-top royal castle on the Forth estuary was used as a prison for Covenanters. It was the base and ammunition dump for General Middleton.

Brunstane House, Edinburgh. This 16th-century tower was remodelled as town house of the Duke of Lauderdale.

Carnwath House. The home of the Dalzell Earls of Carnwath, including Robert from 1639. They were persecutors of Covenanters in 1680s and Jacobites in 1715.

Callendar House, Falkirk. This was the seat of the Livingstons, including the ex-mercenary General Livingston and ally of Montrose who became Earl of Callendar. The original castle was stormed by Cromwell in 1651 and forfeited in 1715.

Castle Cary. The surviving late medieval keep near Cumbernauld is still in private hands and was owned then by pro-Covenant General Baillie.

Castle Campbell at top of Dollar Glen. With a medieval keep and dramatic location above its gorge, it was the eastern home of the Earl of Argyll, close to his colleagues in Fife. For that reason it was besieged but not captured by Montrose in 1645, then was occupied by Cromwell in 1653 and burned by Monck in 1654.

Castle Craig Cumbernauld – minor remains of house of the Fleming family and scene of signing of Cumbernauld Bond by Montrose and Livingston, etc. It was burned down in 1746.

Dalkeith House. The old castle was incorporated into an 18th-century mansion but was the scene of two dramatic sieges in the Bishops' Wars as it was the main Royalist ammunition depot. It was sold to the Buccleughs in 1642.

Dalzell House. This was the home of Hamiltons, near Motherwell, who were driven out by General Tam Dalzell for harbouring Covenanters. In the grounds is a surviving Covenanters' Oak.

Direlton Castle. The 13th-century castle features in this period as the location for several notorious witch trials. It was later besieged by General Monck.

Dumbarton Castle. The rock-top castle was an important royal fortress and the probable location of the projected invasion of Scotland by Anglo-Irish troops in 1640. It was captured by the Covenanters when they waylaid the governor on his way home from church. It was surprisingly stormed by the Royalists in 1654.

Edinburgh
Edinburgh saw substantial building activity in the period leading up to the Civil wars, including the Parliament House complex, Moray House, the Greyfriars and Tron Churches, Lady Gray's house, Heriot's Hospital and the Tailors Hall. With a population about 25,000 crammed into a relatively small area, many now lived in tenement blocks up to seven storeys high. Not surprisingly there were plagues such as those of 1634 and 1645. In 1674 came a major improvement with the first proper supply of fresh running water and the first coffee house opened a year later. The provision of sewage down-pipes did not spread till 1760; waste was allowed to be ejected from upper windows after 10pm. There were also from 1660 regular stage coaches to London and Glasgow. Previously it took around 14 days on horseback.

Blackfriars Wynd. This was the site of attempted murder of Archbishop Sharp by Mitchel in 1668. **Warriston Close** records the house here of Lord Warriston.

Cowgate. It had the townhouse of Earls of Haddington.

Craighouse, Edinburgh. The altered 16th-century tower-house was once owned by the Edinburgh Lord Provost and extremely wealthy Sir William Dick who lost his entire fortune supporting the First and Second Bishops' Wars.

Edinburgh Castle. It was besieged for three months and captured by Covenanters in 1640, besieged again by Cromwell 1650, refurbished by Charles II and besieged and captured from Royalists in 1689. Cromwell staged a diplomatic banquet in the Great Hall. Argyll allegedly spent his last night before execution in the cell above the portcullis.

Granton Castle, outside Edinburgh. Little is left apart from gates and doocot, bought by Royalist lawyer Sir George 'Bluidy' Mackenzie, later Earl of Tarbat, later by Campbells in 1739.

Holyrood Palace. It was used by Charles I in 1633 during his coronation, later by Charles II and James II when Duke of York. The latter used the tennis court both for tennis and as a theatrical venue. It was rebuilt in its current quadrangular format in 1670–78 for Charles II by William Bruce.

Inch House. It is the surviving 17th-century mansion home of the Winram family.

Leith Walk. It was originally a pathway laid on top of the entrenchments dug to defend Edinburgh and Leith by General Leslie in 1648. In 2018, the bodies of many victims from the 1645 plague were discovered during road works.

Liberton House. This is a restored 17th-century tower associated with George Winram, negotiator of the first Breda treaty who was killed at Dunbar.

Liberton Tower. Now restored, it was involved in some of the Cromwell skirmishes.

Mary King's Close. Deep underneath the City Chambers and still open to the public, are the buried remains of parts of the old town, including this close that was possibly walled up during the 1645 plague. It is allegedly haunted by a young plague victim called Annie Blackfriars.

Merchiston Castle. Now part of Napier University, it was the home of the Napier family, two of whom were strong supporters of Montrose. Their ancestor's invention of logarithms was published in 1614.

Moray House. It was built in 1622 by the wealthy widow of Earl of Home and lender of large sums to the Covenanters in 1640. The house was later the scene of Argyll's heir Lord Lorn's wedding and the mocking of Montrose on his way to execution. It was used by Cromwell from 1650 to 1651.

Netherbow Port. It was rebuilt in 1606 and demolished 1764 but bits incorporated in other buildings.

Parliament House. Originally built in 1632 on the orders of Charles I to house the Scottish Parliament, the Privy Council and the Courts of Session, it was badly damaged by fire in 1700.

Potterrow. It was the site of Dear Sandy Hamilton's cannon factory.

Strichens Close. This is the site of the home of the lawyer Sir George 'Bluidy' Mackenzie.

Tailors' Hall. Built by the Tailors Guild, this was the scene of the pre-assembly meeting of 27 February 1638; it is now a hotel.

The Grassmarket. It was the scene of Covenanter executions where they were 'sent to glorify God'. A monument marks the spot.

Hamilton Palace. Built for the Dukes of Hamilton in the early 18th century on the site of Hamilton Castle but it is now totally demolished apart from Chatelherault hunting lodge designed by William Adam.

Linlithgow Palace. This fine but now roofless Renaissance Royal Palace was used in 1633 by Charles I and later his second son James when Duke of York in the 1680s, garrisoned by Cromwell, used again by Bonnie Prince Charlie in 1745 and the Duke of Cumberland a year later after which it was severely damaged by a fire accidentally caused by soldiers.

Menstrie Castle near Alloa. It was bought with his Swedish army earnings by the ex-mercenary Colonel James Holbourne; it was trashed by Montrose, against whom Holbourne fought, and who was eventually responsible for his capture.

Preston Tower. It was the family home of the Hamiltons of Preston including Sir Robert Hamilton, leader of the Covenanters at the Battle of Drumclog Moor and Bothwell Bridge. The tower was torched by Cromwell in 1650 and again in 1663, then abandoned. Now NTS.

Stirling Castle. It was almost the only remaining Scottish stronghold after the defeat at Dunbar in 1648 and was given additional fortifications by David Leslie. It had been used by Charles I in 1633 and was again by Charles II in 1650, was surrendered to General Monck in 1651 after the garrison had mutinied, then was manned by the Jacobites in both 1715 and 1745.

Tantallon Castle. This medieval stronghold of the Red Douglas Earls near North Berwick was sacked by the Covenanters in 1639 and badly damaged in 1651.

Tyninghame House near Dunbar. It incorporates the original castle bought by the new Earls of Haddington in 1628. The succeeding earl was killed in the huge ammunition explosion at Dunglass in 1640. His brother, General Sandy Hamilton, commanded the artillery at Marston Moor.

Fife and Kinross

The heavy concentration of large estates owned by Covenanter lairds in the 1640s including their two most experienced generals illustrates the importance of Fife in the first stages of The Wars of Three Kingdoms.

Airdrie House. It is still occupied, near Crail, and was the home of the Lumsdens including three brothers, all successful mercenary officers from the German wars.

Arnot Castle near Loch Leven. This was the home of ex-mercenary Covenanter general Charles Arnot.

Balcarres House, 3 miles inland from Elie. It still includes a restored medieval tower and was home of the Lindsay Earls of Balcarres, prominent during the wars of religion. Alexander of Balcarres married the ward of Leslie of Rothes, was a close friend of Richelieu's agent Moray and led his own regiment at Marston Moor. There was a large conventicle on the crag nearby in 1670.

Balgonie Castle. This large three-storey medieval courtyard castle by the River Leven was bought in 1635 by Alexander Leslie, field marshal in the Swedish army, later made Earl of Leven, commander of the Scottish armies during two Bishops' Wars and for the 1643 invasion of England, then commander-in-chief of the Parliamentary armies at Marston Moor. He was captured after Worcester in 1651, spent time as a prisoner in the Tower of London and died here in 1661. The castle was ransacked by Rob Roy Macgregor in 1716.

Ballinbreich Castle, near Newburgh. It was a medieval courtyard castle built for the Leslies of Rothes.

Balmerino Abbey. It was badly damaged by the Earl of Argyll in 1559 and again by angry Protestants before being handed over to James Elphinstone in 1605 when he was James VI & I's secretary of State in Scotland. The 2nd Earl of Balmerino was a prominent supporter of the Covenant and joint chief promoter of the Fife Conspiracy, but the abbey remained half-ruinous and he had other homes including Barnton Tower outside Edinburgh. He had arguments with the king over the revenue of the former abbey lands, as he did also with regard to the former monastery at Lindores, a problem he shared with the Earl of Rothes. His son was at Marston Moor.

Balwhinnie. It was the home of one of the Lumsden brothers.

Burleigh Castle, near Kinross. This was home of Lord Robert Balfour (born Arnot) the prominent supporter of the Covenant who was chosen president of the Scottish Estates in 1640 and helped negotiate the Treaty of Ripon. He was less successful as a general as he was twice involved in defeats by Montrose, but he remained highly respected, even by Cromwell.

Dunfermline Palace. It was given by James VI as a wedding present to his new wife Ann of Denmark and was the birthplace of their second son, the future Charles I, in 1600, who visited it again briefly in 1633. Charles II also visited briefly before the Battle of Inverkeithing in 1650.

Earlshall. A 16th-century castle near Leuchars, it was the home of Sir Andrew 'Bloody' Bruce whose father fought at Worcester and who himself was one of more brutal generals during the Killing Times. It was he with his men who killed Richard Cameron at Airds Moss and brought his dismembered body back to Edinburgh for display. The castle is still inhabited and reputedly still haunted by Sir Andrew.

Fordell. This castle north of Inverkeithing was associated with another of the Fife ex-mercenaries Sir John Browne, victor at The Battle of Carlisle Sands, but loser at Inverkeithing, where he was captured by Cromwell's troops.

Innergellie House, by Kilrenny. It replaced an older castle associated from 1642 with General Sir James Lumsden the ex-mercenary who fought at Dunbar and other battles.

Kinloch. This was the home of John Balfour of Kinloch, one of the Sharp murder team.

Kinnaird House, near Newburgh. It was the home from 1630 of Sir James Balfour, made a baron of Nova Scotia by Charles I, author of the *Annales of Scotland* and probably also part-author of the Covenanter propaganda ballad *Stoneyfield Day* about Jenny Geddes.

Kirkforthar House. Ruins remain of parts of the former house and castle of the Lindsays at Markinch, who were strong supporters of the Fife Conspiracy in 1637.

Leslie House or Palace, near Glenrothes. It was the large stately home of Leslie Earls, briefly later Dukes of Rothes, designed by William Bruce with gardens by Adam with minimal remains of earlier castle; suffered severe fire in 2005. John Leslie was the prime mover in the Fife Conspiracy and his castle here was just 3 miles from that of Alexander Leslie, the chief organiser of the wars, whose son married Rothes' daughter. John was also the guardian of Anna Mackenzie who married

Lindsay of Balcarres, the third most supportive of the Fife grandees in 1638.

Lindores Castle. Nothing remains of the castle owned by the Leslies of Rothes and possible birthplace of General David Leslie if it was not at Pitcairlie. The defunct Abbey of Lindores was a controversial part of the estates of both the Leslie and Balmerino families.

Lordscairnie Castle, near Cupar and originally on an island. This now-ruined four-storey keep was a major base of the Lindsay Earls of Crawford.

Mountquhanie Castle. This ruined 16th-century tower, near Cupar, was owned by Robert Lumsden, who was killed when governor of Dundee when it was stormed by Monck.

Mugdrum Island, Lindores Loch. It was bought by Colonel Ludovic Leslie, ex-mercenary brother of General David Leslie, and himself in charge of supplies as Marston Moor.

Newark Castle. This now-ruined clifftop castle on the Fife coast by St Monans, was bought in 1649 by General David Leslie, who became Earl of Newark.

Noughton Castle. There are minimal remains near Balmerino, home of Peter Hay, one of those who aided the intellectual justification and propaganda for the Covenant wars.

Pitcairlie House, near Auchtermuchty. It is on the site of the ancestral home of David Leslie's branch of the family and an important point of contact for the Fife conspirators. Still occupied.

Pitcruvie Castle. A now-ruined keep, near Lower Largo, was owned by the Lindsay Earls of Crawford.

Pitcullo Castle. The restored tower near Leuchars, was the home of the mercenary general Sir William Balfour who, after a career in the Dutch army, fought for the king at La Rochelle, was made governor of the Tower of London but then became a successful general of cavalry in the Parliamentarian army. His strong Presbyterianism may be linked to the fact that Alexander Henderson was the minister at Leuchars. The castle is still occupied.

Pitlochie Castle, near Auchtermuchty. It was the now-vanished home of George Scott of Pitlochie (d. 1685) a keen Covenanter who was imprisoned on the Bass Rock and at Dunnottar. He was also questioned about his neighbour, Balfour of Kinloch, with regard to the murder of Archbishop Sharp. He wrote the *Model of Government* for the proposed settlement of East New Jersey and was granted 500 acres there but both he and his wife died whilst crossing the Atlantic in 1685 on the *Henry and Francis*. His father Sir John Scott (1587–1670) of Scotstarvit Tower near Cupar was a St Andrews trained lawyer who signed the Covenant at Ceres in 1638 and served on the war committees from 1640-1649 but suffered great losses under Cromwell. The tower is well preserved and open to public.

Pitscottie. It was the family home, near Ceres, of later major general Colin Pitscottie, a trusted commander at all the main battles

Rathillet House, north of Cupar. It is a more recent mansion sitting on the site of the castle of David Hackston of Rathillet, an extreme Covenanter who was in the group that murdered Archbishop Sharp in 1679. He fought at Bothwell Bridge, was captured and had his hands cut off before being executed.

Rennyhill House. This was the home of youngest of three Lumsden mercenaries, William, near Anstruther.

Rossie Castle. This was the home, near Ladybank, of James Scott, ex-mercenary in Venetian army who helped lead Covenanters at Tippermuir and other battles, handed over castle to son-in-law and fellow ex-mercenary Browne of Fordel.

Struthers Castle, near Cupar. Itis a now ruined 16th-century L-plan tower-house, which was the main base for Lindsay of the Byres, later both Earl of Lindsay and of Crawford, who played a significant role in the Covenanting wars including fighting at Marston Moor. Charles II stayed here in 1651. The family churches were at Ceres and Markinch.

Wormiston House, near Crail. It is a surviving tower-house, which from the 1620s was the base for the Earls of Crawford who played an erratic role in the civil wars and famously installed the future Archbishop James Sharp as their minister in Crail Church in 1648. Before that it was the base of the remarkable Sir James Spens who pioneered the recruitment of young Fife men to join the Danish and Swedish armies.

Perth and North East
Airlie Castle. It was the main seat of the Ogilvys, supporters of Montrose and bitter enemies of the Campbells who infamously trashed it in 1640 allegedly with the pregnant mistress of the house looking down on the attackers whilst her husband was away. Later rebuilt.

Auchindoun Castle. This ruined Gordon tower, 2 miles from Dufftown, was captured by Covenanters in 1640.

Ballindalloch Castle. A large restored castle near Aberlour, was the home of Grants, sacked by Gordons in 1640 and burned by Montrose in 1645.

Balvenie Castle, near Dufftown. It was used as a base by Montrose in 1645. Nearby is the site of a major battle, won by Leslie against Royalists in 1649 when he took 900 prisoners.

Balfuig Castle, near Alford. The 16th-century tower of the Forbes family, which was torched by Montrose.

Bamff House. A tower near Alyth, it belonged to Gilbert Ramsay, who was made a baronet for helping defeat of Covenanters at Rullion Green, not exactly a difficult task.

Banff Castle. Only the outer walls survive of the 12th-century home of the Sharps and the birthplace of Archbishop Sharp.

Beldorney Castle, near Keith. Now restored, it was Gordon property that was trashed by Jacobites.

Blair Castle. From 1629 belonged to Murrays of Tullibardine and was scene at the Tuidhe of Montrose raising his standard in 1644. It was captured and partly destroyed by Cromwell's forces in 1652, then used as a base by Bonnie Dundee before Killiecrankie in 1689. He was buried in the now ruined church.

Bog of Gight or Gordon Castle. The original castle of the Gordons, near Fochabers, it was badly damaged by Montrose in 1645 and was the place where his eldest son, aged sixteen, died of a fever; he was buried in Bellie Kirk, now ruinous, nearby.

Brodie Castle, near Elgin. It was owned by Covenanting family of Brodies so was torched by the episcopalian or Catholic Gordons in 1645.

Callander Castle, by River Teith. Just a few fragments are left of the tower-house of the Livingstons.

Cardross House. The still-occupied 16th-century tower, near Lake of Mentieth, was used by Cromwell, and was the home of a Covenanting family, the half-Royalist David Erskine, who fought for Charles I at Preston. His heir, Henry, who was imprisoned as a Covenanter, later fought with the Cameronians at Dunkeld and Henry's half-brother John, known as the Black Colonel, landed at Torbay with William of Orange.

Castle Fraser. A huge, well-preserved Z-plan tower-house from the 1630s, belonging to the Frasers who, unlike most other families in this area, were pro-Covenant, so their lands were ravaged, in 1638 by the Gordons, and in 1644 by Montrose. Later they became Jacobites.

Corgarff Castle, near Ballater. Held by Erskine Earls of Mar, including the leader of the 1715 rebellion, it was burned by Jacobites 1689 and by Wade's men in 1715, was used by Jacobites in 1745, and also used as a base by Montrose in 1645.

Drummond Castle, south of Crieff. This remodelled 15th-century keep was home to the Drummonds who played a major but at times ambivalent role in the Montrose campaigns but then emerged as prominent Royalists after the Restoration. It had been damaged by Cromwell in 1650. The Drummond brothers, the Earls of Perth and Melfort, were to dominate Scotland with Lauderdale in the late Stuart period.

Drum Castle. Alexander Irvine, the 10th Laird, was an ardent Royalist who was excommunicated by the Church of Scotland. In his absence, his wife surrendered the castle to General Monro, who had significant artillery. It received a Covenanter garrison and the estates were severely damaged several times during the Montrose campaigns in which Irvine's two sons also fought. Later the castle was captured again by the Campbells and severely damaged. It has now been restored by the National Trust.

Claypotts Castle. An impressive Z-plan tower-house, 3 miles east of Dundee, it belonged to the Grahams of Claverhouse. Nothing remains of Claverhouse Castle, 3 miles north of Dundee.

Delgatie Castle. This restored medieval tower near Forres was owned by Sir William Hay, who supported Montrose and was captured at Philiphaugh and executed in 1650.

Dudhope Castle, Dundee. It was the home of Scrimgeour family including Viscount Dudhope, a Royalist who was killed at Marston Moor fighting for Charles I. It was bought by Claverhouse in 1668 for £6,000 and became his family home, entitling him to be sheriff of Dundee, which he later took as his title.

Duffus Castle, near Elgin. This fine medieval motte-and-bailey castle was captured by Montrose in 1645 and was briefly used as a base by Claverhouse.

Dunkeld House, by the River Tay. It was the home of Murray Earls of Atholl so was blown up by Cromwell in 1653. Then it was rebuilt and restored as part of a hotel.

Dunnottar Castle. Now a substantial ruin, the 12th-century courtyard castle on the clifftops south of Stonehaven was one of the strongest fortresses in Scotland. Montrose failed to storm it in 1645, as did Lambert in 1652. It was used as a place of safety by Presbyterian ministers and as a prison for 167 male and female Covenanters, many of whom were tortured and nine of whom died; eight are buried in Dunnottar Church. Another seventy died whilst being transported to Barbados. Charles II was entertained here in 1650 and, a year later, the Scottish Crown Jewels were brought here for safety

Esselmont Castle, near Ellon. This now-ruined tower was owned by the Hays from 1623, and was where the local Covenanters were besieged in 1646 with 36 deaths.

Glamis Castle. It was the home of the Lyon family. John Lyon, Earl of Kinghorn was a Covenant supporter and close friend of Montrose till the latter changed sides. He raised a local regiment for Marston Moor.

Glencairn or Abergairn. The ruins of a tower-house near Ballater was where a Covenanter force under Colonel Herries had a skirmish with Macphersons of Cluny during Montrose campaign.

Haddo House, north west of Ellon. A fine mansion was built on the site of Haddo Castle, which was besieged in 1644 as Sir John Gordon Haddo had aided Montrose. He was imprisoned in the tiny dungeon under St Giles Cathedral, which became known as Haddo's Hole.

Hatton Castle, Coupar Angus. This ruined 16th-century tower was garrisoned by Crawford Covenanters in 1645 but captured by Montrose.

Huntly or **Strathbogie Castle.** A magnificent semi-ruined castle, it was the main seat of the Royalist Gordons. The Marquis of Huntly was an intermittently active Royalist who was eventually hanged. The castle was captured three times, in 1640 by the Covenanters, in 1644 by Montrose and in 1647 by General Leslie, whose men slaughtered the garrison after a long siege. The Duke of Gordon surrendered Edinburgh Castle in 1689.

Inchbrakie Castle, near Crieff. A ruined former home of Montrose's friend and cousin, it was destroyed by Cromwell's troops in 1651.

Inverquharity Castle, near Kirriemuir. The medieval keep of the Ogilvys, it was the home of Alexander Ogilvy who was captured fighting for Montrose at Philiphaugh and executed. It is till occupied.

Kincardine Castle, near Gleneagles. There are scant remains of 14th-century castle, which was the main home of the Marquis of Montrose and was trashed by the Campbells in 1646.

Old Montrose Castle, 3 miles west of Montrose. Nothing remains of the ancient seat of the Grahams and birthplace of the Marquis of Montrose.

Pitcaple Castle, near Inverurie. It is still occupied and was the home of one of the Leslies killed at Worcester.

Pitfichie Castle, near Monymusk. It was the home of Urie or Hurry family, which produced the serial traitor Sir John Hurry and his brother William, both ex-mercenaries; it has now been privately restored.

Rothes Castle, near Aberlour. The original 13th-century seat of the Leslie Earls of Rothes was trashed by Montrose and demolished 1660.

Towie Barclay. This restored tower-house was the scene of the skirmish between Covenanters and episopalian Royalists during the First Bishops' War 1639.

South East Scotland
Blanerne Castle, near Duns. There are minimal remains of the ancestral home of the Lumsdens who produced several successful mercenaries. *See* also Airdrie in Fife.

Buckholm Tower, by Galashiels. A ruined 16th-century tower of the Pringles, particularly the Pringle who became the ruthless hunter of Covenanters during the Killing Times and allegedly still haunts the ruins.

Broxmouth House, near Dunbar. A replacement mansion, the original was used as HQ by Cromwell for the Battle of Dunbar.

Byres Castle, near Haddington. A ruined keep, owned by John Earl of Lindsay from 1633; he fought for Covenant at Marston Moor.

Cavers House/Castle, near Hawick. The huge ruined five-storey tower was home of the Douglas of Cavers family who, unlike the rest of the Douglases, were strong Covenanters. William Douglas of Cavers having been a prominent negotiator during the English Civil War; seven of his sister's sons were killed at Auldearn fighting against Montrose.

His wife, known as 'the good Lady Cavers', was imprisoned in Stirling Castle in 1682 for obstinate opposition to episcopacy.

Douglas Castle. Douglas village itself turned out to be a Covenanting hotbed and whilst its masters were away, the Covenanters took over the castle. Now only one tower of its later rebuilding survives. Not surprisingly, the Douglas earl and his family became active supporters of Montrose, though embarrassingly he was captured just before the Battle of Kilsyth. Nearby is the monument to the founding of the Cameronian Regiment, which fought at Dunkeld in 1689. Its first official commander, the young Earl of Angus, was killed with his men at Steinkirk.

Drumlanrig Castle. It was the home of the most politically active branch of the Douglas dynasties, including James Douglas (later known as the Union Duke) and his brother who became persecutors of the Covenanters, several times executing prisoners out of hand. It was occupied by Cromwell's troops in 1650. From 1675 it was being almost totally rebuilt as the stately home for William Douglas, 3rd Earl Queensberry, and later Duke.

Drumlanrig Tower, Hawick. The much-altered tower belonged to the Royalist Douglases; it was stormed by the Covenanters.

Dunglass Castle, near Cockburnspath. Only the church survives as the castle was blown up in 1640 by an English soldier, thus killing most of its Covenanter garrison, including it's commander, the Earl of Haddington, and two of his brothers.

Lethington/Lennoxlove. It was the birthplace of John Maitland, future Duke of Lauderdale. His mother was a Seton from Fife so he was a regular visitor to Balcarres during the First Fife Conspiracy.

Newark Castle. The ruined five-storey keep on the Tweed, was the scene of the massacre of a considerable number of Royalist survivors after the Battle of Philiphaugh. Numerous skeletons have been dug up in the field known as Dead Men's Lea.

Polwarth Castle, near Duns. Only the site remains of the home of Patrick Hume who fell foul of James II and hid in his own family's burial vault, with scraps of food brought by his daughter Grizel till he managed to escape to Holland, where he became a key negotiator with William of Orange.

Thirlestane Castle. The ancestral home of John Maitland, later Duke of Lauderdale, it is a superb Palladian mansion designed by William Bruce.

Traquair House, near Peebles. It was the home of the Stewart Earls of Traquair, one of them a major negotiator for Charles I during the Bishops' Wars. Montrose rested here after his defeat at Philiphaugh. Bonnie Prince Charlie also visited.

Yester House. This is an Adam mansion, built in 1699 by the Hay Marquises of Tweeddale, replacing Yester Castle near Gifford.

Argyll and North West
Ardvreck Castle, by Loch Assynt. The now-ruined keep belonged to the Macleods, it was where Montrose sought shelter after losing Battle of Carbisdale; he was betrayed by its owner to the Covenanters in 1650. It was trashed by the Mackenzies in 1672.

Asgog Castle, near Tighnabruaich in Cowal. This ruined 15th-century tower was the scene, after a long siege, of the massacre of about 200 Royalist Lamonts, men women and children, by the Covenanting Campbells in 1646, despite a promise of clemency offered in return for surrender.

Auchinbreck Castle, near Loch Riddon. Only the site remains of the original castle of Duncan Campbell of Auchinbreck, the villain of Rathlin, who was killed at Inverlochy. He also owned Castle Sween and Carnasserie.

Brodick Castle, Isle of Arran. The property of Dukes of Hamilton/ Earls of Arran strategically sited on Firth of Clyde, it was captured by the Campbells in 1639 to pre-empt any landing of troops from Ireland and was later occupied by Cromwell's troops. Now National Trust.

Carnasserie Castle, near Lochgilphead. Now impressive ruins, it was held by Campbell of Auchinbreck and used as an armoury during

Argyll's campaign of 1685 against James II. It was blown up to avoid falling into hands of enemy but is still impressive.

Carrick Castle, on Loch Goil. It is the Campbell tower that was torched in 1685 to avoid its ammunition store being captured by government troops after the Earl of Argyll's rebellion was put down.

Castle Loch Heylipol, on Tiree. Little remains of the Macdonald/Maclean stronghold stormed by Campbells in 1678.

Castle Sween, on Loch Sween. Scotland's oldest surviving 11th-century castle had been granted to Campbell of Auchinbreck, who acted as Argyll's general in the Rathlin and Inverlochy campaigns, and was executed after losing the latter. It was torched by MacColla on his way back to Ireland in 1647.

Duart Castle, Mull. It was the home of Red Hector Maclean, killed along with many of his clan in the Battle of Inverkeithing against Cromwell's troops under Lambert.

Dunaverty Castle, on the cliff near Mull of Kintyre. Minimal ruins remain; it was famous for sheltering Robert the Bruce before his escape to Ireland, and for the massacre here in 1647 of about 300 Macdougals and Macdonalds after they were forced to surrender due to lack of water; they were promised quarter by General David Leslie, but this was overruled by the clergyman John Nevoy of Loudoun, hence the name Blood Rock. The castle was dismantled along with several others after the failure of Argyll's rebellion in 1685.

Dunstaffnage Castle, north of Oban. It was besieged by David Leslie and between 100 and 500 Macdougall survivors from the Montrose campaign were allegedly killed. It was blown up in 1685 by its owner the Earl of Argyll to prevent its stores falling into government hands. Nearby Dunolly Castle was also sacked.

Dunyvaig Castle, on south coast of Islay. It belonged to the Macdonalds including briefly Kolkitto, who made his last stand here, before being captured and executed.

Gylen Castle, on the island of Kerrera. This picturesque ruin was another Macdougall Royalist outpost besieged by David Leslie in 1647; the Covenanters were unlikely to have spared the garrison.

Inveraray Castle. The original castle was part trashed by Montrose in 1645 but remained the main powerbase of the Marquis of Argyll, though trashed again by the Macdonalds in 1685. It was replaced by new ducal residence from 1744. There is a monument in the garden for 17 Campbell adherents, hanged in 1681, including Colin Campbell and a Major Campbell.

Invergarry Castle, west of Fort William by Loch Oich. It had fortifications improved by Macdonalds of Glengarry in their support for James II in 1688; it is now dangerously ruinous.

Inverlochy Castle. It was the scene of the heavy defeat of the Campbells under Auchinbreck by Montrose and the Macdonalds in February 1645. Nearby, at Fort William Station, are the ruins of the original Fort William founded by General Monck in the 1650s as part of a defensive line of forts and given its name when reconstructed by General Hugh Mackay in 1690.

Loch Gorm, in western Islay. This tiny island castle was the site of one of the Irish Macdonalds last stands, along with Dunyvaig.

Scourie House, on the north west coast near Handa. This remote location was the birth place of General Hugh Mackay, the successful mercenary general who fought for William of Orange but suffered defeat by Dundee at Killiecrankie and was killed at Steinkirk in 1692.

Toward Castle, on the southern tip of Cowal. The ruined 15th-century keep belonged to the Royalist Lamonts who were massacred here, or executed at Dunoon, by the Campbells in 1646. The castle was ransacked but a large hoard of silver coins survived till it was discovered in 1821.

Ayrshire and South West
Auchans Castle, near Troon. A ruined tower, it had been the home of Colonel James Wallace, leader of the Pentland Rising, who was at the Battle of Rullion Green in 1666. He died in exile.

Barmagachan, near Kirkcudbright. It was the home of Robert Maclellan, keen Covenanter, who was banished to America after Rullion Green.

Barscobe Castle. The 17th century castle, now restored, was the home of John Maclellan of Barscobe, a prominent Covenanter involved in the capture of General Turner and who was at the subsequent Battle of Rullion Green in 1666. There are several conventicle sites nearby.

Bonshaw Tower, near Annan. This still-occupied tower was owned by Irvine of Bonshaw, persecutor of Covenanters.

Caerlaverock Castle, on Solway coast. This major fortress at a possible landing place for the expected Irish invasion in 1640 was stormed by Covenanters after a 13-week siege, then partly demolished.

Caldwell Tower, near Neilston. It was the home of William Mure or Muir, an active Covenanter who fought at Bothwell Bridge, was a prisoner in Greyfriars and, as some accounts suggest, survived shipwreck off Orkney when the convict ship *Crown of London* sank on its way to the colonies.

Carmichael House, near Lanark. It was built on site of the 14th-century home of Carmichaels, who fought for the Covenant at Marston Moor and against Montrose at Philiphaugh.

Cassilis House, 3 miles from Maybole. Now privately restored, it includes a 14th-century tower and was the home of the Kennedy family, Earls of Cassilis, particularly John, the 6th Earl, who played a prominent part in the Civil Wars and whose chaplain was the Fife minister George Gillespie The family seat was later replaced by the more modern Culzean Castle.

Castle Kennedy, near Stranraer. The now-ruined tower-house was rebuilt by the Earl of Cassilis in 1607, but the family lost money during Civil Wars; they paid for a regiment at Marston Moor, so it was sold to the Dalrymples who rose to power after 1688. It was burned down in 1716.

Cessnock Castle. This impressive castle above a ravine is still occupied and was the former home of Sir Hugh Campbell, one of planners of a Carolina colony with religious freedom; he was punished for allegedly allowing Covenanter activity on his estates despite not being a Covenanter himself. He had also been linked to the Rye House Plot against Charles II.

Corsock Castle, near Castle Douglas. This is the ruined home of the Covenanter Robert Neilson, who was hung, drawn and quartered after Rullion Green. His monument is in Kirkpatrick-Durham kirkyard.

Dundonald Castle, north of Troon. This substantial ruined castle, the former important seat of royal Stewarts with its 13th-century keep, later became the home of the Royalist Sir William Cochrane, who was made Earl of Dundonald in 1669.

Earlstoun Castle, near Dalry. Now privately owned, the 16th-century tower-house was the home of the Covenanting family of Gordons, who were badly persecuted. William Gordon was shot at Bothwell Bridge.

Eglinton Castle. These are the ruins of a more modern castle which replaced the former home of Montgomery Earls of Eglinton, long term enemies of the Cunninghams of Glencairn. Montgomery featured with Cochrane in the messy Jacobite plot of 1694.

Johnstone Castle. Surviving though remodelled, the 16th-century L-plan castle was occupied by the Cochrane family, including Sir John of Ochiltree, supporter of Argyll in 1685 till defeated at Muirdykes nearby.

Kilmaurs Place, 2 miles north of Kilmarnock. Built in 1620, it is the now-altered former home of the Cunninghams, Earls of Glencairn, prominent Royalists despite Ayrshire being mainly Covenanter territory.

Kirkcudbright Tolbooth. It was used as a prison for Covenanters but a number were released when it was stormed by their friends in 1684.

Loudoun Castle. The original castle, later incorporated in a major mansion, was the home of John Campbell, Earl of Loudoun, prime mover in the original Covenant campaign and close associate of the Fife Conspiracy, imprisoned in the Tower of London, chief negotiator for the Solemn League. He fought at Marston Moor and became Chancellor of Scotland till the Restoration. It is now in a theme park.

Ochiltree Castle. Now almost vanished, it was bought by the Cochrane Earls of Dundonald and was the scene of the marriage of General John Graham of Claverhouse, later Viscount 'Bonnie' Dundee.

Newmilns Tower. The ruined tower-house was a former home of the Campbells of Loudoun that was then used as a prison for Covenanters in the 1670s. It was the scene of a famous raid by 60 Covenanters who overcame the guards and freed all the prisoners in 1684, with the loss of only one man. Their leader was John Low or Law, whose gravestone is in embedded in the walls.

Skelmorlie Castle, on a cliff overlooking the Firth of Clyde south of Greenock. A still-occupied 14th-century tower-house, it was the home of the somewhat unstable Sir Robert Montgomery, instigator of the Montgomery Plot in 1694.

Strathaven Castle. It was used as a prison for Covenanters; two were shot here. It was also the base for Colonel Graham of Claverhouse during some of his campaigns. Strathaven has its Trumpeter's Well at Hillhead Farm, commemorating the death of Claverhouse's trumpeter at Drumclog.

The Lee, 2 miles from Lanark. A large surviving mansion, it was home of the Royalist turned Republican Lockhart, who was one of only two Scots on Cromwell's council governing Scotland till 1658. His descendant George Lockhart was an ardent Jacobite.

Fortifications
Aberdeen. There are only tiny fragments left of the citadel built by Cromwell.

Ayr. It is a hexagonal fort or citadel built 1652–3 but largely dismantled in 1660. Cromwell used the St John the Baptist Tower as a lookout post.

Duns Law. Surviving vestiges of Alexander Leslie's entrenchments of 1639 can still be seen on Duns Law. There is a Covenanters' Stone here.

Fort William. Only minor ruins survive of the fortress begun by Monck on orders from Cromwell in the 1650s and then rebuilt as Fort William by General Hugh Mackay in 1690.

Inverness. The so-called Oliver's Fort was built by Monck in 1652, using stone from local churches, including Fortrose, as a star-shaped fort capable of holding a garrison of 1,000 men and part of the Fort William system. It was demolished in 1660 and the site has now been built over but is remembered in the local name Citadel.

Leith, Edinburgh. The pentagonal Citadel was built for Cromwell but partly demolished in 1660. Leith Walk runs along the site of earlier earthworks built by General Leslie against Cromwell.

Stirling. Stirling's defences were extended by David Leslie after the Battle of Dunbar with earthworks to Torwood.

Battlefields
Aberdeen. The battle between Montrose for the Royalists against Burleigh and Lewis Gordon for the Covenanters on 14 September 1646 took place in what is now Aberdeen Retail Park.

Airds Moss, near the River Ayr. The site of this battle, on rough moorland by the road approaching Muirkirk from Cumnock, is marked by the tombstone of the Covenanting preacher Richard Cameron (Cameron's Stone), who died here on 22 July 1680. There is also a cairn at the Muirkirk lay-by. Also nearby was Priesthill where John Brown was shot in 1684. Hackston of Rathillet was captured at Airds Moss and allegedly tortured before being executed.

Alford. The precise location of this battle by the River Don is disputed amongst Montgarrie Ford to the north of the village, Gallows Hill and Boat of Forbes. Montrose's Royalists heavily defeated Baillie whose judgment was overruled by committee. The Gordon Stone survives.

Auldearn. The surviving motte was used as a vantage point by Montrose in his victory over Sir John Hurry and the battle area has a sign and car park. The church has a Covenanter memorial.

Bothwell Bridge. The old narrow bridge over the Clyde where the battle took place has been superseded by a wider carriage-way but there is a memorial for the battle in which General Tam Dalzell and Graham of Claverhouse heavily defeated the Covenanters in June 1679 after which many prisoners were force-marched to Edinburgh and kept in harsh conditions in Greyfriars Churchyard before being transported to the colonies.

Bridge of Dee. A skirmish atook place here against the Royalist Gordons outside Aberdeen while Montrose was still fighting for the Covenant in 1640.

Cadzow Burn-Hieton, by Hamilton. It was the site of a skirmish between Cromwell's troops and hard-line Covenanters under Strachan in 1650. A plaque is on Cadzow Bridge.

Carbisdale, by the River Shin – it was the site of the last battle of Montrose when he was easily defeated in April 1650 by Covenanter troops under Colonels Strachan and Monro.

Cromdale, by the Spey. It is where the Jacobites under Buchan and Cameron were heavily defeated by the pro-Orange forces under Livingston on 30 April 1690.

Drumclog. A monument marks the approximate site of this remarkable victory of the Covenanters against the government dragoons under Claverhouse in June 1679 near Loudoun Hill. The Drumclog Memorial Kirk is of later date. William Dingwall, one of the group which had murdered Archbishop Sharp, was killed here and allegedly had a vision of Paradise as he lay dying of his wounds.

Drummond, near Evanton. The site of a skirmish between the Earl of Glencairn's Royalists and Monck's troops in 1653.

Dunbar. In September 1650 a large Scottish army under David Leslie, fighting on behalf of Charles II and the Royalist/Covenanters, was heavily defeated by Oliver Cromwell, despite his reduced numbers. The unexpected disaster was blamed on the interference with Leslie's plans by the Estates Committee and its clerical members who ordered Leslie to take his troops downhill from a safe position to confront Cromwell near the shore. The site is south of Doon Hill and the road over the Brox Burn. Cromwell used Broxburn House as HQ. The site has been marred by more recent quarrying.

Dunkeld. The town saw an epic battle between the Cameronians under William Clelland and a much larger Jacobite force shortly after the Jacobite success at Killiecrankie in 1689. Clelland was killed but he and his troops had effectively ended the Jacobites' hopes for success.

Inverkeithing/Pitreavie. Cromwell's aid Lambert attacked the Covenanter/Royalists under Sir John Browne of Fordell here and inflicted a major defeat where many of the Maclean clan were killed making a last stand and Browne was taken prisoner. There is a monument to the fallen.

Inverlochy, near what was later called Fort William. This was the site of a bitter battle between the largely Macdonald force under Montrose and a largely Campbell one under Duncan Campbell of Auchinbreck as the Marquis was apparently recovering from a fall. Montrose's force surprised the Campbell Covenanters by a remarkable forced march through snowbound passes. Duncan of Auchinbreck was killed or executed at the end of the battle and more than 1,000 Campbells were killed.

Killiecrankie. It has a visitor centre on the site of Bonnie Dundee's death and his impressive but costly victory over General Hugh Mackay and the Scottish government troops supporting William of Orange in 1689. Nearby is the Soldier's Leap over the River Garry.

Kilsyth. The site of a crushing defeat of Covenanting army under General Baillie by Montrose and MacColla in 1645, it is partly covered by the man-made Banton Loch but also Auchinrivoch Farm, Baggage Knowe, Slaughter Knowe and Bullet Knowe. There is a monument on the banks of Banton Loch, a reservoir built on the battle-site, to feed the Forth and Clyde Canal.

Lagganmore, in Argyll. This was the scene of the so-called Barn of Bones Massacre of locals by the departing Irish troops of MacColla in 1647. The Campbells had reportedly been herded into a barn, which was then set on fire.

Lochgarry. Monck's troops under Morgan defeated the remains of the Glencairn rebellion in 1653.

Mauchline Moor. This was the site of a small battle between two branches of Covenanters, Engagers and Kirk party in 12 June 1648.

Muirdykes and Muirmont, above Howwood in Refrewhire. This was the site of final defeat of the surviving troops from Earl of Argyll's invasion of Scotland against James II in 1685. The Earl had already been captured, as was the commander Cochrane of Ochiltree, after the battle.

Philiphaugh. The site of disastrous defeat of Montrose's depleted army near Galashiels and Harehead Wood was here. There is a 20-foot high cairn for Covenanter casualties, which were far fewer than the Royalists.

Rhunaharoine. The site in mid-Kintyre of MacColla and his Irish troops making a penultimate stand against Leslie as they retreated down Kintyre towards Dunaverty looking for ships to take them to Ireland or Islay.

Rullion Green, in the Pentland Hills south of Edinburgh. This is where Colonel Wallace and a group of extreme Covenanters were heavily defeated by Tam Dalzell, on 28 November 1666. A monument marks the site.

Stoneyhill. It was the site of serious skirmish by Scots under Montgomery against Cromwell's troops near Musselburgh prior to Dunbar in 1650.

Tippermuir, 3 miles south of Perth. This is where Montrose achieved his first major victory on 1 Sept 1644 against a much larger Covenanter army under Lord Elcho. Some 300 Covenanters were buried in the churchyard.

Other Monuments

Auchengilloch. A monument to Covenanters is on a remote site of conventicles south of Strathaven near Lesmahagow.

Carluke. It has the grave of the Covenanter minister Peter Kid who was imprisoned on the Bass Rock.

Clachan of Campsie. The churchyard has the Martyr's Stone of William Boick, killed in 1673; the grave was supposedly tended by Richard Paterson, the model for Walter Scott's 'Old Mortality'.

Covington. It has a monument for Donald Cargill.

Cumnock. Near the scene of a conventicle held 1,200 feet up on Carsphairn 1685, Duns and Paterson were executed. There is a new Cumnock monument to George Carson and John Hair, the Waistland Martyrs, shot on Knipes 1685 here; also Martyr's Moss and John Maclellan of Barscobe.

Dalry, in Dumfries. It has a monument for the start of the Pentland Rising, site of conventicles, and where Robert Stewart was accused of murdering the curate of Carsphairn, as a result, three women drowned tied to stakes in Solway. There are memorials to Captain John Paterson, executed 1684; Richard Cameron, killed at Airds Moss; and John Brown, shot by Claverhouse.

Douglas. The monument near Douglas Castle marks site of the raising of the Cameronian Regiment by the young Earl of Angus in 1689. The village also has a cairn to James Gavin, a Covenanter who had his ears cropped on the orders of Graham of Claverhouse and was then transported to Barbados, but survived to return. Nearby was supposedly a cave used by Covenanters to evade capture.

Garmouth. A plaque on a cottage recalls the place where Charles II signed the Solemn League and Covenant after landing from Holland in June 1650 at the mouth of the Spey.

Irvine. It has a surviving gunpowder store built on royal orders just before the start of the Civil Wars.

Loch Trool. A monument by Caldons Farm to six Covenanters surprised at prayer in 1685 and shot by Cornet Douglas, the future Duke of Queensberry is here.

Inchinnan. A plaque beside St Conval's Stone commemorates the arrest here of the Earl of Argyll in 1685.

Kincardine. In the nearby Devilla Forest is the gravestone of two children who died of the plague in 1646. Many towns in Scotland lost about thirty per cent of their populations during the plague years 1640–49.

Kirkintilloch. There is a Martyrs' Monument on the Kilsyth road commemorating James Smith and John Wharry who were both executed for supporting the Covenant.

Kirkwall, Orkney. Here and at Scarva Taing are monuments for the 211 Covenanter prisoners drowned when the *Crown of London* sank off Mull Head by Deerness, east of Kirkwall, en route from Leith to the West Indies or Boston. The captain had locked the prisoners below deck.

Magus Muir. A monument marks site of the murder of Archbishop Sharp outside St Andrews in 1679. Ironically, close by is the tomb of some of the innocent local Covenanters who were hanged to avenge the murder.

New Cumnock. Carsgailoch Hill was the site of the murder of three Covenanter martyrs.

St Andrews University. The building now referred to as Parliament Hall was completed with money provided in 1642 by Alexander Henderson and was used for meetings of the Scottish Parliament in 1645–6 because Edinburgh had been hit by plague.

Sorn. This was an area of persecution by Bloody Reid of Daldinning, including George Wood who was shot aged six in 1685.

Wigton. A Martyrs' Monument, commemorating amongst others the two women tied to stakes to drown at high tide in the nearby Solway Firth is here.

England

The Battles

Boldon Hill, near Durham. It was an indecisive skirmish in March 1644 between the armies of the Scots Covenanters under Leven and the English Royalists under the Earl of Newcastle. Cannon fire was exchanged but the Royalists withdrew due to the unfavourable conditions.

Carlisle Sands. Scottish cavalry under Sir John Browne defeated English Royalist troops under Marmaduke Langdale in 1645 after the capture of Carlisle by the Scots.

Marston Moor, between Tockwith and Long Marston. A monument marks the site of this hugely important battle in which the Scottish Field Marshal Alexander Earl of Leven was given supreme command of the Parliamentary forces and the Scottish troops made up more than half of the victorious army that defeated Rupert and the Royalists.

Newburn. The highest point on the Tyne reached by the tides and therefore the lowest part suitable for fording is here, so the Royalists had set up earthworks to help prevent a crossing by the Scottish army under Leven in 1640. The tower of St Michael and All Angels Church, built in 1170, was used as an artillery position by the Scots.

Preston. The precise site of the various episodes of the first Battle of Preston in 1648 are hard to identify as the Scottish invading army was badly spread out and therefore vulnerable to piecemeal attack; much of it was near Walton-le-Dale and the Ribble Bridge. The second Battle of Preston in 1715 was far more of a town battle, fought street by street, between the Jacobites and the Hanoverian force.

Worcester. Much of the battle between the Scottish Covenanter/ Royalist army led by the young Charles II was in the main town after the Scots had failed to hold the bridges over the Teme and Severn.

St Martin's Gate survives, also White Ladies Priory. There is a Scots memorial by the River Teme.

The Sieges

Carlisle. The Scottish army, after it crossed the border on its way to Marston Moor in 1644, failed to capture the heavily fortified city but succeeded after a six-month siege in June 1645, by which time the garrison were running out of food. Carlisle was captured again by the Jacobites 100 years later. Significant remnants of the city walls, 16th century citadel and castle survive.

Hereford. The Scottish siege of Hereford was unsatisfactory as the Earl of Leven complained he was neither given the promised supplies, or wages for his troops, and his efforts to mine under the city walls cost many lives due to his sappers drowning as the tunnels were flooded. In the end he was instructed to abandon the siege and take on that of Newark instead. Little survives of the castle except the moat.

Newark. It was an important walled town dominating the north-south road and easily defended, as it was surrounded by the River Trent on three sides. It was besieged three times during the Civil War, the third time by the Scots who had been directed here from Hereford after the Battle of Marston Moor. It was during this siege that Charles I surrendered to the Scots army and Newark surrendered immediately afterwards. One of two huge sconces built to withstand the siege still stands in a public park.

Newcastle. The Scots captured Newcastle from the Royalists after a long siege during the Solemn League and Covenant campaign, which climaxed at Marston Moor. James Livingston, Earl of Callendar, was in charge most of the time. Charles I was brought here after his surrender near Newark and was subjected to attempted re-education to accept Presbyterianism by Alexander Henderson.

South Shields. Remains of the Roman fort still survive but there is little sign of the Civil War fort the Scots stormed at the second attempt as they headed south in 1644. It dominated the Tyne estuary and therefore was important prelude to capturing Newcastle itself.

Castles, Churches and Houses

Boscobel House. An English Heritage property in Shropshire, which has its third generation Royal Oak Tree in the grounds, offered brief shelter to Charles II after his defeat at Worcester, followed by his near capture as he headed for the south coast looking for a ship to France.

Carisbrooke Castle. A strong medieval castle, near Newport, Isle of Wight, is where Charles I was kept prisoner for 14 months prior to his execution. He was visited here by the leading Engagers such as Lauderdale prior to the ill-fated Preston campaign.

Durham Cathedral. This is the site of recent excavations revealing mass graves of Scottish prisoners of war, marched here after Battle of Dunbar, sick and ill-fed.

Gouthwaite Hall. Now submerged beneath a reservoir in Nidderdale, North Yorkshire, it was the birthplace of David Leslie's wife Janet Yorke, whom he possibly met when the Scottish army were camped at Appleby before Marston Moor.

Ham House, south of Richmond. It was built by the Murray Earl of Dysart, known as Charles I's Whipping Boy, inherited by his extravagant daughter Elizabeth, mistress and eventual wife of Lauderdale.

Hampton Court. This was the scene of Charles I's short-lived escape, which ended with his incarceration at Carisbrooke.

Holmby or Holdenby House, near Northampton. It is a large Tudor manor house bought by James I in 1607 and used as lodging for Charles I in 1647 after his surrender to the Scottish army besieging Newark. He was kept here till his abduction by Cornet Joyce, acting for the New Model Army. The house is still in private hands and used for functions or as film sets.

Tower of London. It featured frequently as prison for Campbell of Loudoun, Balcarres, Kilmarnock, Seaforth, Earl of Leven, David Leslie, Robert Monro, et al. In 1640 it had a Scottish Presbyterian governor.

Westminster Abbey and Hall. They were the scene of an Assembly lasting four years, from 1642, arising from English Parliamentarians wanting reform of the Church and Scottish envoys demanding Presbyterianism as a condition for a Scottish army helping to fight the Royalists. The Scottish ministers attending most of the time were Roberts Baillie and Douglas, George Gillespie, Alexander Henderson and Samuel Rutherford. The elders included the two Campbell Earls, Argyll and Loudoun; Lords Balmerino, Warriston, Cassilis and Maitland; plus George Winram of Liberton. The Assembly produced the Westminster Confession, which was accepted without alteration by the Scottish Parliament but only with amendments by the English.

Ireland

Castles and Church sites
Ballycastle. Built about 1625 to help defend the Protestant Plantations, it survived three assaults.

Bellaghy Bawn. It was built in 1619 as a typical defensive bawn to protect Plantation Protestants.

Carrickfergus Castle, on north shore of Belfast Lough. This massive Norman castle dating from 1177 was captured by Monro and Scots from the Earl of Antrim in 1642 and used as his HQ, later lost and besieged by General Schomberg in 1689. It was a landing place in Ireland for William III.

Derry. The walls of Londonderry were built 1613–18 as part of the protection of the Stuart Plantations, they stretched 1.5 kilometres and withstood two major sieges; St Columb's Cathedral was built as an Anglican-Protestant focal point in 1633, and had a peel of eight bells added by Charles I in 1638.

Donaghadee, near Bangor. It was the parish of the prominent Covenanting minister Andrew Stewart.

Dunluce Castle, near Portrush on the Antrim coast. It is a massive clifftop medieval castle, ancestral home of Macdonalds/Macdonnells, exiled from Scotland since 13th century; seat of Royalist Earls of Antrim, who organised invasion of Scotland in 1644, and the siege of Londonderry; surrendered to General Monro and Scots in 1641.

Fort Stuart, on Lough Swilly. It was built by Stuarts in 1611 to help protect Scottish Plantations.

Glenarm Castle. It was built in 1636 as a more up-to-date stately home for the Macdonnell Earls of Antrim.

Groomsport. It has the harbour from which the local minister James Hamilton, in 1636, attempted to sail to America with fellow Covenanters in the ship *Eagle Wing* (her name taken from the Book of Exodus). The 150-ton ship was forced to turn back more than half-way across the Atlantic due to stormy weather but the event is still celebrated by Ulster Scots in the USA. Later as minister of Ballywalter Church, Hamilton went around with a copy of the Solemn League and Covenant and gathered 30,000 signatures.

Laymore. This is the largest conventicle site in Antrim, known as the Round Hole; both Peden and Steel preached here in the 1680s. There is a memorial.

Monea Castle, in Fermanagh. Built in 1618 by a Plantation Scot, Malcolm Hamilton, it was captured briefly in 1641.

Ramelton Castle, in Donegal. Now a ruinous castle, it was built by the major Plantation supporters, the Stewarts, in 1609.

Battles and Sieges

Benburb, 7 miles from Armagh in County Tyrone. This was the site of defeat of Robert Monro and Scottish army by the Irish Confederates under Owen Roe O'Neill in 1646. Benburb Castle was built in 1611 as a typical Plantation bawn.

The Boyne. The Battle of the River Boyne on 12 July 1690 was where William of Orange finally defeated James II; it marked the end of Stuart plans to impose episcopal Lutheranism or even Catholicism on Scotland and England.

Drogheda, in the English Pale, in County Louth. This well-defended walled port town was where Cromwell conducted a siege with subsequent massacre; St Lawrence's Gate, Millmount Fort, and St Mary Magdelen Friary, survive.

Dungan's Hill, in County Meath. This is where 900 Highland Scots, the survivors of the MacColla-Montrose campaign in Scotland, were involved in this defeat of the Irish Confederate forces in 1647, the majority of them were killed or captured.

Glenmaquin, in County Meath. The battle was won by Lagan volunteer force under two Scottish brothers, Stewarts of Ramelton, against Irish Confederates in June 1642.

Knocknanus, near Rock of Cashel County Cork. The final battle of Alexander MacColla Macdonnell in 1647; MacColla was killed after being taken prisoner.

Lagan, rural area near Lisburn. Heavily settled by Scottish Presbyterians sent across by James VI & I; it was home to the two Stewart brothers who formed their own private militia, the Laganeers and won the Battle of Glenmaquin. The Lagan River flows into Belfast Lough.

Londonderry. It was attacked by Irish Confederates in 1641, besieged by Scots in 1649, and by the Earl of Antrim with 1,200 Redshanks in 1688, for six months.

Newry. This important strategic town in Ulster was captured by Monro and Scots troops 1642.

Portrush. Local Presbyterian Scots, recent immigrants encouraged by James VI & I were slaughtered here at start of Irish Confederate Wars.

Rathlin Island. The scene of the massacre by Campbells of Macdougal and Macdonald descendants, followers of Earl of Antrim.

Holland

Breda. It features as the favourite city for political refugees from Scotland, both Covenanters and Royalists, though it was only taken over by the Netherlands in 1648, after many sieges. It was also the home for some years of the future young king Charles II and gave its name to two of the treaties that preceded his Restoration 1650 with the Covenanters and 1660 with the English Royalists and General Monck.

Breda Castle was a moated fort transformed into a Renaissance Palace by the family of Orange/Nassau. The Great Church, or Grote Kerk, became a Protestant church only in 1637. Many old houses around the harbour survive from this period and were doubtless rented by Scottish asylum seekers and visiting delegations.

Huis ten Bosch. It was a favourite residence of the first Mary Stuart to marry into the House of Orange.

Het Loo Palace, Veere. This was the married home of Charles I's daughter Mary, William's mother.

The Hague. Elizabeth, ex-queen of Bohemia, sister of Charles I and mother of Prince Rupert, stayed here. It still has its Grote Kerk, Noordeinde Palace, Mauritshuis and Escher Palace, and was a regular meeting place for many political and religious refugees from Scotland till 1688.

Veer. This town has its Kastel Sandenbutch and the Schotse Huizen or Scottish merchants' quarter.

Belgium

Steinkirk. The battle fought south of Brussels in 1692 was lost to the French, casualties included a number of the Cameronian Rifles regiment, their founding commander, the young Earl of Angus, and many of Mackay's Regiment including General Hugh Mackay.

Germany

In Germany were formed the bonds that turned the future Fife conspirators – particularly the Leslies and Lumsdens plus the Leslie son-in-law Hugh Fraser and Sandy Hamilton – into a confident, compact group.

Lützen. In this battle near Leipzig in 1632 the newly promoted Field Marshal Alexander Leslie and James Lumsden played a key role in a major victory over the Imperial army, marred by the death of Leslie's patron, King Gustavus Adolphus of Sweden. David Leslie was at this time still fighting for the Russians at Smolensk.

Stralsund. Scots had been involved for some time in the defence of this key Hanseatic port on the Baltic coast of Germany from 1628 and being appointed its governor was a major step in the rise of Alexander Leslie to become one of Sweden's top generals. He also successfully captured the nearby island of Rügen.

Wittstock. This well-preserved fortress town in north Brandenburg is where Alexander Leslie, despite still recovering from a wound sustained near Hamburg, was joint-commander of the Swedish army in this important victory over the Holy Roman Empire in 1636. It sealed his reputation as a general capable of winning big battles and led to his being chosen as commander-in-chief at Marston Moor. David Leslie also played a key role here cementing their relationship.

Czech Republic

Nove Mesto. The castle was given to the Aberdonian mercenary Walter Leslie, who murdered Wallenstein.

United States of America

Large numbers of both Royalist and Covenanter Scots suffered transportation or were driven into exile from the 1650s onwards, most of them indentured to plantations in Virginia and the West Indies

Port Royal, South Carolina. Sir Hugh Campbell of Cessnock in Ayrshire, despite not himself being a Covenanter, had been prosecuted for failing to persecute those in his neighbourhood, was imprisoned on the Bass Rock, had his estates forfeited and, with his son George, set up a small colony in the island town of Port Royal in Beaufort County, where parts of the Old Village survive.

Saugus, Massachusetts. Surviving historic site of Lynn Iron Works, founded in 1646, to which Scottish prisoners were transported and indentured after the Battles of Dunbar in 1650 and Worcester in 1651.

Stuartstown, North Carolina. This was the site by the Ashley River of the failed Covenanter settlement, founded by Lord Neil Campbell (1630-92), son of the executed Marquis and brother of the executed Earl. It lasted about twenty years, from 1680. He made a second successful effort in 1682 when he bought a segment of East New Jersey, of which he became deputy governor for a year.

Woodbridge, East New Jersey. Covenanter survivors of the *Henry and Francis* landed at Perth Amboy and settled in this area. George Scott of Pitlochie, a strong Covenanter who had been imprisoned on the Bass Rock and in Dunnottar, was responsible for writing the *Model of Government* for the new colony but sadly both he and his wife died of disease whilst on board the *Henry and Francis*. Neil Campbell, in 1685 after the failure of the Monmouth-Argyll rebellion, organised a new settlement at Perth Amboy, opposite Staten Island.

West Indies

Barbados. The island had been largely bought by James Hay, Earl of Carlisle, and during the Civil War period became one of the favourite destinations for convict ships, particularly prisoners after the Battles of Dunbar and Worcester. Most of the indentured labourers sent to the new sugar plantations did not survive, but some, such as Gavin of Douglas, did. The capital, Bridgetown, was founded in 1628 and some of the buildings from the period when large numbers of Scots prisoners arrived here, can still be seen.

Jamaica. The island was captured from Spain by Cromwell in 1655 and became a dumping ground for about 4,000 prisoners, mainly Irish. Many Scottish prisoners taken after the collapse of the Argyll Rebellion of 1685 were shipped as indentured labour, the start of what became a substantial Scottish settlement there. For example, four men all called John Campbell from Kintyre, Lorn, Cowal and Carrick were shipped to Jamaica from Leith in 1685.

BIBLIOGRAPHY

Adams, Sharon and Julia Goodare, *Scotland in the Age of Two Revolutions*, Woodbridge, Boydell & Brewer, 2014.

Balfour, James, *The Annales of Scotland*, Edinburgh, W. Aitchison, 1824.

Blackadder, John, *Memoirs*, Edinburgh, William Tait, 1826.

Buchan, John, *Montrose*, London, Thomas Nelson, 1928.

Bulloch, J., *George Jameson, the Scottish Van Dyck*, Edinburgh, David Douglas, 1885.

Coventry, Martin, *The Castles of Scotland*, Musselburgh, Goblinshead, 2001.

Cowan, I.B., *The Scottish Covenanters*, London, Gollanz, 1978.

Crookshank, William, *The History of the State and Suffering of the Church of Scotland*, London, J. Oswald, 1749.

Divine, T.M., *The Scottish Nation 1700-2000*, London, Allen Lane, 1999.

Dobson, David, *The Original Scots Colonists of North America*, Baltimore, Genealogical Publishing, 2008.

Donaldson, G., *Scotland: James V to James VII*, Edinburgh, Oliver and Boyd, 1961.

Fissel, M.C., *The Bishops' Wars*, Cambridge, C.U.P., 1994.

Fraser, Antonia, *Cromwell*, London, Weidenfeld and Nicolson, 1973.

Fraser, Murdo, *The Rivals-Montrose and Argyll*, Edinburgh, Birlinn, 2015.

Furgol, Edward, *Religious Aspects of the Scottish Covenanter Armies*, (Thesis 1982).

Gilfillan, George, *The Martyrs, Heroes and Bards of the Scottish Covenant*, London, Cockshaw, 1832.

Granger, John D., *Cromwell against Scotland*, East Linton, Tuckwell, 1997

Guthrie, H., *Memoirs of Henry Guthrie late Bishop of Dunkeld*, Glasgow, 1747.

Hewison. James K., *The Covenanters*, Glasgow, J. Smith, 1913.

Howie, John, *Lives of the Scottish Protestant Worthies*, Edinburgh, 1863.

Hutton, Ronald, *Charles II*, Oxford, Clarendon, 1989.

Leslie, John, *A Relation of the Proceedings Concerning the Affairs of the Kirk of Scotland*, ed., D. Laing, Edinburgh, Ballantyne Club, 1830.

Linklater, Magnus, *Bonnie Dundee*, London, Weidenfeld and Nicolson, 1989.

Love, Dane, *Scottish Covenanter Stories*, Glasgow, Neil Wilson, 2005.

Love, Dane, *Scottish Kirkyards*, London, R. Hale, 1985.

Macaulay, Thomas, *History of England*, London, J.M. Dent, 1906.

Macgibbon, D., and D Thomas, *Ecclesiastical Architecture of Scotland*, Edinburgh, Mercat Press, 1991.

McGrigor, Mary, *Anna Countess of the Covenant*, Edinburgh, Birlinn, 2008.

Macinnes, Alan, *Clanship, Commerce and the House of Stuart*, East Linton, Tuckwell, 2006.

Macrae, Alastair, *How the Scottish Won the English Civil War*, Stroud, The History Press, 2011.

Murdoch, Steve, *Scotland, Scandinavia and the Bishops' Wars*, in A. Macinnes, ed., *Stuart Kingdoms in 17th Century*, Dublin, Four Courts Press, 2002.

Murdoch, Steve and Alexia Grosjean, *Alexander Leslie and the Scottish Generals in the Thirty Yeas War*, Leiden, 2003.

Oldmixon, John, *History of England Under The Stuarts*, London, 1880.

Omand, Donald, *The Fife Book*, Edinburgh, John Donald, 2000.

Patterson, Raymond, *King Lauderdale*, Edinburgh, John Donald, 2003.

Paterson Raymond, *A Land of Affliction*, Edinburgh, John Donald, 1998.

Paul, G.M. Ed., *The Diaries of Archibald Johnston*, Edinburgh, 1896.

Paul, J. Balfour, *Scots Peerage*, Edinburgh, David Douglas, 1904.

Reid, Stuart, *Crown, Covenant and Cromwell*, Barnsley, Frontline, 2012

Royle, Trevor, *The Civil War*, London, Abacus, 2009.

Scott, Hew, *Fasti Ecclesiae Scoticanae* Volume V, Edinburgh, Oliver and Boyd, 1825.

Scott, Walter, *Tales of a Grandfather*, London, Adam and Charles Black, 1898.

Scott, Walter, *The Tale of Old Mortality*, Edinburgh, Caxton, 1826.

Shukman, Ann, *Bishops and Covenanters*, Edinburgh, Birlinn, 2000.

Smout, T.C., *A History of the Scottish People 1560–1830*, London, Collins, 1969.

Spalding, John, *Memorials of the Troubles in Scotland*, ed. J Stewart, Edinburgh, Spalding Club, 1856.

Stephen, Thomas, *Life and Times of Archbishop Sharp*, London, Joseph Rickerby, 1839.

Stevenson, David, A*lastair MacColla and the Highland Problem,* Edinburgh, 1980.

Stevenson, David, *The Scottish Revolution,* Edinburgh, John Donald, 2003.

Stevenson, David, *Revolution and Counter Revolution 1644–51,* Edinburgh, John Donald, 2003.

Stevenson, David, *The Origins of Freemasonry in Scotland,* Cambridge, C.U.P., 1996.

Stevenson, R.H., *Chronicles of Edinburgh,* Edinburgh, Whyte, 1852.

Terry, C.S., *The Pentland Rising and Rullion Green,* Edinburgh, 1905.

Thomson, D., *The Life and Times of George Jameson,* Oxford, O.U.P., 1974.

Thomson, Oliver, *The Great Feud,* Stroud, Sutton, 2000.

Thomson, Oliver, *The Rises and Falls of the Royal Stewarts,* Stroud, History Press, 2009.

Watson, Robert, *Peden – Prophet of the Covenant,* Glasgow, 1983.

Wedgewood, Veronica, *The King's Peace,* Harmondsworth, Penguin, 1955.

Wedgewood, Veronica, *The Thirty Years War,* London, Pelican, 1957.

Whitley, Lawrence, *A Great Grievance: Ecclesiastical Lay Patronage in Scotland,* Oregon, Eugene, 2013.

Wodrow, Robert, *The History and Sufferings of the Church of Scotland,* Glasgow, Blackie, 1829.

Wright, Thomas, *History of Scotland,* 6 vols, London, London Printing and Publishing Company, 1850.

INDEX